Not Automat ...

D0686611

Not Automatic

Women and the Left
in the Forging of the
Auto Workers' Union

**SOL DOLLINGER AND
GENORA JOHNSON DOLLINGER**

Monthly Review Press
New York

Copyright © Sol Dollinger 2000
All Rights Reserved

Library of Congress Cataloging-in-Publication Data
Dollinger, Sol, 1920–
    Not automatic : women and the left in the forging of the Auto
Workers' Union / Sol Dollinger and Genora Johnson Dollinger.
        p.   cm.
    ISBN 1–58367–017–3 (cloth). — ISBN 1–58367–018–1 (paper)
    1. International Union, United Automobile, Aerospace, and
Agricultural Implement Workers of America—History.   2. Trade-
unions—Automobile industry workers—Organizing—United States—
History.   3. Women in trade-unions—United States—History.
I. Dollinger, Genora Johnson.   II. Title.
HD6515.AR215735   2000
331.4'781292'0973—dc21   99–38833
                                                                CIP

ISBN 1–58367–018–1 (paper)
ISBN 1–58367–017–3 (cloth)

Monthly Review Press
122 West 27th Street
New York, NY 10001

Manufactured in Canada
10   9   8   7   6   5   4   3   2   1

Contents

Acknowledgments   vii

List of Illustrations   viii

Foreword
by Kim Moody   x

Preface   xiv

PART I   ORGANIZING THE AUTO INDUSTRY, 1934–1948

Chapter 1   The Toledo Auto-Lite Strike, 1934   3

Chapter 2   The Toledo Chevrolet Transmission Strike, 1935   16

Chapter 3   Homer Martin Leads the UAW   27

Chapter 4   Factional Warfare Breaks Out, 1937–1938   36

Chapter 5   A Program for Peace   45

Chapter 6   R. J. Thomas Elected Leader as Recession and
             War Preparations Hit   53

Chapter 7   The UAW Organizes the Ford Motor Company,
             1940–1941   63

Chapter 8   Equality of Sacrifice?   71

Chapter 9   Anti-union Forces Take Revenge   82

Chapter 10   Briggs and the Mafia   93

Chapter 11   Reuther Slams the Door on Union Democracy,
              1947–1948   105

PART II   ORAL HISTORY

Chapter 12   Striking Flint
              Genora Dollinger Remembers the 1937 Sitdown   123

PART III   PUTTING THE RECORD STRAIGHT

Chapter 13   Good Housekeeping Seal of Approval   163

Chapter 14   Who Led the Flint Sitdown to Victory?
              On the Rewriting of History   173

Epilogue   The Auto Unions Today   189

            Notes   195

            Bibliography   205

            Index   208

Acknowledgments

Grateful acknowledgment is due to the following for their assistance: Nancy Bartlett, Bentley Historical Library, University of Michigan. Dean Braid (Education Director, 1995) and Gene Ridley (Education Director, 1996), Buick UAW Local No. 599, Flint, Michigan. Oscar Bunch, President, UAW Local No. 14, Toledo, Ohio. Dave Finkel, editor of *Against the Current*, for permission to reprint Chapter 11, which appeared in the May–June 1996 issue, with modifications. Margaret Anne Fortier, Learning Center Coordinator, Labor Museum and Learning Center of Michigan, Flint, Michigan. James C. Marshall, Manager, Local History and Genealogy Department, Toledo–Lucas County Public Library, Toledo, Ohio. *Militant*, 1947, 1948; *New Militant*, 1935. *Nation*, 1934, 1935. *New York Times*, April 1934–June 1935; May 1935–June 1935. *Socialist Call*, 1938, 1939. Tom Whalen, editor of *The History of Region 2B*. United Automobile Workers Local No. 12, Toledo, Ohio. *Workers Age*, 1937, 1938, 1939.

My deep appreciation goes to Dr. Leslie Hough and Thomas Featherstone of the Archives of Labor and Urban Affairs, Wayne State University, Detroit, Michigan—repository of the oral histories of Joseph Ditzel, James Roland, Genora Dollinger, and many others.

A special debt of gratitude is due to Anne Fox, without whose editorial assistance, encouragement, and advice this book would not have seen the light of day.

List of Illustrations

1. Electric Auto-Lite strike, 1934: Troops lead the charge behind a tear-gas barrage. *Toledo–Lucas County Library Archives.*

2. The National Guard returns fire against strikers with stones from the street. *Toledo–Lucas County Library Archives.*

3. Electric Auto-Lite strike: a strikebreaker, stripped of clothes, is marched down the street. *Toledo-Lucas County Library Archives.*

4. Picket line at Toledo Chevrolet Transmission strike, 1935. *Archives of Labor and Urban Affairs, Wayne State University.*

5. A. J. Muste, National Secretary of the American Workers Party. *Archives of Labor and Urban Affairs, Wayne State University.*

6. John McGill, president of the Buick local 1940, 1945, 1946. *Archives of UAW Buick Local No. 599.*

7. Roy Snowden, Genora and Sol Dollinger in 1944. *Dollinger collection.*

8. John Anderson, President of Fleetwood UAW Local No. 15, standing in front of the factory. *Courtesy of Minnie Anderson.*

9. Roy Snowden wielding bat at the Ford 1940–1941 organizing campaign. *Photo: Milton Brooks, © Detroit News Archives.*

10. Emil, William, Ernest, and Emil Mazey. *Courtesy of William Mazey.*

11. Genora Johnson and son Jarvis at the 1937 children's picket line. *Archives of Labor and Urban Affairs, Wayne State University.*

12. Genora and some of the five hundred women inspectors in Mack Avenue Briggs in 1944. *Dollinger collection.*

13. Flint, 1937: Car blockade of Fisher Body 2, site of the Battle of Bull's Run. *Flint Journal Photo.*

14. Strikers at Fisher Body 2 repulsing tear-gas attack at the Battle of Bull's Run. *Flint Journal Photo.*

15. Women's Emergency Brigade marching in front of Chevrolet Plant 9 after breaking the windows to release the tear gas. *Flint Labor Museum and Learning Center.*

16. Chevrolet Avenue after the capture of Plant 4. *Flint Labor Museum and Learning Center.*

17. Genora Johnson with members of the Women's Auxiliary. *Socialist Appeal.*

18. John Lamesfield, recording secretary; Kermit Johnson, president, Chevrolet Division UAW Local No. 156. *Dollinger collection.*

Foreword

Kim Moody

In writing *Not Automatic*, Sol Dollinger has set out to put the record straight. In doing so he has brought us a wealth of new material and insights into how America's industrial unions were organized and won their first victories. This is not a memoir or personal account, but a well-researched history of the early years of the United Automobile Workers, told through the eyes of a participant. Covering the period from the early 1930s through the late 1940s, *Not Automatic* brings to life many of the worker activists whose roles in creating the UAW have been passed over or trivialized in much of the literature on America's most studied union.

As Dollinger recounts the struggles, the factional fights, the heroism and savvy of "regular" working-class men and women, the cowardice and false wisdom of old-guard union bureaucrats, and the perfidy and plunder of corporate giants still on the prowl, the lessons for today leap out and demand our attention.

The unorganized were not "organized"; rather they organized themselves or were recruited by fellow workers, sometimes with help from the best of the contemporary officials. Dollinger writes:

> The battles for unionization engaged tens of thousands of rank-and-file auto workers, who volunteered hours, days, and weeks of superhuman, self-sacrificing activity. After their normal shift work, these union warriors waged a battle against the country's biggest corporations.

There was no organizing institute or legion of well-paid professional organizers. When these did appear from the tired hierarchy of AFL officialdom, they often did more harm than good. The real organizers of the UAW were rank and filers or local officials like Charles Rigby, a press operator who initiated the union in the stamping department of the Auto-Lite plant in Toledo, Ohio that would explode in one of the first successful strikes in the industry; or like Kermit and Genora Johnson, later Genora Dollinger, who would play key roles in the great Flint sitdown of 1936–1937.

After years of failed "blitz" drives by professional organizers, we are hopefully witnessing the return to this kind of unionizing as we see Teamster members volunteering to recruit workers at Overnite Transportation and Continental Airlines, or Communications Workers' members from telecommunications signing up thousands of airline reservation clerks at USAir. Once again, it seems, more and more U.S. workers are willing to put in the "hours, days, and weeks" of volunteer efforts needed to do the job.

Dollinger reminds us of something else, as well. It was corporate America's relentless pressure on the workforce that set people in motion, but it was a bigger vision that brought tens of thousands into the streets to defend and support one another in struggle after struggle. While we certainly have an excess of relentless pressure on working people as corporate America pushes for lean and mean industries and society, the vision of what a vibrant, democratic labor movement could do is hobbled by a commitment to labor–management "partnerships," hierarchical methods, and an obsession with media and PR techniques. As welcome as the new vitality at the AFL–CIO is, it suffers from a distrust of the rank and file that is not qualitatively different from that of the AFL old guard, or even many CIO leaders in the 1930s.

The vision that inspired workers in the 1930s as well as much of the tactical and organizational know-how that made these activists so effective was typically provided by workers who first acquired a bigger world-view, and frequently a pretty good political education, in one of the many organizations of the socialist and communist left of that period. Historians have tended to focus on those who rose to high places, even if momentarily, in the UAW and other CIO unions. This has favored well-known national leaders like the Reuther brothers and, oddly enough given America's thirty-year Cold War anti-Communist obsession, leaders and activists associated with the Communist Party of the Depression years.

Without trying to deny the role played by these better-known figures, Dollinger redresses some of the imbalance. Much of his "lost history" is that of rank-and-file leaders who made history but didn't make the history books. In particular, he tells the stories of those militant workers affiliated with a number of non-Communist left organizations: followers of A. J. Muste, Socialist Party members, and Trotskyists.

The focus on the Socialist Party of the mid-1930s is interesting because of the contradictory nature of that organization. On the one hand, the Socialist Party contained an ossified "old guard" that included a number of top-level union leaders in both the AFL and the CIO. On the other hand, the one-time party of Eugene V. Debs had seen rapid growth in the early 1930s as young workers and students joined its ranks. Their leader was Norman Thomas. Into that renewed party in 1936 flowed the militants from the Workers Party. This itself was the product of a regroupment of Trotskyists who led the 1934 Minneapolis Teamsters strike, and members of Muste's American Workers Party who had led the great Toledo Auto-Lite strike of 1934. Thus, the Socialist Party that Dollinger writes about was bubbling with working-class militancy and a radicalized brand of anti-Stalinist socialism. With this multi-tendency vitality came a certain amount of factionalism within the party and between it and the Communist Party, the Lovestoneites, liberals, and others. And it all spilled over into the UAW.

Not Automatic reminds us of two remarkable facts about political debate, struggle, and conflict in the labor movement. First, when the chips were down, as in Flint in 1936 and 1937, these various political currents worked together to shape a single unbeatable army capable of tumbling a giant corporation like General Motors. Contrast today's almost (save the oppositional UAW–New Directions Movement) single-party regime in the UAW, its stifling internal life, and its increasing ineffectiveness in bargaining with such corporations.

The second consequence of those days of internal union factionalism was a level of genuine democracy not seen since in the UAW. Democracy, we are reminded, isn't just about good structures or appeals systems; it's about membership involvement in setting the union's course. The many political groups in the UAW in the 1930s provided a line of communication from the leaders to the members; they sharpened policy debates and brought them into the open; they mobilized members to support their side; and they moved the union along even while its top leaders, almost from the start, were trying to centralize power and control debate. They couldn't do it for years because the members were offered alternatives and issues to debate and mobilized to fight for them.

Not Automatic is not, however, a rerun of factional fights. Rather it emphasizes the role of political rank and filers and local officials, many in the Socialist Party at one time or another, in the big events of that time. It sets the record straight, especially in relation to Henry Kraus's

1993 *Heroes of Unwritten Story,* which recalls the same period from the point of view of a one-time Communist Party member.

There is a lot more lost history here than that dealing with forgotten heroes or those workers who saw the left as a way of giving contemporary struggles direction and meaning. Read *Not Automatic* to fill in the holes left by other accounts, but most of all read it for what it tells us about the kind of unionism we need now more than ever.

Kim Moody is director of *Labor Notes,* and author of *Workers in a Lean World* (Verso 1997).

Preface

The history of the United States labor movement from the 1930s into the 1940s and beyond has, in many respects, been well documented. Nevertheless, what has been either lacking or presented in a skewed manner in the history book accounts is a faithful record of those original workers who made labor victories possible—class-conscious union militants such as Sam Pollock, Ted Selander, James Roland, John McGill, Bill Mazey, John Anderson, Ernest Mazey, my late wife Genora Dollinger, and many other valiant fighters.

The chapters that follow detail the history of three important strikes—the Toledo, Ohio, 1934 Electric Auto-Lite strike; the Chevrolet Transmission strike in the same city the following year; and the sit-down strikes of 1936–1937 in Flint, Michigan. These and other landmarks of labor history reveal the courage and devotion of the early standard-bearers, their pioneering struggles and strategies to unionize the auto industry, and the reasons for their obscurity in history. Finally, consideration is given to the reasons for the later decline in militancy, power, and influence of the unions.

The movement to the right in the United States has resulted in unbalanced reports about labor militants, or indeed in their eradication from the historical literature altogether. In this regard, the words of historian Edward Hallett Carr have great meaning for us: "The past is intelligible to us only in light of the present; and we can fully understand the present only in light of the past." I believe this book will illuminate both the past and the present, and possibly even cast a light on the future, by its disclosure of facts long blurred or actually misreported or erased—not only by historians but also by the unions themselves.

The book also records the dramatic details of the inspiring, complex, and intrepid role played in the labor movement by my wife of fifty-four years, Genora Dollinger, who died in 1995. Side by side with her union

activity was a lifelong involvement with socialism. At the age of seventeen Genora became a charter member and organizer of the Flint
Socialist Party. In 1938 she joined the Socialist Workers Party; fifteen
years later she was a charter member of the Socialist Union of America
(which disbanded in 1959). Her commitment to politics led her to
become a founding member of the new Labor Party. Genora's work in
the 1937 sitdown strikes has only been given full credit in recent years.
During the Second World War she played an important part in the
leadership of the Briggs local. After the war, she was actively involved
in the Flint branch of the National Association for the Advancement of
Colored People (NAACP), then in the Detroit and Michigan American
Civil Liberties Union (ACLU), Women for Peace, and other significant
social and political movements. As late as 1987 she unflinchingly confronted Henry Kraus at the fiftieth anniversary meeting of the Flint
sitdowns with her criticism of his failure to document the role of the
women in the strike. She received resounding cheers from the packed
hall. Wherever Genora lived and worked, she made something better
in the world. Her dynamic spirit, her bravery and resolve, will live on
in the annals of labor history and love.

Part I

Organizing the Auto Industry, 1934–1948

Chapter 1

The Toledo Auto-Lite Strike, 1934

Rise like Lions after slumber
In unvanquishable number
Shake your chains to earth like dew
Which in sleep have fallen on you—
Ye are many—they are few.

Shelley, *The Mask of Anarchy*

By 1934, the worst Depression in United States history had entered its fourth year. It was a period of tremendous hardship for working people. Record unemployment and the resulting economic deprivation had produced suffering and social dislocation on a scale hitherto unimagined. The conditions for successful strike action in the automobile industry could not have been less auspicious. Nevertheless, against all the odds, in the spring of that year the workers at the Electric Auto-Lite factory in Toledo, Ohio, won a historic partial victory over the company, following a bruising six-day struggle that involved hand-to-hand combat with the Ohio National Guard.

The ferocity of this struggle was a warning that the auto empire would not surrender control without great sacrifice by the union workers. The auto industrialists could rely on strong financial reserves, police forces, private detective agencies, and the undisguised support of government courts and committees. This formidable combination confronted the newly organized Toledo auto union, which had emerged when small groups of workers from City Auto Stamping, Bingham Stamping, Dura, Spicer, and Logan Gear received a charter for federal Local No. 18384 from the American Federation of Labor (AFL). The local was at the forefront of historic strikes in 1934 that led to the founding of the International Auto Workers Union (IAWU).

The auto industry had experienced sporadic labor conflicts throughout the Depression, attended by wage reductions and speed-ups, the notorious system introduced by Frederick Winslow Taylor. Speed-ups were a stopwatch timing method that increased productivity without new mechanical processes, simply by increasing the assembly-line speed with incremental adjustments.[1]

Attempts to organize had occurred in six different states. In 1933, Briggs, Motor Products, Murray Body, and Hudson had plant shutdowns in Detroit; Fisher Body was struck in Flint; Nash and Seaman Body in Wisconsin; General Motors in New York, Ohio, and California. The immediate cause of the strikes was employees' resistence to the efforts of the corporations to increase productivity beyond endurance. The previous four years of the Depression had seen auto workers' wages severely reduced. Unfortunately the auto workers had no experience of dealing with great corporate institutions: they lacked direction, basic resources for sustaining pickets, knowledge of public relations to counter hostile company propaganda, and awareness of elementary procedures of negotiation.

The Lessons of the 1933 Briggs Strike

The Briggs strike of 1933 had exemplified these problems. As in most of the strikes in that year of labor discontent, spontaneous action arose when the corporation attempted to cut the wages of the hourly and piece-rate workers. Six thousand workers marched out of the plant. An inexperienced committee—which included members of the Socialist Party (SP), the Proletarian Party, the Industrial Workers of the World (IWW), and the Communist Party (CP)—found it necessary to seek help from the Automobile Workers Union (AWU), asking Phil Raymond, the secretary, who had previous strike experience, to provide direction.

With the assistance of the AWU, Raymond directed the establishment of the Briggs strike committees. The strikers demanded union recognition, the restoration of the previous wage scale, and a more tolerable line speed. The company's response was to withdraw the wage cuts but also to launch an attack on the Communist leaders of the strike. Briggs had an easy target, linking the AWU with the Trade Union Unity League (TUUL), which the Communist Party had established in 1929 to help build unions in industries independent of the AFL. Under unrelenting attack, the strike committee of twenty-five requested the removal of Raymond and his CP assistants. After two months the dispirited Briggs workers trickled back to work.[2]

Briggs workers learned that accepting aid from the AWU cut them off from the mainstream of the union movement in the United States, which still flowed through the AFL, the country's major union. The AFL's strength resided in the craft unions, a fact that weakened their appeal to the large concentration of auto workers in factories where skilled craft workers were only a small part of the workforce. In the few instances where the auto workers established local unions—as they did in Cleveland, Ohio; South Bend, Indiana; and Kenosha, Wisconsin— local union leaders opposed AFL efforts to split the skilled workers into the various crafts.

The AWU leadership stood for industrial unionism and counterposed their program to that of the AFL, but the superiority of a program could not overcome the prejudice of workers toward the left-wing leaders. The average worker chose a union to deal with basic shop problems of wages and working conditions. Red-baiting was a divisive attack by the corporations that successfully divided the union ranks. Workers sought a trusted, untainted political leadership. Some turned to company-dominated unions, influenced by Father Charles E. Coughlin. The AWU and the company unions remained paper organizations.

In the period following the 1929 stock-market crash, the record of periodic rebellions reveals that labor did not accept the pain of wage cuts, intensified speed-ups, and short hours in the industrial plants without resistance. At this time, millions of workers wandered the country in search of jobs. Their experiences on the road broadened their political horizon so that many lost faith in the capitalist system. In the subsequent period of the New Deal, the upturn in employment and the policies of a reform government—introduced by political representatives who feared the possible destruction of the capitalist system and a redress of the balance between capital and labor—inspired workers to seek change in the workplace itself.

Some of the strikes took place because the strikers incorrectly thought the government had provided a legal basis in the National Recovery Act (NRA) for workers to join unions of their own choice without interference from industry employers.[3] These auto workers sought out the AFL, even though AFL strength was in craft unionism and its leadership under William Green was conservative. Although Green spoke from a national pulpit for labor, in most of the country the AFL had been reduced in size and influence; it nevertheless represented a starting point for organization. As things developed, however, in Detroit and other centers of the auto empire the Green representatives led the auto industry to repeated defeats.[4] The half-hearted assignment of organizers by the AFL, failure to mobilize strike support, and the policy of relying on government boards in union organization, were all factors disarming the incipient movement to unionism in Detroit.[5]

Federal Local No. 18384

Toledo, the center of an auto parts and glass industry, depended on the larger auto companies for its prosperity. When the large companies sneezed, the auto parts companies caught pneumonia. The largest manufacturing company in Toledo, Willys-Overland, had employed 28,000 workers before the stock-market crash. In 1932 it closed its doors. This in turn forced the closure of the Ohio Bond and Security Bank: thousands of depositors lost their life savings.

The manager of the Ohio Bonds and Security Bank was one Clem Miniger. It later emerged that before the default, key depositors from the parts industry had shifted their funds to secure repositories. The citizens of Toledo would subsequently vent their wrath on Miniger. The violent middle-class reaction against the rich financier, an admired figure before the Depression, illustrated the precipitous decline in the reputation of the capitalist class nationwide. For decades the public had believed that the prosperity of the country had been produced by the captains of industry, and unlimited praise was heaped on the Mellons, Duponts, Morgans, and Rockefellers. Following the credit default and economic collapse, the rich—the mighty industrialists, the millionaires, America's sixty families—were seen as damaged goods.

Clem Miniger was also the head of the Electric Auto-Lite Company, which, under his leadership, had become a major force in the parts sector. The plant manufactured ignition, lighting, and electrical parts systems for the auto industry and supplied Chrysler, Ford, Willys, Packard, and Nash. It employed 1,800 men and women, with 400 in the stamping division.[6] A relation of interlocking ownership existed between Auto-Lite, Bingham Tool and Stamping, and Logan Gear.

High unemployment in Ohio, at a record 37 percent, and in Toledo, at 80 percent, did not deter workers at the Electric Auto-Lite Company from attempting to organize the company. To this end, they sought help from the Central Labor Union (CLU) of the AFL, which represented twenty-three different crafts. The action was initiated by Charles Rigby, who was to play a central role in the strike, and several others working in the punch press stamping department. Rigby and his committee were told that Auto-Lite workers came under the jurisdiction of Federal Labor Union No. 18384. (The AFL had chartered auto locals throughout the country in federal locals to avoid conflict with the craft unions.) The Toledo auto union charter covered Willys and five plants in the parts industry.

Charles Rigby's father had idolized Eugene Victor Debs and brought his son up to share his own socialist philosophy. Rigby joined the Industrial Workers of the World when he worked on the Northwest railroad, and gained an understanding of unionism. When he returned from his travels around the country, Rigby went to work at Auto-Lite. He convinced the union officers of Local No. 18384 that his committee in the punch press stamping department occupied a strategic position at Auto-Lite. A walkout of the four hundred press stamping workers would shut down the rest of the plant, which was dependent on his department for parts. The officers of the local accepted his analysis and during the next few months planned to shut four auto parts plants. From August until the first strike, many secret meetings were held as the insurgent group of unionists expanded their influence. Nearing the moment of decision for strike action, they held public meetings that attracted several hundred workers from the parts industry.

Rigby, the elected shop committee chairman, requested a meeting with the management of Auto-Lite. He informed the company that the union committee was requesting a meeting under the provisions of Section 7(A) of the NRA, which guaranteed them the right of collective bargaining. The committee presented management with the following demands: union recognition, a 10 percent wage increase, seniority, and the establishment of a regular bargaining procedure. The company rejected the demands outright and informed the committee it had a million-dollar fund to fight any attempt at unionization.[7]

On February 23 the union stopped work at Auto-Lite, Bingham, Logan, and Spicer, affecting four thousand workers. The strike was effective at Bingham and Logan, but at Auto-Lite, in spite of a small picket line, production continued without interruption. The union declared that there would be no settlement at any of the plants until all of the strikers were protected.

Federal mediators entered the dispute, proposing a 5 percent wage increase. Auto-Lite, Bingham, Logan, and Spicer accepted the proposal but refused to grant union recognition or seniority. In further negotiations the mediators suggested holding the remaining issues in abeyance for future negotiation. The union agreed to accept the mediators' recommendation to return to work and negotiate the outstanding issues on April 1, the understanding of the strike committee being that the companies had agreed to adjudication on the outstanding matters. The terms of the strike settlement, as reported to the members, expressly included further negotiations on substantive matters at a later date. The proposal to end the strike was submitted by Thomas Ramsey, the local union business agent, to the membership meeting. The union voted to return to work.[8]

Bloody Confrontation

The record does not indicate whether the mediator actively misled the strike committee. The fact is, nevertheless, that the inexperienced union negotiators failed to get concrete agreement from the company for more talks. The auto parts companies subsequently made it quite clear they had no intention of bargaining further. Instead, they prepared for another strike by hiring replacement workers and purchasing a supply of tear gas. Local No. 18384 used the 35-day period to enroll members. They were convinced they had won a victory in the February strike. When the two sides met, the company ruled out negotiations. In response, strike votes were carried at Bingham, Auto-Lite, and Logan. Bingham struck on April 12, with an almost complete shutdown of the plant. Auto-Lite struck the following day and several hundred workers walked out, primarily the stamping department; nevertheless the strike failed to close the factory, which kept working with hired replacement workers. Logan walked out on April 17, with less than a majority supporting the picket line.

The Auto-Lite strikers, reinforced by members in the parts industry, and with support from the Unemployed League and the CP-led Unemployed Councils, maintained picket lines around the plant. From the beginning, the police attempted to prevent the pickets from keeping scabs out of the factory. On May 3 Auto-Lite asked the Lucas County Court for an injunction, which was granted by the Common Pleas Judge, Roy R. Stuart. Stuart's injunction restricted the number of pickets at Auto-Lite to twenty-five, and the same at Bingham. The injunction also barred members of the Socialist Party, the Unemployed League, and specific strikers and sympathizers from the picket line. Sheriff David Krieger, a political ally of Auto-Lite boss Miniger, was assigned to enforce the injunction. Both men were active in the Republican Party.

Furthermore, Miniger had given financial support to the sheriff in his campaign for office. Auto-Lite authorized Krieger to hire extra deputies, and the company advanced money for their wages. These vigilante deputies, dressed in street clothes, wore armbands and badges. James Roland, a member of the Unemployed League, gave the following account:

> We, in Toledo, at least a small group of us, felt that unless the Auto-Lite strike was a winning strike the labor movement would be set back for quite a few years in Toledo. There was this strike being conducted by Tom Ramsey for quite some time. A group of us felt that it was a lost strike. So we decided to do something about it. There were five of us who assumed leadership. I do not say that we were elected, although there were probably about 25 or 30 people at a small meeting which we had to decide on what we can do to change the situation at Auto-Lite regarding the strike. It was decided at that small meeting, excluding Tom Ramsey, of course, that five of us that would more or less volunteer and we were acceptable to the small group there that we would try to do something about violating the injunction which was granted and was killing the strike. So these five people were Earl Stucker, from the Auto-Lite, Sam Poleck [*sic*—Sam Pollock] and Ted Seamyer [*sic*—Ted Selander] at that time were from the Unemployed League in Toledo, and I was from Chevrolet. The five of us were trying to direct the strike and the first thing we did was to violate the injunction.[9]

On May 5, Sam Pollock, secretary of the Lucas County Unemployed League, wrote to Judge Roy R. Stuart:

Honorable Judge Stuart:

On Monday morning May 7, at the Auto-Lite plant, the Lucas County Unemployed League, in protest of the injunction issued by your court, will deliberately and specifically violate the injunction enjoining us from sympathetically picketing peacefully in support of the striking Auto Workers Federal Union.

We sincerely believe that this court intervention, preventing us from picketing, is an abrogation of our constitutional liberties and contravenes the spirit and the letter of Section 7a of the NRA.

Further, we believe that the spirit and intent of this arbitrary injunction is another specific example of an organized movement to curtail the rights of all workers to organize, strike and picket peacefully.

Therefore, with full knowledge of the principles involved and the possible consequences, we openly and publicly violate an injunction which, in our opinion, is a suppressive and oppressive act against all workers.

Sincerely yours,
Lucas County Unemployed League
Anti-Injunction Committee
Sam Pollock, Sec'y[10]

Thus, the day after the injunction, Louis Budenz, executive secretary of the American Workers Party, Ted Selander, an officer of the Toledo Unemployed League, and forty-six of the Auto-Lite strikers appeared on the picket lines, calling for the resumption of mass picketing. They were duly arrested for contempt of the injunction. They were defended by Arthur Garfield Hayes of the American Civil Liberties Union of New York and Edward Lamb, a prominent attorney from Toledo. Members of the Unemployed League jammed the courtroom. Judge Stuart released the defendants without a sentence and they returned to the picket line. News broadcast on the radio that the union was fighting the injunction traveled through the city. Thousands joined the pickets. Each day the lines grew larger, from one thousand to ten thousand, as Louis Budenz and A. J. Muste, founder and chairman of the American Workers Party, addressed the pickets in front of the factory gates.

Auto-Lite exerted pressure on the sheriff to prevent the strikers from harassing those crossing the picket line. Again, Budenz was arrested along with many others. The court singled out Budenz, Selander, Pollock, Rigby, Roland, and several others. Before sentence was passed, the workers in the courtroom rose and told the judge: "We all are guilty of the same offense." This action of solidarity by the union members persuaded the judge to release the defendants. The court was unable to handle mass arrests and in any case hesitant to inflame further the growing strike movement.[11]

On May 23, at the urging of the company to stop the harassing of replacement workers, the ranks of deputies, scabs, and police tried again to smash through the lines. The company police fired tear gas from the roof of the four-story brick Auto-Lite plant and tossed down metal generator brackets, which injured pickets. Clashes between pickets and scabs grew more violent. Strikers invaded the parking lot and overturned cars belonging to strikebreakers. Fights broke out inside the plant in the early hours of the morning when the pickets entered and engaged in hand-to-hand combat. The strikers broke windows of the plant and threw the tear gas canisters back into the plant. A picket line ten thousand strong ringed the plant and refused to allow the scabs to leave. Office workers, management, and plant police were also kept inside the plant until daybreak.[12]

The *New York Times* filed the following report on these violent scenes witnessed by its reporter:

The crowd had been assembling in territory adjacent to the factory since noon. Piles of bricks and stones were assembled at strategic places and a wagon load of bricks was trundled to a point near the factory to provide further ammunition for the strikers.

Suddenly a barrage of tear gas bombs was hurled from upper factory windows. At the same time company employees armed with iron bars and clubs dragged a fire hose into the street and played water on the crowd.[13]

On the evening of May 23, the sheriff made frantic calls to the governor to have the National Guard rescue the imprisoned nonstrikers and the security men, who were by then isolated on the fourth floor. Shortly thereafter, the National Guard arrived at the plant, where they set up gun emplacements and planned the release of the 1,500 trapped men and women.

The sheriff had advised the governor that Guardsmen living in nearby counties should not be deployed. Thus, young recruits from counties distant from Toledo made up the National Guard that night. Many strikers were veterans of the First World War and had no fear of the young men with rifles. The Guard tried to disperse the huge crowds on Champlain and Chestnut streets. After each of the several charges, the pickets regrouped and advanced down Chestnut. Some National Guard units wearing gas masks shot tear gas into the ranks of the strikers, who immediately picked up the canisters and threw them back. A filmed scene shows members of the Guard corps in a Kafkaesque rock-throwing contest with the strikers. The battle lasted for two full days.

The Guard commander asked in due course for reinforcements: eight rifle companies, three machine-gun units, and a medical unit. Reinforced with his additional troops, he instructed the Guardsmen to fix bayonets. The strikers and some ten thousand sympathetic supporters gathered again. Orders to fire at the strikers were issued following a two-hour barrage of tear gas. The commander later claimed that he had issued instructions to fire over the heads of, and not into, the crowd. Nevertheless, two strike sympathizers were killed and thirty-five wounded. Later that afternoon the Guards again fired on the strikers, wounding many more.[14]

The Threat of a General Strike

That night the Central Labor Union met to consider two issues: the abrupt shift in the course of the Auto-Lite strike, and the refusal of Toledo Edison Electric to bargain with the International Brotherhood of Electrical Workers (IBEW), who were threatening a strike for union recognition and a 20 percent wage increase. The IBEW was a craft union and normally would not have considered acting in solidarity with the Federal Workers Union. However, the strike at Auto-Lite, engaging thousands of workers and the unemployed, had escalated to the point where the face of unionism had changed in Toledo. Meanwhile, on the bosses' side, the Merchants and Manufacturers Association and the automobile industry leaders informed Miniger that he had their full support in resisting unionization of the parts industry. The issue came to a head when the twenty-three craft unions in the CLU, perceiving an open-shop threat in Toledo, represented by the Auto-Lite strike, reacted by voting for a general strike. A strike by the electrical workers alone would bring the city to a standstill. The employers' intransigence had escalated the strike to a dangerous and unanticipated level of confrontation.

The same evening the CLU proposed to intervene in the strike, Charles Taft, son of the former U.S. president, met with the Auto-Lite workers. Frances Perkins, Secretary of Labor, had sent Taft to mediate. Taft proposed that the disputed issues be sent to the Auto Labor Board in Detroit for mediation. This proposal was rejected by a meeting of the union, a defeat that Taft blamed on the influence of Rigby and his committee. The union countered with a request for the National Guard's removal and the shutdown of the plants. The Guard had arrested Louis Budenz early in the week and Ted Selander on the Saturday. Selander was held incommunicado; Muste's efforts to obtain his release were refused. The government negotiators wanted the two AWP leaders removed from the strike arena so that Taft and other government mediators could advance new proposals to the less experienced local union leaders.[15]

Taft told A. J. Muste, syndicated columnist Heywood Broun, and E. R. Lamb, attorney for Ted Selander, that the "strike should never have been called," and claimed that it was the work of "outside agitators." Similar sentiments appeared in the *Toledo Bee*, a Scripps–Howard paper. The response of Muste and Lamb was to wire Roosevelt, demanding the removal of Taft. Writing in the *New Republic* after the strike, Muste underlined the bias of the special mediator selected by Perkins: "Taft called all the newspapermen into his room, and in the presence of Lamb and Muste, demanded that they suppress any information about his antiunion statements. Heywood Broun refused to be gagged."[16]

Auto-Lite company negotiators grudgingly agreed to submit the dispute to binding arbitration, but the idea was rejected by the union. Too much blood had been spilled to make this a viable proposal. Instead, in response to the growing pressure, the CLU voted for a general strike, with representatives of 93 of the 103 unions present; of these, 88 were in favor of the strike. The mediators, for their part, were working around the clock to prevent such action, and Taft succeeded in negotiating a temporary postponement. The picket line was quiet on Friday, but on Saturday clashes again broke out. The National Guard commander ordered all of the plants shut.

A Hard-won Victory

Throughout the strike, including the six-day period when the action resembled a riot, the American Workers Party, led by Louis Budenz and A. J. Muste, was passing out handbills to the strikers on the picket lines and making speeches. The independent posture of the AWP enabled the backers of Muste to find support in the Auto-Lite local, which had like-thinking supporters in Charles Rigby and his committee. Obviously, many others in the local were influenced by the political direction of the AWP. Even the more conservative or nonpolitical leaders preferred the radical ideas of the AWP to those of the Communist Party. The Auto Workers Union opposition to the AFL compelled the leaders of the Federal Workers Union to shun their offer of aid. However, members of the Unemployed League were joined on the picket line by the CP-dominated Unemployed Council, who were welcomed gratefully.

The strikers accepted the handbills passed out by the Muste supporters but rejected those of the CP, although the messages of the two left-wing organizations had a similar political content. The Muste/AWP pamphlets make common ground with AFL Teamster strikes in Minneapolis.

> On to the general strike!
>   There must be no delay!
>   Every minute that action is delayed is a golden minute for Miniger, the bank robber, for the Toledo Edison, for the Merchants and Manufacturers Association....
>   On to the general strike! ...[17]

> The workers of Toledo realize, as their brothers in Minneapolis realized, that there is strength for them only with their own class. Even the president of the United States cannot or will not help....
>   Man the picket lines at Bingham and Logan Gear Plants.
>   The militia must go!

Call the general strike!
No compromise settlement in the Auto-Lite strike!
Auto-Lite, Toledo Edison, all employers must recognize the right of workers to organize.[18]

Another handbill alerted the union to the dangers of mediation by the Automobile Union Board, established in March by Roosevelt when William Green of the AFL threatened a nationwide strike of the auto industry. The two deaths and the wounding of pickets was seized upon by the Muste forces to drive a wedge between the AFL and Roosevelt, and to protest his appointment of the Auto Labor Board (ALB) to resolve disputes between labor and the auto industry. The threat by William Green of a general strike in auto expressed the unions' dissatisfaction with the procedures of the ALB in arranging votes that included representatives of company unions. The threat by Green evaporated after Roosevelt met with him to resolve the dispute. No new procedures emerged from the meeting in Washington. Muste drew the lesson for the auto workers with a new handbill:

Firmness in dealing with the employers will not come from the president or anyone else. Firmness must come from our own ranks. The Detroit Labor Board and like agencies only let the workers down.[19]

With the plants closed, negotiations held off the threat of a general strike. Meanwhile, Toledo Edison referred the recommended contract proposals to City Service power system, which had a controlling interest in Toledo Electric. They eventually conceded, granting union recognition and a 20 percent wage increase. With the settlement of the Edison strike, the threat of a general strike was removed.

The mediator moved swiftly to draft an Auto-Lite contract with Local No. 18384, which called for the union to agree that the local and the company union Auto Council share the benefits of the settlement. This union compromise was then put to the union in Auto-Lite; it was subsequently put to Toledo Chevrolet in 1935, and to Flint General Motors in 1937. However, the auto industry refused to accept the principle that majority rule in a strike meant the exclusion of company union minority groups from the bargaining process. The recall of workers applied first to all employees hired before the strike; the strike replacement workers were called back after all the strikers had been recalled. The fact that all the strikers were recalled without penalties was vindication of the union's declaration of victory. The 5 percent wage increase applied to all workers.

Rigby indicated that hard feelings existed in the plant between the strikers and nonstrikers. The union's declared goal of winning over the nonstrikers was duly accomplished the next year. Furthermore, Local No. 18384 embarked on a vigorous membership drive and in a short time had signed up eighteen parts plants in Toledo. The one exception was the Toledo Chevrolet Transmission Plant. The Auto-Lite strike had sent a message to the entire industry that the auto workers could no longer be denied an international union of their own choice.

Local No. 18384 later became the powerful Local No. 12 in the UAW–CIO, with a wartime peak membership of 35,000. Nearly three decades later, Richard Gosser, an early organizer for Local No. 18384, former president of UAW Local No. 12, former regional director of Region 2B, and former vice president of the UAW, negotiated a contract with Auto-Lite that was rejected by the workers. As a consequence, the plant shut down and moved its operations out of the state. That, however, is another story. In 1934, following the Auto-Lite strike, auto workers set their sights on the lone remaining unorganized parts plant: the General Motors Chevrolet Transmission Plant.

Chapter 2

The Toledo Chevrolet
Transmission Strike, 1935

Let no one underrate his own power, or imagine that one more or less makes no difference. No one not even the weakest can be dispensed with for furthering the advance of humanity. A continual dropping hollows out the hardest stone. And many drops make the brook, and brooks make the stream, and streams the great river whose majestic course can be stopped by no object in nature!

August Bebel, *Women under Socialism*

Following the 1934 Auto-Lite strike, the Central Labor Union sought the aid of the Unemployed League in two strikes. The combined force duly achieved signed contracts at Armour and Swift and Larrowe Milling. In February 1935, a committee representing the Buildings Trades Council, Unemployed League, and the Workers Alliance embarked on mass picketing of building-trades projects. The "March of Labor," a concept of Sam Pollock, brought the projects to a standstill and soon resulted in victory for the building trades locals.[1]

Organization of the eighteen auto parts plants had meanwhile brought about structural and political change in the leadership of Local No. 18384. The enlarged executive committee of the local union expanded to reflect the growth in membership. Future events would reveal the committee to be more conservative than the founding group that directed it in the Auto-Lite strike. Following the success in making Toledo a union town, the remaining obstacle was the Chevrolet Transmission Plant. It was recognized that a victory at the Transmission Plant would require a herculean effort. With its deep pockets, General Motors (GM) was one of the most powerful corporations in the world, employing 191,000 in 1934 and handling a payroll of $191 million.

Local union leaders had tracked the 1934 Cleveland Fisher Body Strike against General Motors. The plant employed over eight thousand. This strike precipitated similar actions at other GM plants; a few were led by independent unions, but most were charted by the AFL. Workers from Flint, Atlanta, Baltimore, Janesville, Tarrytown, and Kansas GM plants walked off the job. Cleveland Fisher Body, with over 4,500 on the picket line, attracted the most attention. AFL director William Collins and his small staff, who represented locals in Ohio, Indiana, Wisconsin and Michigan, were overstretched by the responsibility for auto corporation plants spread over so many states. Logic therefore dictated that Collins appeal to the Auto Labor Board (ALB) for aid in arranging a central site for negotiations with GM.

General Motors accepted the proposal put forward by the Board. Automobile production had increased substantially in 1934 and the corporation was obviously anxious to end the strike. Nevertheless, William Knudsen, president of Chevrolet, set conditions before negotiations began, insisting that the striking workers return to work before discussions started. He also informed the ALB that GM's policy against the "closed shop" was inviolate; therefore negotiations had to include all employee organizations, including the company-sponsored unions. Furthermore, the unions were required to furnish a list of all members so that the company could determine proportional representation.

Union leaders derided the idea of company unions sitting at the bargaining table with legitimate unions. The AFL insisted that this would stack the table against the AFL because the company union representative would side with the corporation. Knudsen set additional ground rules: each plant had to meet with local management to settle that plant's problems. The ALB sided with Knudsen. Collins capitulated to the GM conditions and ordered the Cleveland workers back. Collins's action dealt a body blow to the AFL union: the returning workers tore up their union cards.

Elections and Strike Plans

To overcome the problem of company union representation at the bargaining table the ALB ordered elections, with the plant divided into districts. Workers had to run without a union designation. Since the company arranged the elections in the plant, the use of foremen and supervisors to influence balloting was a foregone conclusion. The AFL denounced the ballot procedure and asked union supporters to boycott the vote.

In more than half of the elections held between December 1934 and April the following year, 200,000 ballots were cast. A total of 85 percent of these voted without listing an organizational affiliation—fewer than 4 percent listed the AFL or company union. Analysis of the vote pointed to despair on the part of the workers. Notwithstanding the inordinate degree of pressure by the corporation to support the puppet company union, the vote represented a defeat of company-sponsored organization. Nevertheless, prospects were also bleak for the AFL, who had boycotted the election.[2]

At the request of the Toledo Chevrolet Transmission Plant management, the ALB scheduled an election for April 9, 1935. General Motors sought to capitalize on the union setback in the elections by promoting the company union. Toledo Local No. 18384 voted to contest the scheduled ALB election, a decision contrary to AFL policy. In contrast to the disarray of the AFL in Detroit, the Toledo union movement was riding a rising crest of union organization. Indeed, within a year the AFL had consolidated its organization in the auto parts industry and had also expanded significantly in the traditional craft industries.

The local had a well-organized committee in Chevrolet, headed by 23-year-old James Roland, a charter member of the local, holder of union card no. 5 and a trustee of Local No. 18384 from its inception in 1933. Roland had been a participant in the struggle to defeat the injunction brought against the Auto-Lite strikers. He had in fact been fired before the strike and appealed his discharge to the Automobile Labor Board. His reputation soared following a brave and daring act described by Art Preis, a participant in Chevrolet strike activities:

> One year ago Toledo Chevrolet officials were looking out of plant windows, extremely irritated.
> They were watching Jimmy Roland marching around the factory gates with picket signs on his back. A one-man picket line around a factory employing 2,500 men!
> Brazen, insane, unprecedented—but successful. The regional Labor Board decided in his favor....
> So, Jimmy was rehired.[3]

Roland had advised the ALB in advance of his intention to picket the factory. The sign he carried asked for an immediate hearing by the Labor Board. Two days later, Roland was told that a hearing would be held. He abandoned picketing and in due course was granted an appearance before the three-man Board headed by Leo Wolman representing the public, Nicholas Kelly representing management, and Richard Byrd representing labor. A month passed without word of a decision. Roland again alerted the ALB to his intention to resume picketing the plant. The next day, the ALB instructed Chevrolet to return Roland to employment. Chevrolet put Roland in the accounts payable department, far away from the production workers. He remained in the front-office job even after his election as chairman of the shop committee and of the strike committee.[4] Serving on the shop committee with Roland was Robert Travis—his first appearance in the history of the auto union.

The decision by Local No. 18384 to contest the ALB election allowed little time for preparations. They nominated business agent Fred Schwake on the ballot in all eight districts. The union held a successful meeting the night before the election and elected Roland chairman of the nine-member strike committee. This committee also served as the shop committee. The members voted the committee authorization to call a strike. The AFL carried every district, with a vote of 1,300 votes out of the 2,100 cast. The ALB scheduled a runoff vote; the union, however, acted quickly to make this unnecessary. The union then met with management and submitted demands for union recognition, seniority, and a 10 percent wage increase.

The company, in the meantime, was making its intentions clear. As Roland related in an interview in 1960:

> To us it looked like they were preparing for a showdown strike and were making preparations so that there could not be another Auto-Lite ... they put up screens around all their windows, heavy wire screens.... From all indications it looked as if they were planning ... [to] make a long battle of it.[5]

The shop committee tried to keep secret the final strike-date decision. On April 22, GM sent in a special crew of negotiators headed by William Knudsen, Charles Wetherald,[6] and M. E. Coyle, who kept the strike committee in session for twelve hours, considering the company's counter-proposals. The union rejected GM's position; the decision was made late that night to strike the following morning. Much to the consternation of the committee, GM greeted the workers on the morning shift with a handbill listing the company's proposals for a settlement. The union leaders learned that a leak in their group had made it possible for management to react overnight and embarrass the committee. General Motors proposed the following: a 5 percent increase in wages; rigid enforcement of the seniority rules established by the government; each employee to be given access to his seniority record; layoffs and rehiring according to seniority; meetings with accredited representatives of employees to resolve remaining grievances.

The company pointedly refused to concede to a "closed shop"; also glaringly absent were union recognition and a signed contract.

The union responded three days later with the publication of *Strike Truth*, co-edited by James Roland and Joseph Ditzel, with George Addes as executive committee representative and Arthur Preis as associate editor. The paper answered GM point for point, but focused on the "closed shop":

> By the afternoon of that same day it slowly dawned upon the management of Chevrolet that the "closed shop" was one of the conditions not demanded by our union in this instance; and, fearing lest further mention of it might put notions into our heads, the company conspicuously refrained from including the statement in its full page advertisements in the afternoon papers.[7]

The union paper hit hard at the ALB-sponsored election won by Local No. 18384. The unsigned articles expressed the belief that organization of the union in Chevrolet resulted from the company's attempt, in collusion with the ALB, to rig the election in favor of a company union. The paper also called for a meeting to reject Chevrolet's counter-proposals and told the members to bring a receipt showing union membership to gain admission to the meeting.

In a sharp reversal of their policy of abstention, AFL president William Green and Francis Dillon (appointed National Representative to the Automobile Industry by Green in October 1934 after the removal of William Collins) endorsed the strike. The AFL officials warned that neither the company nor the public realized how serious the situation was in Toledo. Dillon indicated that conditions like those in Toledo existed elsewhere and suggested that the strike might spread, even to Detroit. The nine-man strike committee greeted the strikers, insisting that their cause was just—"On to an Organized Auto Industry."

The about-face by Dillon and Green contrasted with the weak position of the AFL in Detroit, where, lacking the organized force, the AFL refused to challenge any of the auto companies for union representation. In Toledo, of course, the local union, organized a year earlier, was able to lend material support and the practical experience it had gained in the Auto-Lite strike.

The prominent Chevrolet strike committee members and their political orientation were described thus by Henry Kraus:

> The Toledo Chevrolet strike was led by an extraordinary group of radicals, who were in revolt throughout its duration against the ultraconservative AFL

officials, particularly Francis Dillon. Its three outstanding leaders were James Roland, Robert Travis and Joseph Ditzel. Roland was unquestionably a disciple of A. J. Muste, cofounder of the American Workers Party, who was in Toledo through that entire period. Ditzel was an active Socialist Party member, Travis was unaffiliated despite later attempts to link him at the time to the Communist Party by what one might call "association by anticipation." I met Travis during the Chevy strike (as I did Roland, Kenny Cole, and other Chevrolet leaders) and saw him two or three times, once in my home, in the period directly following it. He never gave the slightest intimation that he was a Communist nor that he was a Musteite, either, however highly he praised Roland for his trade union know-how and guts.[8]

The local strike committee led by Roland had no difficulties with Dillon in the first days after the strike, but as the strike progressed their perspectives diverged sharply. The committee's primary objective was a signed contract with union recognition, never before granted by General Motors. The strike committee, strongly influenced by Muste, believed it was the right of the local union committee to make the decisions in the strike. This was an important lesson they had learned in the Auto-Lite strike of the previous year.

Muste himself considered the greatest threat to the strike to be internal—a view that influenced many strike leaders. Muste's record in support of labor strikes, dating back to the famous Lawrence textile strike of 1912, gave him stature in the strike. Muste opposed unions' reliance on government institutions to help settle strikes.[9]

Dillon shared the committee's objective regarding a contract. He, however, came from the school of unionism that looked for help from government agencies. He wanted the strike confined to Toledo; an enlarged strike would create political and organizational difficulties and make maneuvering difficult. Dillon "declared in a statement that once a strike conflagration started, 'you could never tell where it will go.'"[10] He worried, furthermore, that an enlarged strike would empty the International's coffers.

Dillon asked the local to arrange a meeting to vote on the GM proposals: this took place four days into the strike. In the meantime, the company shut down the plant and made no effort to hire replacement workers or to ship transmissions by railroad. The company adamantly refused to meet with Dillon and the strike committee until the workers returned to work. Art Preis, writing in the *New Militant*, claimed that the Chevrolet strike committee's publicity matched that of the corporation. Every GM press release was answered by the union. The publication of a strike newspaper was a first-time event for a Toledo union. It was a major effort to counter the propaganda of GM and the major newspapers.

Expanding the Strike

Without waiting for concurrence from Dillon, the strike committee sent telegrams, signed by Roland, to all the federal AFL locals in General Motors, asking them to strike for higher wages, seniority, and a signed contract. The telegrams urged the locals to remain on strike until all the demands were met and to inform Local No. 18384 of the results. Members of the committee were divided into groups, which took the strike message to other plants. The group that went to Detroit to distribute *Strike Truth* were arrested by the Detroit police.

In Norwood, Ohio, Roland's reception was friendly, but the GM workers there were hesitant to take action. He informed them they would be shut down for lack of auto parts: "Why don't you go on strike so that you are a part of it?" Two of the GM plants in Norwood were persuaded to strike. Then Roland made three trips to Flint. On the first visit, having been in town only two hours, he was arrested and put in jail. The police had warrants for his arrest on charges of armed burglary. Although they made no effort to make the charges stick, they nevertheless threatened to hold him for thirty days unless he left town immediately. On his second visit, he made speeches to groups of Buick workers. Joe Ditzel was with him on these visits and recollects:

> We wanted to expand the strike, and we even went up to Flint and talked to the leadership up there about striking some of the Flint plants. We met with their executive board up there. Later we were told that most of those we were meeting with on the executive board were stool pigeons. It was more or less a paper organization. When we left Flint that night, we sent Jimmy Roland out on the back roads back to town because we heard they were going to waylay him and he would come to great bodily harm. I know there were individuals around there looking for him then. Something might have happened to him if he had not. It was a member of the Teamsters Union who tipped us off to get him out of town by the back roads so nobody would find him.[11]

While Roland was carrying the message to the other GM plants in the region, he came under attack within Local No. 18384. A campaign of Red-baiting had begun after the arrival of Dillon. Fred Schwake, the local business agent, was under pressure from Francis Dillon and T. N. Taylor, representing William Green in Toledo. Local No. 18384, which controlled the funds of the amalgamated local, made the decision to cut off support for the publication of the Chevrolet strike bulletin. They wanted Art Preis removed as associate editor. Furthermore, in local meetings, conservatives in the amalgamated local made an effort to control the influence of the Chevrolet strike committee. On one occasion a small group of workers chased distributors of radical papers from the picket lines. The attack was directed primarily against the Communist Party. Art Preis wrote:

> Members of the Workers Party reported these reactionary actions to the Joint Action Committee, which immediately sent a strong protest to the strike committee and the union executive board. The Workers Party members continued to distribute leaflets in the name of our party, which were widely accepted by the strikers and read with keen interest. The strikers shortly made a distinction between W.P. literature and that of other groups...[12]

Meanwhile, General Motors took action in the second week of the strike to set up a transmission line in Muncie, Indiana. Most workers were not too concerned at this development: it would take months to bring a new plant into operation. More disturbing to the Chevrolet workers was GM's sponsorship of the company union, called the Independent Workers Association (IWA). The IWA held a meeting, which was attended by 1,600, the majority of whom approved the corporation's proposals submitted to the Chevrolet workers on the morning of the strike. The company union went further: it asked for a secret ballot of Chevrolet workers on the proposals to end the strike. The IWA concluded its meeting with a proposal to petition the government to conduct such a ballot on what it termed the company's "strike settlement concessions."

The Workers Party handed out leaflets mocking this latest GM-sponsored action:

> Where does this so-called workers society hold its meeting? In the Chamber of Commerce hall! In the stronghold of the bosses and bankers! In that Chamber of Commerce which President Roosevelt himself has just denounced and flayed as hopelessly reactionary.
>
> True, they could not have gotten a union hall for their anti-labor meeting. But they chose the Chamber of Commerce as a meeting place! Any doubt that this is nothing but a strike-breaking, anti-union move has been removed.[13]

The IWA soon announced the success of its petition campaign for a government-backed ballot, claiming that over half the signatures were from GM employees. Dillon urged the strike committee to accept the

IWA proposal but insisted the vote be conducted by the Department of Labor. Roland's strike committee acquiesced in this action; nevertheless, it maintained that expansion of the strike was the surest way to a successful conclusion.

The Chevrolet Transmission strike crippled GM plants in several cities, as the plant was the source of gearboxes destined for Chevrolet and Pontiac cars. The first plants affected were the assembly plants in Atlanta, Kansas City, St. Louis, and Janesville. The press reported that another half-dozen plants were in danger of closing. It was clear that GM would suffer a major economic blow from the closure of the Flint Buick Plant. Consequently Roland tried to convince the union workers and their leaders to participate in the strike. He met with some encouragement. The leaders reacted to the attempt to shift transmission production to one of the plants in Pontiac, Michigan: the union workers indicated that while the Chevrolet Transmission strike was in progress they would not handle transmissions produced by a scab plant in Michigan. Dillon, nevertheless, persuaded the Buick union officials to refrain from taking action in support of Toledo until the Department of Labor vote was held.[14]

Betrayal

The Chevrolet strike committee concentrated on winning the vote conducted by the government. Prior to the vote, the Workers Party held a meeting attended by six hundred people. Muste, the main speaker, attacked Dillon's attempt to prevent the spread of the strike; however, he also emphasized the need for a strong vote in support of the AFL. As it turned out, the vote was a major victory for the AFL: 1,261 rejected the company's proposal; 605 were in favour. This was in sharp contrast to the response of the company union, which had accepted the offer. General Motors agreed to meet with the union, thereby reversing its previous stand of not negotiating with striking workers. In this second round of talks, however, the corporation again refused union recognition, though it made some small concessions. The committee voted eight to one to reject GM's terms.

Under pressure from Dillon, another membership meeting was called for May 13 to vote on the new company proposal. Before the meeting, the committee and Dillon had agreed that no public statement would be made. Dillon, however, broke the agreement and issued a press statement accepting the company's proposal and suggesting that the members of the strike committee were under the influence of "Reds." The meeting at first refused to give Dillon the floor. A motion was agreed that only strikers and members of the strike committee could speak. Dillon threw a tantrum and stormed from the hall, yelling that the charter of the local would be withdrawn. Writing soon after the strike, Muste said:

> Francis Dillon, leading A.F. of L. figure in the federal automobile unions, was barred from speaking last night, by unanimous vote, at the meeting of Chevrolet strikers called to consider a compromise settlement. Dillon had prevented the General Motors workers in Flint from coming out in support of the Toledo strikers and had even condoned their working on scab transmissions. A chorus of boos shook the rafters as Dillon stalked out of the hall and shouted that their A.F. of L. charter was withdrawn and that, if a personal reference may be made, they could "let Muste run their union for them."[15]

The leaders of the local were in fear of Dillon's threat to withdraw their charter. They pleaded with Roland to persuade the members to allow Dillon to speak. Roland gave way and George Addes went to the hotel to plead with Dillon to return to the meeting, assuring him that he would be heard. Three times the meeting booed Dillon, but finally the workers listened to his presentation for the acceptance of the GM proposal. He was now backed by Fred Schwake, who had supported the strike from the beginning, and who earlier in the day was reported to have said that he would rather lose an arm than advise the men to accept the company offer. Schwake's acceptance broke the united front of the local leadership and opened the door to a yes vote, even though Roland spoke against acceptance of the GM offer. Louis Stark, labor reporter of the *New York Times*, noted:

> Mr. Roland, disappointed with the vote to go back to work last night, tried to stem the tide but in vain. Today he went to the Chevrolet factory where some unauthorized pickets were stationed and ordered them to disband.[16]

Another meeting was held soon after the workers returned to work. Leaders of the local and representatives of the Central Labor Body denounced Dillon's role in the strike. A resolution passed by Local No. 18384 asked Green to remove Dillon.

General Motors, like the other auto corporations, recognized AFL locals without signing a contract. The company union soon disappeared. A series of small strikes subsequently facilitated the resolution of the problems in the plant. Yet GM had the last word: within a year, the company had transferred production to the Muncie plant, cutting the Toledo workforce by half.

For all their weaknesses, the Toledo Chevrolet workers, led by a group of class-conscious—indeed, Socialist—leaders, broke new ground. In doing so, they set the stage for what would be the classic struggle of the 1937 sitdown strikes. Auto workers owe a considerable debt of gratitude to Roland, Ditzel, and Travis.

Chapter 3

Homer Martin Leads the UAW

> History does nothing, it possesses no immense wealth, fights no
> battles. It is rather man, who does everything, who possesses and
> fights.
>
> Karl Marx and Friedrich Engels, *The Holy Family*

The Toledo Chevrolet Transmission strike convinced William Green,
president of the American Federation of Labor, to establish an international auto workers' union. To accomplish this a convention was held
in Detroit on August 25, 1935. Toledo delegates, the largest group in
the convention, were joined by a majority in demanding agreement on
two principles. They insisted on an industrial union covering all workers
in the factory. Equally important to the delegates was the right to elect
their own officers. The debate on the latter was fractious, with many
of the Toledo delegates threatening to walk out when Green overruled
a request for a democratic vote and reappointed Francis Dillon as
president. Among the other appointees was Homer Martin, former
president of the Kansas Chevrolet assembly plant.

Eight months later, on April 30, 1936, Dillon opened the second
convention, in South Bend, Indiana. Homer Martin was elected
president of the International Union of United Automobile Workers.
George Addes was elected secretary-treasurer. Elected to the board were
Wyndham Mortimer, president of the White Motor Company Cleveland union, and Walter Reuther, who would later take the lead in
organizing the large Detroit amalgamated Local No. 174. The International subsequently ended its affiliation to the American Federation
of Labor (July 1936) and joined the newly formed Committee for
Industrial Organization (CIO).

Mortimer was assigned the task of organizing General Motors. He
chose Robert Travis from the Toledo Transmission plant to head the
campaign in Flint, Michigan. Mortimer had been attacked as a member

of the Communist Party from his early effort in organizing the White
Motor Company; nevertheless his political beliefs were not a factor in
his appointment. Nor was any objection raised to his appointment of
Robert Travis to lead the General Motors organizing effort in Flint.
Travis's union experience consisted of his participation in the Toledo
Transmission strike of 1935 as a member of the strike committee led by
James Roland, and his later election as president of the local. Mortimer's
selection of Travis suggested a strong political affinity; however this
only became apparent during and after the sitdown strikes.

Sitdown Strikes at Flint, 1937

Another eight months on, and what would turn out to be historic
sitdown strikes erupted. They started in the Cleveland Fisher Body
plant and spread first to Fisher Body 2 on December 30, 1936, and
soon after to Fisher Body 1, both in Flint, Michigan. With the strike
deadlocked for a month, on February 1, 1937, the UAW moved boldly
to break the stalemate by capturing and sitting down in the Chevrolet
Motor Plant in Flint, Michigan, that supplied engines to the Chevrolet
assembly plants nationwide. On February 2 the corporation sought
injunctive relief. Judge Paul V. Gadola handed down a draconian ruling
against the Flint auto workers and demanded the evacuation of General
Motors' private property by the union. The penalty for unlawful occupation was $15 million, with enforcement left to the police forces of the
city, county, and state. Sheriff Tom Wolcott was dispatched to read the
provisions of the injunction to the sitdown strikers.

Robert Travis, the union strike leader, responded to the injunction
by calling for help from organized labor in Michigan and Ohio. Union
sympathizers rallied to Flint and formed a massive picket line around
the Fisher Body Plant on South Saginaw Street, which normally
employed eight thousand workers. Reinforcements duly came from
Detroit, Toledo, Pontiac, and Lansing. The mile-long picket line, six
abreast, surrounded the huge plant. Thousands of Flint spectators
watched the union pickets, who were armed with clubs, hammers, steel
bars, and other weapons. Political officials in the city and the state felt
the dramatic impact of the demonstration.

The Women's Auxiliary of Flint, about a thousand strong, and its
Emergency Brigade, organized by Genora Johnson after the Battle of
Bull's Run on January 11,[1] wore their red berets and distinctive EB
armbands. Women's Auxiliaries from other cities, also armed with

clubs, augmented the Flint Auxiliary. Flint's police force disappeared from the streets; the union maintained traffic control. Union women marched through downtown Flint, waving banners and shouting union slogans.[2]

John Barringer mobilized his small Flint force of 125 police, deputizing an additional 500 for a vigilante squad, many of them from the Pinkerton detective agency. He took this action when the governor failed to call for the mobilization of the State Police and the National Guard to evict the strikers from the Fisher Body plants. His action sent an ominous signal to the union. A similar event had led to the riots of the Electric Auto-Lite strike of March 1934. The lessons of the 1934 strike explain Travis's urgent call for help from outside labor forces.

Sidney Fine captures thus the chaotic events of February 3, 1937:

> When word spread in Flint that the municipal government was mobilizing a force of vigilantes that might eject the strikers, there was "near panic" in the city and considerable apprehension that the dreaded confrontation of striker and nonstriker was at hand. Strikers and strike sympathizers streamed back to Fisher Body No. 1 by the hundreds and once again took "complete possession" of the area. It was later to be alleged that the UAW had even stationed men armed with rifles in a room above the restaurant across the street from the plant.[3]

General Motors shied from the use of force and acted to restrain the city manager, John Barringer, who wanted the Flint police to evict the sitdowners. GM moved cautiously for fear of damage to property and life.

The writ issued by Judge Gadola hung like the sword of Damocles over the negotiations. The intense bargaining sessions continued for the next eight days, after the union had captured the Flint Chevrolet Engine Plant 4, with the participation of John L. Lewis and CIO officials, effectively closing down the GM Chevrolet operations. It was reliably reported that, behind the scenes, President Roosevelt urged a settlement. Although he avoided direct participation in the talks, he was in constant communication with Governor Frank Murphy.

At a later stage in the negotiations, Murphy showed Lewis a copy of the decree he had drawn up for the expulsion of the sitdowners from the plants. The Murphy decree was designed to induce further modifications of the union position, which was to be the sole bargaining agency for the sixty-nine GM plants. Early on, Lewis had modified the proposal and suggested recognition in only twenty of the corporation's auto plants.[4]

General Motors Recognizes the UAW

On February 11, 1937, a historic agreement was reached by the UAW and the General Motors Corporation. The settlement, set out on a single page, gave the union recognition as the bargaining agency for its members. The corporation agreed not to bargain with any other agency during the six-month agreement without the approval of Governor Frank Murphy. The intricate terms included an about-face by the corporation on its long-held and steadfast policy not to give the union exclusive bargaining rights. The corporation further agreed not to discriminate against any union member. All employees previously fired for union activity were reinstated in seventeen plants, which employed 105,000 workers. GM also agreed to meet five days later to bargain collectively over wages, hours, and working conditions.

The agreement was signed by Wyndham Mortimer, John L. Lewis, and Lee Pressman for the UAW. Homer Martin, president of the union, had been dispatched on a speaking tour to key auto centers early in the negotiations. No effort was made to delay the signing of the agreement until Martin returned. He was not happy with this slight to his office and authority. Universal praise was heaped on Governor Murphy for arranging a peace without bloodshed. A cautionary observation came from the *New York Times* reporter Russell Porter, writing three days later, that the pact "was not a peace from a long-range view but a truce."

General Motors, which had misread the new social relations in the country, and was accustomed to making policy without consulting with an outside entity, had reluctantly conceded in order to get its employees back to work. The corporation had no notion that the strike would begin a social upheaval that ultimately would transform all future labor relations.

The sitdown phenomenon caught the imagination of the working class. Strikes spread like a firestorm, sweeping out of Flint into Detroit and across the country. The media trumpeted new strikes in a variety of industries. A month later the Steel Workers Organizing Committee reached a pact with US Steel covering 250,000 steel workers.

Obviously US Steel and General Motors drew different conclusions from the strike wave. When the negotiations for implementing the agreement at GM were under way on February 16, the corporation made it clear that its policies had not changed; it intended no significant concessions. GM rejected the union proposal for a steward system;

it would allow only five committeemen in small plants and nine in large plants. The result was that an informal steward system developed without corporation recognition. The failure to arrange a formal grievance procedure would come back to haunt the corporation. The position of GM seemed bolstered by editorials in major newspapers, which reviewed the contract signed by the auto corporation and concluded that the union had failed to achieve its goal in the epic strike. John L. Lewis lost no time in responding to the union critics:

> The situation boils down to this—seven weeks ago General Motors would not deal with or recognize a labor union—it never had and it had publicly proclaimed it would not do so in the future. Now, after seven weeks it has made a contract that is entirely satisfactory and that paves the way for an adjusted relationship in the industry that is rational and constructive.[5]

The Flint workers were empowered by the sitdown strike. In the absence of a formal procedure, the workers in a department simply pulled the switches and sat down, and within minutes the plant had stopped work. A long, involved process of negotiation became unnecessary: foremen and supervisors found an immediate solution to the grievance in order to get the men back to work. Hundreds of these quickie strikes occurred in the five Flint GM Plants. This was not the bargaining process that GM understood, and the company's executives insisted that Homer Martin enforce union discipline and bring an end to the local strikes.

An End to the United Front

Victory brought a rapid increase in membership. When the sitdown strikes began, the UAW had only a few thousand members among the forty thousand GM workers. The strike was won through a united front of the leading political groups: Communists, Socialists, Lovestoneites, and followers of the Proletarian Party. Nevertheless the quickie strikes contributed significantly to the internal union conflict that threatened the UAW in the spring of 1937. The pact signed on February 11 by the union and General Motors Corporation brought an end to the undeclared united front. In a matter of a few weeks the muted dissension, the submerged political differences, surfaced and erupted into political warfare that in two years would lead to a split in the union, the ousting of Homer Martin as president of the UAW–CIO, and the ascent of Walter Reuther.

Red-baiting had not been an effective weapon while the left tendencies were united. After the strike, however, the Martin group made
Communists in the union the big bugaboo. Many Martin followers in
Flint and elsewhere were only too ready to keep Communists from the
leadership. Their largest concentration was in Chevrolet Plant 9, which
was led by Ted LaDuke, and in Fisher Body 1, which was led by Bert
Harris. Whereas LaDuke was motivated by political solidarity with
Lovestone, Harris was a conservative—fighting the Reds in the union
was his anthem and battle cry. The two made strange bedfellows.

Martin was politically incapable of dealing with the UAW Communist and Socialist union forces. He was an expert on the Bible and had
been a Baptist minister before becoming an auto worker in a Kansas
GM plant. As an eloquent speaker, Homer had great appeal for the
southern migrants who worked in the auto plants of the north. Although he could quote chapter and verse with the best, he had only
begun to learn the lexicon of Socialists and Communists. Bert Cochran
worked closely with Homer Martin during one period of the union's
factional struggle. This is his description:

> He was an orator of the evangelical, stem-winding school, and had some of
> the talents associated with the public orator—facile intelligence, flashiness,
> an ability to draw fire from an audience, and an actor's adaptability to alter-
> ing circumstances. In the formative period, his popularity with the ranks, his
> image of ex-minister devoted to the cause of social justice, were invaluable
> assets to the young struggling union.[6]

Cochran's own rise to prominence in the UAW resulted from leading
several auto union locals under contract with the Mechanics Educational Society of America to break away and join the UAW. He played
a significant role in the hectic factional period that marked Homer
Martin's administration. He was a counterbalance to the Lovestone
forces in the UAW.

The Role of Jay Lovestone

Lovestone advised Martin to keep organizational control firmly in his
own hands. His authority stemmed from his majority on the UAW
Board; yet he was aware that his opponents in Detroit and Flint con-
stituted a formidable force in the union. Flint Local No. 156 was the
largest in the International and a battleground for the opposing groups.
Martin's opponents controlled Local No. 156. Lovestone advised Martin
to wrest control of the local from the SP and CP leaders.

Martin's working relation with Lovestone was apparently established as early as March 1937. This aspect of the union war was hinted at by Martin's employment of known Lovestoneites but was not officially confirmed until much later in the factional battle. Martin first moved discreetly by replacing Henry Kraus with William Munger as the editor of the *United Automobile Worker*, the official paper of the International Union, following with a number of other administrative changes. Eve Stone was put in charge of the women's department; George Miles coordinated activities in Flint and worked to counteract the influence of Bob Travis and Roy Reuther. The new appointees were followers of Lovestone; none had worked in the auto industry.

Jay Lovestone's critical role in the UAW remained murky for some time; the full impact of his actions would not be understood until 1939. Many top union leaders knew that Lovestone had been a founding member of the Communist Party and much later elected to the post of national secretary. He directed the expulsion of the followers of Leon Trotsky from the Communist Party. In 1929, while in Moscow for the sixth world congress of the Comintern, Stalin engineered Lovestone's removal from office and would not permit his departure from the USSR until this had been achieved. On his return Lovestone organized a new group called the Communist Party Opposition, and later the Independent Labor League of America.

The new appointments that Martin made, especially those directed against UAW Local No. 156, left the opposition in no doubt that they faced a bloody struggle with Martin, who controlled all the union levers. While the opposition leaders were aware of the Lovestone–Martin connection, the vast majority of the membership knew little of the left-wing politics involved. They had no understanding of the political divide that arrayed the two union groups against each other; nor did they know that the Martin–Lovestone connection came about soon after the sitdown strikes in Chrysler in March 1937.

One of Lovestone's top lieutenants, Charles Zimmerman of the International Ladies Garment Workers Union and a vice president of the union, was to make the political transition from supporter of Lovestone to loyal supporter of David Dubinsky. Dubinsky, president of the ILGWU, and Lovestone both became advisers to Homer Martin. They showed a fear of the Communist Party that bordered on paranoia. That fear was reinforced by the Moscow show trials, at which Stalin framed and executed the leaders of the Russian Revolution. Paradoxically, those far-off events reverberated in the ranks of the political leaders of the UAW. Although the crisis of leadership in the UAW remained focused on the continuing strikes in the Michigan plants, international politics contributed to the problem of controlling the auto workers, who resisted the efforts of the top brass to restrain them in their relations with the auto corporations.

In March 1937, sixty thousand Chrysler workers sat down in the plants. The union submitted demands similar to those proposed to General Motors a month earlier. The settlement, also similar to the GM agreement, did not meet with the approval of the Chrysler workers, however. Chrysler's company unions had affiliated en masse to the UAW in 1936; the UAW now claimed to represent 95 percent of the workers in the plants. Communist Party executive board members and chief stewards were particularly strong in some of the plants and actively opposed the settlement. When the Chrysler plants had been occupied for two weeks, Lewis and the top leaders of the Communist Party prevailed on the workers to leave the plants; however, some Communist militants dragged their heels. The delayed departure from the plants gave Martin the opportunity to charge that Communists were preventing the union agreeing to a contract.

Meanwhile, the struggle in General Motors continued, adding to the maelstrom. Strikes had broken out repeatedly in Flint—the corporation claimed 160 as the number from February to June. Martin, for his part, attacked the Flint CP and SP leaders.[7] The UAW president assured GM that he intended to bring the leaders of these strikes under control. Martin appointed an interim committee of five to guide the affairs of the Flint local until the UAW Milwaukee convention in August 1937. Three of the five were from the Martin caucus. Anticipating that Roy Reuther would be removed from the Martin staff, motions were presented and carried to place Roy on the payroll of Flint Local No. 156.

In an effort to gain control of the Flint UAW Local No. 156, the largest local in the international union, Martin's supporters launched an attack on Bob Travis after the strike contract settlement, accusing him of Communist Party affiliations. However, Martin's caucus had a difficult time with the attacks on Bob Travis's CP membership because of his reputation with the auto workers. Since his success in obtaining a contract for the workers with the corporation, his standing had never been higher. In fact, Bob's political affiliation to the Communist Party was not revealed until many years after the strike. His popularity with all of the contending political factions was due to his ability to make sound union decisions and to work in harmony with his political opponents.

Roy Reuther, for his part, was one of the prominent Socialist Party members in Flint. He assisted Bob Travis in leading the strike. Roy was an excellent speaker, much more proficient on the platform than Travis; consequently he became the spokesperson for the union at the many public meetings. Roy came to Flint in October 1934 to teach as part of a government program. A year later his classes were terminated under a government probe instigated by General Motors. During this year in Flint he met many GM workers in his classes; this gave him a head start as a leader of the strike. The association of Travis and Reuther in the strike unified the two largest largest left-wing factions in Flint.

Lovestone's Flint supporters launched a furious attack on Travis, who was referred to as the leader of the Communist Party. His most prominent supporters in Fisher Body 1—Bud Simons, Walter Moore, and Joe Devitt—were also branded as Reds. They never denied their party affiliation. These three had led the sitdown strike in Fisher Body. Four months later their slate was defeated in an election and the conservative, Red-baiting Bert Harris slate swept into office. This was now Martin's strongest base in Flint.

Lovestone enjoyed strong support in Chevrolet Plant 9, which was represented by Ted LaDuke, Tom Klasey, and Melvin Center. Nevertheless, the Lovestoneites faced a more difficult situation in Chevrolet than in Fisher. The leaders of the anti-Martin forces were Socialists: Roy Reuther, Kermit Johnson, Genora Johnson, Bill Roy, and a score of secondary plant leaders. The CPers had not played a major role in the strike, and the anti-CP propaganda didn't carry the weight that it had at Fisher Body. It was difficult for LaDuke to attack the Socialists when he himself had been in the Party just a few days before the beginning of the strike.

Before the strike the left had been united against the common corporate enemy. Yet, as the political tendencies in the union subsequently contested for power, the struggle surfaced and exploded with enormous force. The ongoing factional struggle in the UAW was perceived in the country at large as the workings of a fractious, cantankerous democratic organization. This image remained etched in the mind of the country and gave the union the resolve to confront crises and overcome them. The members were not alienated from leaders: both were engaged in fighting for a cause they deeply believed in.

Chapter 4

Factional Warfare Breaks Out, 1937–1938

> Workingmen unite
> We must put up a fight,
> To make us free from slavery
> And capitalistic tyranny;
> This fight is not in vain,
> We've got a world to gain.
> Will you be a fool, a capitalist tool?
> And serve your enemy?
>
> E. S. Nielson, *IWW Industrial Union Handbook*

C. E. Wilson maintained a drum-beat attack on the union for its inability to control the rash of departmental sitdown strikes in Chevrolet and the other General Motors plants. Homer Martin, in response to Wilson, averred that it was the left's intention to embarrass him and his leadership of the union. Furthermore, he wrote to GM president William Knudsen, promising to bring to an end these strikes by "certain elements."

Martin organized the first meeting of the Progressive caucus in June 1937. Its goal was to centralize control of the union, deal with the wildcat strikes, and replace Wyndham Mortimer and Ed Hall with Richard Frankensteen and R. J. Thomas as vice presidents of the union. Only a change in the constitution at the August 1937 Milwaukee convention could accomplish these changes.

The Unity caucus, organized in response to the meeting of the Progressive caucus, was headed by George Addes, Mortimer, the Reuther brothers, Big John Anderson of Local No. 155,[1] Nat Ganley, Bob Travis, Emil Mazey, Kermit and Genora Johnson, and many others. Its program also called for the control of unauthorized strikes. It stood for the re-election of all the top officers. Not much separated the two platforms. The major conflict was over the president and vice presidents of the union.

Left over from the February sitdown strike were felony charges against Victor Reuther, instigated by General Motors, for his leadership in repulsing the police attack at the Fisher Body 2 plant. GM dropped the charges against Roy Reuther and Bob Travis. UAW Flint Union Local No. 156 let the city officials and the corporation know that all hell would break loose should they try to convict and jail Victor. Roy and Kermit led the campaign to prevent Victor's imprisonment. Two days before the trial, they organized a demonstration of some forty thousand in Kearsley Park—the largest labor demonstration ever held in Flint. When the corporation and the court saw the massive scale of the campaign that led to the demonstration, they dropped the charges. Short work stoppages in the plants mobilized support for Victor. Genora Johnson, reflecting on the events of 1937, made this observation of Kermit's role:

> Kermit was the chairman of the Chevrolet Division of Local 156 up until the time that the local separated into its component parts according to the factories in Flint. They had met at divisions, they had division meetings of the Chevrolet workers, division meetings of the Buick workers, but they were called Buick Division of Local 156. Kermit was the chairman of the Chevrolet Division, and James Lamesfield, another member of the Socialist Party, was elected as secretary of the Chevrolet Division. He was the spokesman for all of the Chevrolet workers in Flint. He was a good speaker, immensely popular, naturally, with everybody in Flint after the heroic culmination of the strike.[2]

The Flint demonstration was a small hiatus in the factional campaign: when the union was in trouble, the members rallied to support the institution and its leaders. Unified displays by the labor movement were rare during the period of factional fighting. Powerful forces were at work driving the groups apart.

For and Against Homer Martin

The observations of auto worker Clayton W. Fountain of Chevrolet Gear and Axle Local No. 235 shed light on the factional battle and the issues that separated the two groups:

> In the spring of 1937 I was drawn swiftly into the raging conflict between pro-Martin and anti-Martin forces, particularly after I joined the Communist Party. It is difficult now to say just how much of that fight was due to a clash

of ideologies and how much was caused by a natural desire of young men for leadership in a youthful dynamic organization.[3]

Many other leaders in the factional battle also held these views. Bert Cochran of Cleveland was the leading Trotskyist in the auto union. In March 1936 the Troskyists were members of the Socialist Party, a sojourn that lasted about sixteen months. Then the leaders of the SP began a process of expulsion: they objected to the issues raised by the Trotskyists concerning the Civil War in Spain. Cochran and Little John Anderson of the Fleetwood unit in Local No. 174 steered an independent course but were more closely aligned with the Martin caucus. Their effort to maintain an independent policy brought them into conflict with the CP-dominated Unity group.

The Trotskyist auto faction looked with disfavor on the political line of the CP, its support of the Moscow show trials, its support for capitalist politicians like Murphy and Roosevelt, its efforts to join with Homer Martin in curbing local union independence, and the endeavor to centralize control over local unions and their publications.

Within the Socialist Party faction there were also divergent views. In early 1937, Walter Reuther embraced the larger CP faction within the Unity caucus (led by George Addes). He saw eye to eye with both their union and their political policies. Emil Mazey, George Edwards, Ben Fischer, Bob Kantor, and even Victor Reuther did not like Walter's close association with the CP.

Much tacking and veering occurred in all the major groups fighting for the leadership of the UAW. Lines were not established with the rigidity later seen in the union. The problems were complex. Young militant union leaders, most of them in their twenties or early thirties, had no illusions and very few icons. They tried to make rational judgments fit the changing complex of forces.

The two camps were gearing up for the August convention. In Flint, the Martin administrators had delayed the elections. They feared early elections and sought to break up Local No. 156 into five separate locals. After several delays, the International Board of the UAW put off the final decision until after the convention. With the election of convention delegates, the Unity slate won overwhelmingly in all divisions except Fisher Body 1 in Flint. Roy Reuther headed the slate. It captured twenty-three of the twenty-five delegates in Chevrolet. The Buick delegation was even more solid for the Unity camp. Far from resolving the factional struggle, the Milwaukee convention postponed a final decision.

When the smoke cleared, the convention of 250 delegates divided 60 percent for Martin and 40 percent for the Unity caucus.

The strike issue had been the major focus of the two caucuses at the convention. The two political forces agreed that the International had to approve the right of a local to call a strike. Mortimer and Martin set out the procedure for strike approval in the convention debate. They insisted that a local had to obtain prior approval for a strike by letter or telegram to the International Union.

Delegate Coleman, an International representative, described the nub of the problem:

> Upon arrival on the West Coast I found the largest aircraft plant in the world out on strike with 50 signed-up members and 5,000 men working in the plant. That [strike] was called without the authority of the International Union, and since that time 347 men have been before the courts for committing a felony and taking possession of a plant by force.

This staff representative had already forgotten the lesson of Flint, just seven months after the "illegal" sitdown strikes that trampled the laws of private ownership of property. His concern was the failure of the newborn union to obtain strike approval before walking out, even though delay in seeking a vote would have resulted in the defeat of the strike.

Bert Cochran tried to protect the rights of locals from the high-handed bureaucrats, who were motivated primarily by their right to exercise authority:

> I think no one will question the fact that during the past year the overwhelming majority of strikes conducted by our union were in violation or at least not completely in accordance with the rules laid down in the constitution on strikes.

The remainder of Cochran's remarks defended the rapid strike action the local union considered necessary for a proper response. He counterposed the action of the local to the long, intricate process set out in the constitution requiring the vote of Board members scattered across the country.

Only the intervention of John L. Lewis and his appeal to the convention for a unified union compelled the Martin forces to compromise on the re-election of the four top officers. Lewis had saved the union temporarily. Nevertheless, the Board was to continue heavily weighted in favor of Martin.

Tactical Retreat

Some pre-convention business awaited action. Three months before the convention, the General Motors union council elected a seventeen-member committee to negotiate a new agreement. The February 11 pact would expire at the same time as the August meeting. This committee, dominated by the Martin forces, was inactive for many weeks because of the conflict over delegates. After the convention, they drew up their wish list of demands to be made to the corporation.

Negotiations did not get under way until fall, by which time a recession had taken hold in the auto industry. In Flint, employment dropped from 40,000 to 29,000. Many workers were put on a four-day week, and matters worsened by the end of the year. The union's demands—for a company-wide seniority system (the company to provide the union with the starting date of all employees; in the event of layoffs, the principle of "last in, first out" to apply), a steward system, a 35-hour week, and sole bargaining rights for the UAW—couldn't have been made at a worse time. The company responded with an emphatic no on all counts. John L. Lewis urged Martin to obtain a temporary agreement.

Martin reacted to the layoffs and Lewis's prompting by proposing to the International Executive Board that General Motors be given the right to fire leaders of wildcat strikes without the protection of the bargaining system. This the Board approved. Martin then presented an agreement he had negotiated with the corporation along these lines to the 280 GM delegates meeting in Detroit. They, however, unanimously rejected it, much to the chagrin of Martin and Reuther, who had expected support for the measure. The president duly withdrew the draft agreement, and he and the other top leaders beat a hasty retreat.

The leaders then tried to outdo each other in the militancy of their speeches to the delegates. They scurried to support a motion introduced by Little John Anderson, president of GM Fleetwood unit of the West Side Local No. 174:

> that all UAW Locals be called upon to hold special meetings on the following Sunday afternoon "establishing the authority of the union." This would be accomplished by proclaiming a "national labor day for General Motors" that would take the form of a short stoppage, the day and hour being kept secret until the last minute, when it would be announced by a strategy committee of Martin, Mortimer and Dowell. The plan met with instantaneous approval.[4]

During the weeks and months following the conference, auto production continued in sharp decline. Companies laid off over 300,000 auto workers. The UAW's loss of members and dues created a financial crunch that quietened the factional war and muted the militant local union leaders.

On January 29, 1938, *Socialist Appeal*, a Trotskyist newspaper, made the following critical observation of a joint resolution submitted by Frankensteen and Reuther to the UAW International Executive Board. The editorial took exception to the union's relinquishing basic rights concerning shop conditions to the corporation. The union, it claimed, had conceded to the company issues that covered some 75 percent of problems between employee and company:

> The union agrees that it is the responsibility of management to maintain discipline and efficiency in the shops; the right of the employer to hire, discipline, and discharge employees for cause is expressly recognized, subject to right of appeal through the grievance procedure.

The massive cutbacks in production and the corporations' unwillingness to make concessions to the weakened but still militant union had taken their toll.

The Ludlow Amendment

At the January 1938 UAW International meeting the Board unanimously adopted a resolution submitted by Homer Martin in support of the Ludlow amendment. The constitutional amendment, to be introduced into Congress by Louis Leon Ludlow, writer and reporter and member of the House of Representatives (1929–1949), called for a referendum on whether the country should go to war. It was an expression of the widespread opposition in the country to U.S. involvement. Among the more prominent leaders of the committee set up to support the amendment were John L. Lewis (president of the United Mineworkers Union) and Norman Thomas (titular leader of the Socialist Party).

It was revealed seven months later that the introduction of this issue was the brainchild of Jay Lovestone, considered by many to be a crafty, unprincipled maneuverer. Wyndham Mortimer received from Detroit attorney Maurice Sugar the Lovestone correspondence with Martin, which Lovestone claimed was stolen from his apartment some months before its public release by Unity caucus representatives. Apparently, an unknown person delivered the purloined material to Sugar's office receptionist.[5] The Lovestone supporters were intent on driving a wedge into the Unity SP faction, since Norman Thomas was a prominent backer of the committee supporting the Ludlow amendment.

On January 29, 1938, *Workers Age*, the official Lovestone publication, reported the ambiguous reaction of the Trotskyists to the Ludlow amendment as published in their paper, *Socialist Appeal*, edited by Albert Goldman.

> Possibly the pacifists of "socialist" persuasion will go to the root of the problem by presenting the bright idea of abolishing war by referring the question of the existence of capitalism to a referendum vote.

The appearance of this editorial comment suggested that the American Trotskyists opposed the Ludlow amendment. Leon Trotsky subsequently wrote to the leader of the SWP, indicating that while it was politically correct to explain that the Ludlow amendment could not end war, even if it passed through Congress, it was nevertheless tactically incorrect to oppose the campaign for the passage of the amendment. This new position was subsequently advanced by Bert Cochran, along with the Lovestoneites.

It would be a mistake to inflate the importance of this battle over the Ludlow amendment, which was not at the top of the auto workers' agenda, even though workers' and popular sentiment strongly opposed intervention into foreign conflicts. Workers had other, more pressing, problems to confront. The SP group, with exceptions, saw the amendment campaign as a maneuver by Lovestone.

The failure of Mortimer and other CP members to oppose the amendment in the International Board meeting raised hackles in the CP. The CP passed the word through the ranks that the People's Front policy required their faithful opposition to the antiwar amendment. A few SP supporters broke ranks with the SP party line to support Martin on the Ludlow amendment. The most prominent was Emil Mazey, president of the powerful UAW Local No. 212. Meanwhile, most of the SPers remained steadfastly opposed to Martin's union program. They were more concerned with mounting unemployment and General Motors' threat to cancel the contract, which, with extensions (new negotiations, due to take place in August, had been shelved), was not a great deal better than the one signed eleven months earlier.

Martin Outmaneuvered

In December 1937 Martin had appointed Richard Leonard as welfare director of the union. The unemployed union evolved into a Works Project Administration (WPA) auxiliary of the UAW. Extensive layoffs in auto manufacture crippled the union. Washington moved quickly to soften the blow by expanding the WPA, with work projects rapidly increasing. The Martin forces reacted to prevent these workers coming under the influence of the Workers' Alliance, then dominated by the Communist Party, even though the director, David Lasser, was a member of the Socialist Party. Leonard approved the setting up of WPA locals affiliated to the UAW.

In Flint at this time, a third to a quarter of the population of the city was on welfare. Kermit, laid off from Chevrolet, and Genora Johnson took the lead in establishing a UAW Unemployed and WPA Local No. 12; this achieved phenomenal success. The UAW dominated the unemployed movement and pushed the Workers' Alliance from the unemployed scene in Flint.

In March 1938 the UAW locals held elections for officers. This resulted in a great shift toward the Unity camp. A key local in Detroit was Dodge Local No. 3, Frankensteen's home local. Frankensteen interpreted the Unity victory as the beginning of the end for Homer Martin. Lured by the siren song of the CP, which promised him support in his quest for the UAW presidency, Frankensteen shifted his allegiance to the Unity caucus. Chrysler No. 7, the home local of R. J. Thomas, joined by Dodge and many other locals, switched from the Martin camp to the Unity caucus. The defeat of International Board members in key regions who supported Martin duly spelled the end of Martin's control of the union.

The only major defeat of the Unity caucus came in Flint, where Roy Reuther, John McGill, and Jack Little were in contention for the presidency of Local No. 156. Chevrolet nominated Reuther; the Lovestone forces supported Little, who was from the Chevrolet Parts and Service Plant 3. Buick local nominated John McGill, who ran in opposition to Reuther, although a member of the Unity caucus. McGill came in third, leading to a runoff election. Although McGill and the Buick group promised support to Reuther in the runoff, the vote suggests that they did not deliver. The vote also indicates that the CP break with Reuther at the April Michigan CIO convention was not a transitory act. Even though both the CP and Reuther opposed Martin, they were nevertheless in contention for the leadership of the caucus and the union.

Jack Little's win was contrary to the union-wide trend, as future elections would reveal. Before the year was over, Flint had shifted into the Unity camp. Roy Reuther was elected president of the Flint CIO Council, which represented all organized labor in the city.

Martin was dealt a further blow at the Michigan State CIO convention in April 1938. His Progressive caucus nominated Richard Leonard for secretary-treasurer, only to see Leonard shift his allegiance to the Unity caucus at the convention. Leonard's opponent, from the Unity caucus, was Victor Reuther. As a result of the March elections, Victor should have been elected without difficulty because of the massive shift from the Progressive to the Unity caucus. It did not happen. This is Clayton Fountain's description of the dramatic turn of events:

> I remember vividly how we comrades were hastily rounded up and called into a caucus to have the party strategy spelled out to us. William Weinstone and Bill Gebert were the commissars in command. All the party-line UAW-CIO leaders from Michigan were there. Thirty or 40 comrades of lesser rank, including myself, sat around listening while the powers of the Party gave us the line. Out of nowhere they came up with instructions to desert Vic Reuther and turn on the heat for Dick Leonard.[6]

Leonard was duly elected. The CP in the Unity caucus had double-crossed the Reuthers. Although Walter Reuther promised revenge, he did not immediately break with his CP allies. Ben Fischer, the SP organizer in Detroit, set forth the SP position:

> Socialists in the UAWA are opposed to a personal fight against Martin. They are ready to oppose Martin when he is wrong, and increasingly this means on the most crucial local and shop questions. Socialists will of course support Martin's war position since he follows the Socialist position.[7]

Chapter 5

A Program for Peace

And I will war, at least in words (and—should
My chance so happen—deeds), with all who war
With Thought;—and of Thought's foes by far most rude,
Tyrants and sycophants have been and are.
I know not who may conquer: if I could
Have such a prescience, it should be no bar
To this my plain, sworn, downright detestation
Of every despotism in every nation.

Byron, *Don Juan*

When Frankensteen and Leonard shifted their allegiance to the Unity caucus, Martin no longer had control of the UAW International Board. Nevertheless, at the May 1938 Board meeting, Martin submitted a twenty-point program drafted by Bert Cochran and others in the Progressive caucus; it was unanimously adopted. The program was designed to unite the warring factions in support of a policy to extend unionism to the rest of the auto and aircraft industries. It provided for the build-up of union funds to finance this drive and to extend the union campaign among the WPA workers. The program promised support of CIO policies and vigilant efforts to oppose anti-union legislation. It called for support of the Ludlow amendment. Finally it asked all International officers to assume responsibility for carrying out the program.

Late in the factional battle, Ben Fischer wrote a confidential report to the SP headquarters in Chicago. His observations show confusion and shifts in position by the major contending left-wing political groups:

Martin's attitude is extremely friendly now. He consults with us. He has recommended that Kermit Johnson be placed as a functionary in the Flint WPA auxiliary. He also recommends George Edwards as WPA director for Detroit, but George was forced to refuse this appointment for personal reasons.

> The general reaction to the board meeting has been a lessening of factional tension; more time to do work and relaxation from a year of factional strife by the Socialist forces. The CPO [Communist Party Opposition—Lovestoneites] is claiming that the SP has now switched its position and is supporting the program of the administration. The fact is that the administration is beginning to give some support to the program which has been advocated by the SP for some time.[1]

The twenty-point program, intended to moderate the factional fight, received the endorsement of Walter Reuther. Wyndham Mortimer and three Board members identified with the CP voted for the resolution. Although Cochran had a hand in drafting the program, it is difficult to discern his part precisely because he left no paper trail. Frank Marquardt cites some hearsay evidence regarding the Trotskyist position:

> I wonder how many UAW historians know that the Trotskyists were in the Homer Martin camp in 1938. I know how it happened: In the spring of 1938, Morris Field, then a UAW Executive Board member and International Education Director, asked me to accompany him to New York to meet union experts....
>
> But I soon learned that Field, who was then a Homer Martin supporter ... had another reason for making the trip to New York—a factional reason. He reported to Jay Lovestone.... Field contacted Jim Cannon, leader of the Trotskyists, and worked out a deal with him. Cannon insisted the Stalinists in the UAW had to be defeated at all costs and agreed that his group would help Martin. Cannon proposed that Bert Cochran, an able member of his group, be put on Martin's payroll.[2]

There are two problems with this story. Field surely visited Cannon, and Cannon would not have hesitated to convey his strong animus toward the CP in the UAW and in the rest of the world. First, Cochran had been employed by Martin months earlier. According to Erwin Baur, who had worked with Cochran in Budd Wheel and had a long association with him, Cochran had been hired and fired several times by Martin.[3]

Cochran had led the fight at the Milwaukee convention in August 1937 in defense of the local union's right to strike. This action was sure to have displeased all the top leaders of the UAW. In the fight between the Martin Progressive caucus and the Addes–Mortimer–Reuther Unity caucus, Cochran steered an independent course, even while employed by Martin.

James P. Cannon, national secretary of the Socialist Workers Party, wrote to the International Secretariat of the Fourth International on February 9, 1938, or soon thereafter:

The second item was the reinstatement of one of our comrades to his position as international organizer of the automobile workers' union at Cleveland. In the reactionary drive of the general executive board of the automobile workers' union, he was removed from his position as international organizer about three weeks ago. Thereupon the locals in his district raised such a furor, bombarded the national office with so many truculent resolutions of protest, that they were compelled to reinstate him in his position.... The comrade, who is still a very young man—only twenty-four years old—got his political education in our New York movement.[4]

This is the second reason that Marquardt's account is off target. The course of action taken by Cochran was followed by Mazey while in the Unity caucus. Fortunately for the union in those days, factional lines were much more fluid than they became when the union was bureaucratized. The union militants—and there were many of them—tried to find some room for maneuver between the two power camps.

There is evidence that Marquardt was misled as to the role of the Trotskyists in auto. A leaflet signed by five unions appeared late in the factional struggle: three were associated with Cochran in Cleveland and two with Little John Anderson in Detroit. The unions were Williard Storage Battery Local No. 88, Weatherhead Local No. 463, Baker-Raulang Local No. 451, Fleetwood Fisher Body Local No. 15, and McCord Radiator Local No. 210. The document indicts the two caucuses:

The UAW faces the worst crisis of its history. Will it destroy itself and bring back the open shop? Or will it survive the crisis and go forward as a fighting organization to improve and protect the interests of the automobile workers?

The answer to this question lies squarely in the hands of the rank and file of the union.

The two factions in the top leadership of the union, the Martin and the Unity groups, accuse each other of betraying the interests of the automobile worker.

It is our considered judgment that the record shows that BOTH OF THESE ACCUSATIONS ARE TRUE![5]

A Widening Rift

Peace and harmony didn't last very long. It ended at the June International Board meeting. For the first time, the Board overturned Martin on a ruling concerning a union insurance program. Martin adjourned the meeting and reconvened it six days later at the headquarters of John L. Lewis. At this meeting Martin accused the opposition of voting for the twenty-point program but having no intention to follow through on the platform. He accused them of violations of the accord intended to slow down the factional struggle. After two days of discussion, Martin suspended Addes, Frankensteen, Mortimer, Hall, and Wells. Martin's press release explained the reason for his action:

> The actions of Richard Frankensteen and his associates in opposing the policies of the UAW administration have come as a complete surprise to us.
> It is an indication of extreme bad faith inasmuch as the last Board meeting unanimously approved and signed a 20-point program to end factionalism in the union....
> When this present Board session first convened Wednesday, the opposition took advantage of the fact that several Board members were absent and tried to stage a coup.

Addes, the International Union's secretary-treasurer, responded by instructing the banks that UAW bank checks required his signature and one other, thereby curtailing the cashing of checks by Martin. Addes further advised the locals to send per-capita dues payments to an escrow account he was setting up. Reuther's local continued to send its dues payments to Martin. Emil Mazey wanted all the top officers thrown out for creating this crisis.[6]

At this time, the Lovestone–Martin correspondence referred to in Chapter 4 was exposed in a blockbuster 23-page document, signed by the suspended officers, indicting Homer Martin as a puppet of Lovestone. The communications between Martin and Lovestone revealed that Martin had followed Lovestone's suggestions from March 1937 until the suspensions of secretary-treasurer Addes and vice presidents Frankensteen, Mortimer, Wells, and Hall. Furthermore, Lovestone had asked Martin to employ key Lovestoneites, and Martin had obliged with the hiring of fifteen in key positions. The revelations of the Lovestone correspondence doomed the Martin forces. As a consequence, the local elections in March 1938 catapulted the Unity caucus into leadership in the factional fight.

Over the summer, the Unity caucus struggled to find a solution to the union rift. A caucus meeting was held in Toledo, the largest ever held by the Unity group; its broad representation assured the Unity caucus of union domination. Reuther and Mazey opposed the call for a special convention. Addes and Frankensteen, for their parts, wanted mediation by John L. Lewis. The latter course was the one chosen by this unusually large gathering of locals.

Lewis sent in CIO monitors Philip Murray and Sidney Hillman, who ordered the reinstatement of the suspended officers. The Board reaffirmed the twenty-point program. The joint statement of Murray and Hillman cut close to the bone:

> Underlying the agreement is the realization that the factional differences in the U.A.W. are, for the most part, due to outside influences. This agreement is aimed at driving from this union for all time those influences, whatever may be their name or whatever their source.

The Board approved the dismissal of key staff supporters of Martin, major Lovestoneite personalities. Among them were William Munger, editor of the *United Automobile Worker*; Eve Stone of the Women's Auxiliary; Bill Taylor of the WPA auxiliary; and Francis Henson, Homer Martin's personal secretary. With the UAW International Board now firmly in control of the Unity caucus, a tight rein was kept on Martin. All press statements had to be reviewed before publication.

In the fall of 1938, Richard Frankensteen and Walter Reuther ran as independents for the City Council in Detroit—a class political expression that mushroomed with the rise of industrial unionism. Throughout the Midwest, Labor's Non-Partisan Leagues (LNPL) sprouted, as leaders of the union movement sought to bring into the political field what they had learned in fighting the industrial corporations' solid control of the two-party political and legal system.

Murphy campaigned for re-election in Michigan; he denounced the sitdown strikes. The CP and the SP had diametrically opposed political positions regarding support for capitalist politicians. The CP found it necessary to choke down political support for Democrats and Republicans following the violent shootings that smashed the Little Steel Strike.[7] John L. Lewis, for different reasons, espoused support of the LNPL. His views expressed the yearning of workers to support class-based politics.

Open Warfare

The election campaign had interrupted the factional conflict, which resumed in earnest when the International Board of the UAW learned in January 1939 that Martin was in negotiation with the Ford Motor Company. When asked to report on the nature and progress of these negotiations, Martin suspended fifteen Board members, accusing them of attempting to turn over the membership, books, and property to the

CIO just as he was about to conclude a deal with Ford. He claimed that Ford had agreed to reinstate six hundred fired workers, although he could not back up this assertion.

This was the last curtain call for Martin. In March 1939 the UAW arraigned Martin on charges, with R. J. Thomas serving as temporary president until the Cleveland convention on March 27. The Martin convention, held three weeks earlier, represented a corporal's guard compared with the CIO convention that followed. The split was fought out in union halls and in the streets with fists, clubs, and blackjacks. Genora Johnson Dollinger was witness to the fight at Fisher Body, a Martin stronghold. The Martin and the Thomas–Addes headquarters were across the street from the plant. Just a few doors down were the rented offices of the Red-baiting ultra-right Flint Bert Harris group, supporters of Martin. Groups of supporters of both camps fought in front of the halls. In one violent confrontation, the police aided the Martin group. On one occasion the Harris group tried to invade the CIO office. Clayton Carpenter, the first financial secretary of Fisher Body 1, ordered the stairwell to be piled high with chairs and desks to keep the invaders from reaching the second floor of the building. Genora found lye in the rear of the hall, which she combined with a pail of hot water:

> When you see a mob mood, it can mean death. To talk about it now, you don't really appreciate that, unless you're right in the middle of it. There is no reasoning when mobs go into action on the basis of emotion alone.... We filled up this pail of hot lye water and we dumped it out the window. I remember one of the policemen, it hit right down his right sleeve. He jumped out of the way.... For the time being, it did deter anybody else because they didn't know how many pails of hot lye water we had up there ... the police knew they had to act a little less biased.[8]

The action in union halls around the country was in defense of the Unity group headquarters. The Addes–Thomas forces controlled most of the headquarters; the Martin forces had residual strength in Detroit, Lansing, and Flint. The division of the union into the two groups led to the staging of separate conventions. Consequently the two groups jockeyed for the election of delegates to the two opposing conventions from January until March. Homer Martin's supporters duly met in Detroit, while the Unity Thomas–Addes group convened in Cleveland. When the smoke of battle had cleared, the Cleveland convention represented the overwhelming majority of UAW workers. The left forces in the union had won a great victory.

The delegates to the UAW Cleveland 1939 convention amended the constitution, first, to ensure the rights of the locals, making a two-thirds vote necessary to revoke the charter of a local union. Second, it was agreed that an administrator over a local could serve in that capacity for only thirty days, after which a new vote of the local had to be held by the administrator. Finally, whereas Martin had threatened locals that published their own newspapers, the convention encouraged the activity. Furthermore, at the suggestion of CIO monitors Hillman and Murray, the convention voted to eliminate the vice presidents, thereby striking a blow against the CP; this resulted in the elimination of Mortimer as a top officer of the union. Conservative CIO leaders had set a pattern of intervention that Emil Mazey, Walter Reuther, and other militants had fought to prevent. Suspicious of outside CIO interference from Hillman, Murray, and Lewis, they opposed it early and often. The CP had sought CIO intervention: they now paid a devastating price for it.

Reuther was elected to the Board and put in charge of the General Motors division, a huge reward by Thomas for Reuther's support after Thomas was selected to replace Martin. Reuther, as a consequence of his calculated maneuver, was now in a position to determine policy as the leader of the largest division in the UAW. More important, Reuther had climbed another important rung on the ladder that would in due course lead to the presidency of the UAW.

The Bureaucratic Impulse

Though Martin and Reuther had traveled quite different roads during this two-year period, in fact their journeys to the same ardently sought goal bore many similarities, ironic as this may seem. The situation can perhaps best be explained with an analogy. In the USSR, it was Stalin, an old Bolshevik and steadfast supporter of Lenin, who ultimately effected the destruction of Lenin's leading Central Committee and deserted Lenin's policies abroad. Reuther, for his part, fought under the banner of greater democracy for UAW members, and yet he became the instrument in the establishment of a tight restrictive union subject to the rule of one person. This, paradoxically, was in contrast to the Homer Martin era, with its galaxy of talented leaders in both the locals and the International Union.

Reuther and Martin shared the desire to muzzle independent local union papers. Whereas Martin failed in this effort, Reuther made the papers toe the line. When a local challenged his rule, he brought it to heel with the threat of appointing a receiver over the local. Similarly, Martin sought a centralized union with the authority to call and prevent strikes, particularly wildcat strikes. Yet neither Martin nor R. J. Thomas ever succeeded in this. Walter Reuther, however, was to bring the union under control in the early years of his presidency.

The UAW had been unique in its creation of a climate where any member could present an idea and advance it from his local all the way to the International UAW convention and receive a fair hearing. Every member under Martin felt he had a stake in the union and its affairs. Reuther, though, imposed a straitjacket over rank-and-file initiative. Workers consequently became alienated from the union as simple payers of dues.

Homer Martin tried to control and subdue his political opposition. He failed. Reuther, admittedly with the help of outside forces that came under the label of McCarthyism, did succeed in eliminating all left-wing opposition. What Martin and Reuther had in common was the bureaucratic development of their careers. Although both men reached their ultimate objective, to become president of the most dynamic union in the country, neither man had a larger vision that embraced using the union as a fulcrum to create social change which would benefit the nation as a whole.

Chapter 6

R. J. Thomas Elected Leader as Recession and War Preparations Hit

No sane man can be satisfied with the present system. If a poor man is happy he is the pick-pocket of happiness. Only the rich and noble are happy by right. The rich man is he who, being young, has the Rights of old age; being old the respect of good people; a coward, the command of stout-hearted; Doing nothing, the fruits of labor.

Victor Hugo, *The Man Who Laughs*

The battles for unionization engaged tens of thousands of rank-and-file auto workers, who volunteered hours, days, and weeks of superhuman, self-sacrificing activity. After their normal shift work, these union warriors waged a battle against the country's biggest corporations. They braved corporation thugs, private hired felons, thousands of Pinkerton agents, police and state troopers armed with weapons ranging from blackjacks to machine guns. Large numbers of workers were beaten; many were wounded and hospitalized.[1]

What motivated these militants to make sacrifices far beyond narrow self-interest? We know from the history books and other publications about this epoch-making decade that the leaders were politically class-conscious Socialists, Communists, Lovestoneites, Trotskyites, and members of the Proletarian Party. Yet the contribution of the thousands who were *union-conscious* has not been reviewed with the same effort by the labor historians. Without the selfless and courageous contribution of rank-and-file workers, the unions would never have achieved success. Yet not all the workers in the movement were simply rank and file. Many were leaders in their local unions. Though they had not pursued a radical political association, they had earned their battle stripes in scores of labor battles years, even decades, before the sitdown strikes. They may not have originated policy, but they were certainly a major influence in its execution or in obstruction of unpopular policy. They served as local union presidents, shop committeemen, and members of the union flying squads. The membership of the flying squad varied from local to local. Budd Wheel Local No. 306, for instance, had written by-laws restricting membership to fifty. A recommendation for membership required a two-thirds vote. The objective of the squad was the defense of UAW Local No. 306, to assist in the defense of other unions; "against any and all anti-labor attacks; ... to organize, maintain and protect picket lines during strikes." Members wore cap, shirt, and uniform bearing the insignia of UAW Local No. 306.[2]

Key Players

In this chapter I shall in part examine the role of the leaders of the larger UAW locals, those whose members numbered in the thousands. Sometimes a small local generated an exceptional leader, such as Frank Donoly, president of Motor Products Local No. 203; Paul Silver, president of Detroit Steel Products Local No. 351; Bill Jenkins, president of Chrysler Local No. 490; and Art Hughes, president of Dodge Truck Local No. 140. These were among the salt-and-pepper cadre of leaders that spiced the upsurge of the UAW. They were key players in the defense of the union, particularly during the war years. Generally, however, the leaders were in the larger locals of the International Union; and it is these that will feature in this chapter.

Unlike the mineworkers, led by the autocratic John L. Lewis with his appointed district leaders, the auto workers' organizational drive was a great volunteer movement unparalleled in the history of labor. The UAW contended with the spontaneous outbreak of union strikes in hundreds of cities across the land. The Midwest was aflame with strikes. Strike activity spread like wildfire as the few top leaders tried to harness the rampaging industrial union movement.

The emerging UAW, coming out of the factional struggle that marked its early years, deposed its first president, Homer Martin, and elected R. J. Thomas in his place. The Unity caucus, of which Thomas was the nominal compromise leader, comprised two disparate political tendencies: the Addes–Frankensteen group, strongly influenced by the Communist Party; and Walter Reuther and his supporters. Reuther was formerly a member of the Socialist Party; many of his supporters remained in the party. In time, the demarcations between the two political groupings within the union would be slight.

One early participant in the affairs of the union, Bert Cochran, made the following observation, a view that was shared by many:

Unauthorized strikes, union discipline, constitutional powers of the inter-national leadership—the three were interwoven, into what one might assume was the one issue of substance dividing the Unity and Progressive caucuses. Any straightforward debate was precluded, however, because both factions succumbed to demagoguery, with the result that programmatic declarations became tactical expedients designed to solve the major question in their favor—the major question being who was going to run the show.[3]

When the consensus divided on votes, it was to gain small tactical advantages. However, on the strategic questions of the day brought into focus by the war, the principals remained united.

Victor Reuther indicates that the rupture in the Unity caucus, the consequence of its battle with Homer Martin, had emerged at the first Michigan CIO convention in 1938. The Progressive and Unity groups had agreed to support Adolph Germer for president. The Unity caucus recommended Victor Reuther for secretary-treasurer. Frankensteen, however, broke ranks and proposed Richard Leonard, president of the DeSoto local, for the post. It is a long-standing tradition that members of a labor caucus accept the majority vote decision. For Frankensteen to nominate Leonard, a strong supporter of Homer Martin, was a callous and shameful break with caucus discipline. During an interlude in the proceedings, Walter Reuther followed Dick Frankensteen from the room and found him closeted with William Weinstone and B. K. Gebert, prominent leaders of the Communist Party, and with the two leading CPers from the auto union, Nat Ganley and Big John Anderson. Victor Reuther described in detail what followed: Walter Reuther under-stood the significance of the meeting; it was a signal that the CP was casting its vote for Leonard.

> Walter exploded. "What are you bastards doing? Don't you realize you are going to destroy the Unity Caucus, which is the only thing that can save this union?"
> "We know what we're doing," Winestone [sic] replied.
> "If you carry through with this double-cross, then count me on the other side, not only in this fight, but from here on out."[4]

Many in the Socialist Party had long been apprehensive about Walter Reuther's collaboration with the Communist Party. They disagreed with the CP on fundamental political policies. Kermit and Genora Johnson of Flint and other members of the SP had urged the party to run Walter Reuther for governor of the state on the SP ticket. Reuther, though, would have no part of these suggestions. He insisted on the party tail-ending his efforts to win the top job in the UAW. Bert Cochran writes:

> With an ex-Socialist like Reuther, ambition is colored by social awareness. Not that social awareness is permitted to inhibit the scramble for posts or the means used; one simply justifies or internalizes the scramble for the purpose of realizing higher social objectives, as an ecclesiastic might explain that his maneuvers are a means to realize the Deity's purposes.[5]

The Problem of Wildcat Strikes

A year after the union had won recognition, sporadic interruptions of production were a frequent occurrence in the General Motors plants. There was no established bargaining procedure to settle disputes. In the absence of a recognized steward system, the union faced the problem of creating a system for the election of official union representatives. Departmental workers found the quickest method of resolving a dispute: they sat down. Plant managers acted with alacrity to keep production running, and concessions brought a swift resolution of problems.

The workers harbored numerous long-term grievances. As "quickie" strikes multiplied, the corporation demanded that the union control these "anarchic" forces. When the time came around for a new contract in General Motors, the company's top priority was the banning of unauthorized strikes. The union, for its part, was eager to establish a recognized bargaining procedure: election of representatives, division of the plant into districts, time off from the job for the routine processing of the grievance, and an orderly procedure for conducting negotiations with the company.

It will be recalled that in the fall of 1937 Homer Martin had led the negotiations for a contract and brought back the results to the International Board of the UAW. The contract gave the corporation the right to sack wildcat strikers. Walter Reuther had joined with the other Board members in unanimously approving the proposals. This, however, was contrary to the position of his home local. Amalgamated Local No. 174—which covered three GM plants: Cadillac, Fleetwood (which made bodies for Cadillac), and Ternstedt—proceeded to wage an intensive campaign against the agreed contract in the local union paper. The GM union local members were incensed over the bureaucratic decision that a strike could take place only with the prior approval of the International Executive Board. The local unions wanted plant grievances thrashed out before strike authorization procedures were approved. They rejected the agreement and sent the negotiators back to the bargaining table with the corporation. This was the first of many times that Reuther would approve a measure, then reverse his position when his troops rebelled.

The tension between the large locals and the International Union over the locals' right to strike was to continue until Reuther was elected president for the second time in 1947. The top officials of the International believed that the power to declare and legitimize a strike was theirs alone. How they envied John L. Lewis and his union marching in lockstep as they did just before and during the war. The miners held out against the most intense anti-union barrage from the press, radio, politicians of both parties, and President Roosevelt. Roosevelt threatened to send in the army and to draft coal miners with a one-way ticket to the front lines. Lewis coolly told the president, "You can't mine coal with a bayonet."

The top UAW leaders coveted Lewis's aura and prestige but didn't understand that these came from great deeds, from leadership and success in great strike battles. Lewis broke the old boundaries of craft unionism, without which the CIO could not have made progress. He broke through in 1937 to gain a contract in coal that made the miners the most powerful union in that momentous year.

Organizing the Unemployed

In the period 1937–1940 few Flint auto workers were employed for a full year at a stretch. The layoffs usually came with the decline in sales in the months before a model change; this allowed for no stability in labor relations. However, even the most militant worker, though he might lack seniority, could gain protection from layoffs by being elected as an officer or committeeman. An agreement with the corporation put elected members of the shop committee at the head of the seniority list—a considerable further inducement to run for these coveted positions.

Those laid off sought work in the Works Project Administration. Every city had make-work programs. Until the eve of the war, with ten million unemployed, the Roosevelt administration could ill afford to stop these programs. When Roosevelt told the country that he would not send "our sons" to fight on foreign soil, many workers treated these "fireside chats" as mere propaganda: they could see the moves to rearm the country advancing with increasing tempo. In Flint, thousands were laid off, waiting for the conversion to war production. However, conversion did not happen at Buick or Chevrolet, the two biggest employers in Flint, despite the country-wide turn toward rearmament. To be without work, without financial reserves, and with no unemployment compensation, brought families to the edge of the abyss.

Ben Fischer, writing in *Socialist Call* (May 28, 1938), reported on the current unemployed crisis and the measure adopted by the UAW in the spring of 1938, pertaining to the thousands of auto workers now employed on WPA projects. The UAW International Board resolution, according to Fischer, "indicates a renewed determination on the part of the union to link the WPA workers, especially in Michigan, to the organized labor movement through a WPA auxiliary sponsored and backed by the CIO movement generally."

Kermit Johnson and thousands of others were laid off from Chevrolet and found employment on WPA. Genora and Kermit set out to organize the WPA projects and the unemployed of Flint. They affiliated the local with the UAW and were chartered by the International as WPA and Unemployed Local No. 12. Many Local No. 12 members learned their unionism at this time; some later became prominent leaders in the UAW following their return to work in the auto plants. Among these militants was Bob Carter, later a president of A.C. Sparkplug Local No. 651, regional director of the UAW, and finally, City Manager of Flint. Pat Murray and his two sons were active in Buick Local No. 599. He was a committeeman and delegate to national conventions. Claude Workman was a prominent Buick shop committeeman. Roy Lawrence was a shop committeeman at A.C. Sparkplug for many years.

To show the plight of the unemployed, WPA Local Union No. 12 publicized a suggested relief budget:

$2.52	Food
$1.00	Milk
$1.50	Fuel
$3.00	Rent
$8.02	Total per week[6]

This was the union's conservative estimate of the cost of maintaining a family on relief. The average wage of a WPA worker in 1938 was $13.20 a week. The budget made no allowance for the modest charges for haircuts, medicine, household necessities, soap, shoes, and apparel. The lack of proper food and clothing for children and their families, the deplorable occasional handout of beans, rice, rancid butter, and oatmeal, impelled the union to organize protest demonstrations. They hanged in effigy the head of the welfare administration, demanding more food from Washington.

Across the street from the welfare offices was a small city park. The welfare building and the park faced Buick Motor Company on Industrial Avenue. The plant stretched for blocks. On the side facing the park were windows that could be opened in hot weather. The WPA local mounted a demonstration in the park when nine hundred families were cut off from relief. The members of the local erected tents to house families. They strung a banner in front of the park reading "This Is a Death Watch." It was a wake-up call to Flint that people were starving, and that if the situation continued they would starve in public so that Flint could see it happen. The demonstration lasted from May 6 to May 15, 1939. Forty years later, Genora Johnson Dollinger commented thus on the Death Watch:

> We were warned and served some kind of notice at the union headquarters. And of course, for electricity, we strung it up on city electrical wires. Men shimmied up these poles and connected the wiring, which was illegal as hell and dangerous. It may have been Consumers Power union men who did this for us. [They] wired them directly to the tents. [There] was a string hanging down with an electrical light bulb from a clothes line or whatever they had hooked it on in front of the tent. At night you could see these bulbs shining inside the tents and then outside. We didn't want anybody sneaking up and setting fire to them.[7]

The press responded by photographing women washing diapers and stringing them on lines hung between trees. The police also came out; their intention was more ominous. However, in the Buick plant was Pat Murray, who had been recalled to work. He mobilized the Buick workers to stand by the windows, armed with wrenches and metal bars. They told the police not to interfere, and that if they did the workers would come out of the plant to protect the unemployed demonstrators. Telegrams flew back and forth from Flint to Lansing, the state capital, and from Lansing to Washington. Within a few days Washington had organized a large distribution of surplus food, bringing the demonstration to a close.

The organizing of the unemployed and affiliating them to the UAW was unprecedented, an example of how pervasive the spirit of the CIO had become. In most cities the WPA workers and the unemployed were affiliated with the Workers' Alliance or the Unemployed and Project Workers Union. WPA Local No. 12 conducted protest demonstrations throughout the year. They organized a one-day strike of four thousand project workers to protest impending layoffs, as well as demonstrations at City Hall to remind city officials of the plight of the unemployed.

Genora Johnson came under attack from Detroit for publishing a handbill with a cartoon critical of Roosevelt. Joe Pagano, formerly employed at Hudson and now on the UAW staff, came to Flint and threatened to put the local under an administrator. He was obliged to retreat when Genora disclosed that the cartoon had in fact been copied from an official CIO publication.

Rallying to Roosevelt

The union officials and their staffs were for Roosevelt. The members, however, who were close to the poverty line, paid little heed to these people, who were more interested in political favors with politicians than solving immediate problems. Rarely had so many crosscurrents been at work. The union leaders wanted to be "labor lieutenants" of capitalism (a catchphrase of John Keracker and Daniel DeLeon, former leaders of the Proletarian Party and the Socialist Labor Party). Though they courted the media to obtain favorable publicity for their new role as labor statesmen, they nevertheless still had to address the unions' basic concerns—an unresolvable contradiction.

In the meantime, the militarization of the country grew more pervasive. While the union leaders joined ranks and supported Roosevelt's drive to involve the country in the war program, the broad ranks of workers were antiwar. Convention proceedings of 1940 speak to the strong antiwar current. John L. Lewis brought a word of caution to the Fifth Annual Convention of the UAW:

> I warn my fellow Americans not to be beguiled into a war hysteria nor the acceptance of a war state of mind merely because some politician or statesman was incapable of coping with the problems of Americans who see in war, or the association of our country with other countries in war, relief from the clamoring of its own people and relief from the dreadful obligation of not being able to submit constructive ideas for national economic reform or bring about national economic stability.[8]

Sentiments of this kind were to be heard frequently in Flint. Across from the huge Fisher Body plant on Saginaw Street were restaurants, bars, and the Fisher Body Local No. 581 union hall. After end of shift, many Fisher Body workers would gather in the corner bar for a few beers before going home. At the back of the bar was a small stage for the band that played on weekends. This writer can well remember Frank Feke, a sitdowner, regaling the audience with a perfect impersonation of Franklin D. Roosevelt: "And while I am talking to you, fathers and mothers, I give you once more assurance. I have said this before, but I shall say it again and again: Your boys are not going to be sent into any foreign wars." After a pause came the punchline: "I'll sink them in the middle of the ocean."[9] The raucous laughter greeting this performance demonstrated the gap between what workers in the shops thought and what their leaders were saying. Not until Pearl Harbor did the flag-wavers take front and center. Even after the start of the war, local union leaders were not willing to give up the gains won in 1937, as would soon be revealed.

During April and May 1941, John L. Lewis and the miners fought for a large wage increase. Two years later, from May to November 1943, the miners' union led the attack against the coal operators and restrictive government regulations. Although the top leaders of the UAW were conspicuous by their silence, the locals expressed their support for the miners' strike by passing resolutions through their union meetings. Lewis could always count on the support of the ex-miners in the UAW, but many other leaders in the UAW locals chose to register their dissatisfaction with the union's International Board by giving support to the miners' union.

Labor leaders played a diverse role during these events that captured the attention of the entire nation. Philip Murray of the CIO and Thomas Kennedy of the United Mine Workers resigned from the tripartite board Roosevelt had set up to moderate disputes between labor and management. The AFL representatives, for their part, sided with the government. The UAW leaders were muted and embarrassed by the militant example Lewis was making in defense of the miners. They cringed at the thought that the auto workers might want them to lead a similar action against the auto corporations and a government determined to resist any labor advances.

Just as the Germans rallied to Hitler when he solved the unemployment problem with war production, so did the same process work in the United States. The WPA and a dozen alphabet agencies did not succeed in bringing unemployment down until the war industries sprouted across the forty-eight states. By the time of Pearl Harbor, most of the labor movement accepted the Roosevelt war build-up. Flint typified the general patriotic fervor. Workers even started putting small

American flags on their car antennae, although after a few days, when
a rumor swept through town that the flags were manufactured in Japan,
they were hastily removed. Such was the strength of feeling that those
delinquent in taking the flags off were in danger of having their cars
overturned.

Local union leaders watched the Big Three auto companies refuse to
convert their plants until they received government guarantees of an
acceptable rate of profit. While the auto plants had many laid-off
workers, the slack was now being taken up by the new plants engaged
in war production. In the midst of these events, new union administra-
tions were trying to cope with new situations.

Chapter 7

The UAW Organizes the Ford
Motor Company, 1940–1941

The whole world is under obligation to the Negro, and that the
white heel is still upon the black neck is simple proof that the world
is not civilized.

Eugene Victor Debs

Following the March 1940 Cleveland UAW convention that ratified the
ousting of Homer Martin, the union turned its attention to Ford's River
Rouge plants in Dearborn. These employed a total of 83,000 workers
in seventeen plants with 325 departments. The Ford empire, spread
over 1,200 acres, looked from the air like an ancient fortress surrounded
by highways and the River Rouge, which transported ore directly to
the factory. Access was by seventeen gates. Protecting the Ford empire
from the inside was a special armed police force, the Ford Service
Department, under the direction of Harry Bennett.

In May 1940, the campaign against Ford began. By agreement with
the CIO and the UAW, John L. Lewis appointed Michael Widman
from the miners' staff to direct the campaign. The CIO and the UAW
agreed to share, equally, an initial fund of $100,000.

The appointment of Widman allayed any fears that factionalism
might carry over from the Homer Martin era. When Frankensteen was
in the Martin caucus, he received the assignment to direct the organization of Ford. However, logic dictated that it should come under the
jurisdiction of Walter Reuther, since the Ford factory lay on the far
West Side of his region. The UAW leaders believed that the organizer
of Ford would become the leading contender for the union presidency.
R. J. Thomas gave Frankensteen the directorship of the aircraft division,
which was growing at a rapid clip with the acceleration of wartime
production. Reuther's assignment, along with responsibility for General
Motors, made his the largest department in the union.

Tackling Racial Division

The task of directing the union effort in the ethnic and African-American communities was assigned to the former president of Briggs Local No. 212, Emil Mazey, whom Widman had appointed as assistant director of the Ford drive. The union established six offices easily accessible to the large Polish, Hungarian, and Italian neighborhoods. The special attention given to the Black ghetto reflected the huge resistance the UAW had to overcome in a community suspicious of a union that hitherto had made no special effort on its behalf.

The leaders of the union had adopted a stand against discrimination, and its policies reflected this. As a consequence, the leaders were in fear of a backlash from the white southern working class that predominated in the recent wave of migration to the auto plants. The customs of northern society were similar to those of the southern communities they had emigrated from.[1] They came north filled with prejudice and hostility to Blacks. The corporations, for their part, bolstered southern workers' prejudices, deliberately pitting African-Americans against whites.

Ford's reputation in Detroit as an employer of Blacks ensured that in its fight with the union the corporation received the support of a large majority of church ministers, the NAACP, and the Urban League. Ford, in effect, developed a system of patronage with these Black ministers, who could in turn obtain employment for church members. Ford was the largest employer of Blacks in Detroit—some fourteen thousand worked at its plants. Most were employed in the foundry, with its arduous, dirty, and dangerous jobs. Roy Wilkins and Walter White, the two most important leaders of the national NAACP, supported the UAW however. Wilkins, writing in the national NAACP's publication *Crisis*, directed his remarks at those church ministers supporting Ford in Detroit who took exception to the national NAACP support of the UAW campaign there:

> If the two greatly disturbed divines in Detroit feel called upon to attack their one great national organization because of their love for Negroes in Detroit, we invite them to Mr. Ford's plants in Edgewater, N.J., Chester, Pa., Atlanta, Ga., Kansas City Mo., and St. Paul, Minn. (where blacks are limited to janitorial work), and ask them if they will find anything in these places to cause them to don the garments of the Lord and preach a holy defense of the 800 million-dollar Ford Motor Company. The spectacle of poor preachers ministering to the needs of poor people whose lot from birth to death is to labor for a pittance, rising to frenzied, name-calling defense of a billionaire manufacturer is enough to make the Savior weep.[2]

Notwithstanding the support for the UAW given by Walter White, Roy Wilkins of the NAACP, and A. Philip Randolph of the Sleeping Car Porters Union, the Black community did not rush to join the UAW. Among the measures adopted by the UAW to overcome the hesitancy of Black workers was the appointment of seven full-time African-American organizers, two from the Ford Foundry. Special issues of *Ford Facts* were handed out in the ghetto and at the Ford factory gates, once the courts had ruled on the legality of such leafleting (see below).

The employment policy of the company carried over to the Ford Service Department, responsible for internal security. Among the three thousand men it employed were several hundred Blacks. The core of this special police force comprised felons paroled from Jackson State prison, members of the University of Michigan football team, as well as boxers and wrestlers. Their task was to create fear in the factory by intimidation, using physical force when necessary. The intimidation extended into the community. Churches, for example, were warned not to provide meeting rooms for the UAW. The few ministers who ignored the warning soon complied with the demands of the Ford representatives when Ford members of the church were fired.[3]

Nevertheless, the union was to build its campaign primarily on the basis of solid support given by Black unionists. Among these outstanding pioneers in bringing the union to Ford were Tanner Perry, a chief steward in the pressed steel department, and Al Johnson, chairman of the glass plant bargaining committee, elected in a department that was predominantly white. In the important foundry was Shelton Tappes, chairman of the foundry building committee and on the negotiating committee during the strike. The leader of the NAACP youth group was Horace Sheffield. He and his father worked in the foundry. Horace was a tall, young, articulate supporter of the UAW in spite of NAACP opposition to the union. During the subsequent strike he obtained a union sound car and cruised the Black neighborhood to drum up support for the UAW.

Ford Suffers Legal Setback

The first indication that the Ford organizers were running out of time in their strike preparations came with a strike at the rolling mill plant. William Allen, writing in the *Daily Worker*, reported:

> March 13 saw for the first time in Ford's history a stoppage on the huge assembly lines in the Rolling Mill, with 3,000 union and non-union workers

standing. Forty-eight minutes later the union committee leaned over the balcony and shouted, "Let her roll, fifteen fired workers will be reinstated."

Allen reported another stoppage in the Axel building five days later, and, a day after the Axel strike, the largest strike of all at the B building. All three incidents resulted in the reinstatement of fired union representatives.[4]

The emergence of a union structure in the Ford plants began following a ruling by Municipal Court Judge Lila Neuenfelt, who in October ruled that Ford at Dearborn had violated the Constitution by banning leaflet distribution. Ford hurried to reverse the ruling, asking for an injunction. Two months later the decision came through from Judge James E. Chenot of the Wayne County Circuit Court. He issued an injunction against the Ford Motor Company for its attempt to use traffic regulations as a means of preventing free speech. The court duly ordered Dearborn officials to respect the right of free speech represented by the handing out of leaflets at the Ford factory gates. The union was at the gates for the next two days, distributing thousands of handbills; this was followed by regular distribution of *Ford Facts*. The Ford union leaders then carried the campaign a step further. They enlisted the aid of all UAW members in Detroit to assist the effort to bring a union to Ford. They solicited active participation of members, suggesting they sign up their neighbors and friends. This was an all-encompassing union effort engaging thousands of unionists.

Ford suffered a further setback when a National Labor Relations Board (NLRB) ruling came down against the corporation. The appeal by Ford had gone to the Supreme Court, which refused to hear the case. Discharged workers in cases going back to 1937 were reinstated with back pay. These multiple rulings, in the space of a few months, had a dramatic impact inside the Ford plants. Ford finally posted notices on bulletin boards spelling out the right to join a union. Bargaining committees were elected; members proudly and openly wore UAW buttons.[5]

The union leaders at first entertained notions of organizing Ford without a strike. To this end, they petitioned the NLRB for an election at the Lincoln plant for union representation. The opportunity was not lost on Harry Bennett of the Ford Service Department, who resurrected the AFL and Homer Martin in another gambit to divide the Ford workers. Following the UAW convention on March 1, 1940, Martin had taken the seceding locals into the AFL. He subsequently resigned from the union to take a job as a chemical salesman. In September the remaining locals gave up their AFL charters and returned to the CIO. Then, in an extraordinary turn of events, at Bennett's request Homer Martin reappeared on the scene from private industry with the charter for an AFL auto union. AFL president William Green gave his approval to Martin's intervention in the Ford drive.

Ford Fights Dirty

The plans of the UAW for a peaceful settlement were shattered on the afternoon of April 1, 1941, when management fired the recently established bargaining committee. In response, ten thousand rolling mill workers stormed out of the factory, followed by a thousand in the open hearth plant and then by fifteen thousand in the B Building. William Taylor, an organizer for the UAW, reported a sitdown in the final assembly, the rolling mill, and the B Building. The foundry workers found their exit barred by the Ford Service Department hooligans. The reports do not indicate if any of them were unwilling to leave. William Allen claimed the foundry workers marched into the superintendent's office to discuss long-standing grievances.[6] The violent nature of the confrontation was captured in a *New York Times* report:

> Scores were hurt as the heavy forged iron shafts were thrown at pickets by nearly two hundred Negroes who made sorties from gate #4 on Miller Road. Hand-to-hand encounters resulted in knifings and beatings to picket and company supporters.[7]

Union leaders were concerned by the Ford Motor Company's calculated effort to use the Black workers as strikebreakers. They called for help from Walter White. At a meeting with the Detroit NAACP, union officials conceded that Ford had given Blacks employment when many other plants had kept their doors shut. They promised Walter White and the local NAACP that henceforth it would be union policy to seek promotion for Black workers, from janitorial to all classifications of work. This promise neutralized the opposition of the Detroit NAACP leaders. That afternoon Walter White toured the Ford plant with a sound car, asking the Blacks to leave the plant and join the strike. Very few heeded him.[8]

Thousands of pickets ringed the plant and barricaded Miller Road with their automobiles. Those inside included the Ford Service Department and strikebreakers, induced to stay with promises of higher pay.

The only way to get supplies into the Rouge plant was by boat. Consequently, after three days most of the workers were forced to leave for lack of food; even some Servicemen exited complaining of lack of food and tobacco.[9]

The flying squads of the major auto locals from city and state came armed to do battle with the Ford Servicemen. They had not forgotten the brutal thrashings administered by Bennett's Service Department to Walter Reuther, Richard Frankensteen, and Robert Kantor as—assisted by other union men and women—they had attempted to pass out handbills in July 1937 at the Miller Road overpass. The UAW men were determined not to let this happen again.

On the first evening of the strike, the AFL auto union under Martin's direction organized a mass meeting. Over three thousand attended, with the audience predominantly Black. The speakers were Homer Martin and Donald Marshall, the African-American who served Ford for many years as the chief liaison with the Black community. They urged Ford workers to cross the picket line and return to their jobs.[10]

Ford's answer to the strike set the tenor for the negotiations:

> The strike, which was begun by a criminal seizure of the rolling mill in a sit-down strike Tuesday afternoon, was abandoned in favor of an all-out communistic demonstration on the highways leading to the Rouge plant this morning. Union members trained by Communists in the Moscow manner were imported from other plants to create a false impression of strength. They threw a double barricade across all important highways, seized control of railroad facilities to block all entrances to the plant, and stopped all employees, by terroristic methods and strong-arm tactics, from entering the factory, in violation of State criminal law.[11]

Martin went on the radio to ask all Ford workers to visit the AFL union office. Frank X. Martel, president of the AFL council in Detroit, reacted swiftly. He wanted the Ford Motor Company organized and refused to scab on the powerful effort of the CIO to end the open shop at Ford. He therefore called on William Green to lift the charter, recently granted to Homer Martin by Green, giving AFL approval to shattering the united union front against Ford. To Frank Martel it smelled of union busting. Green agreed to the request. The UAW and the AFL respected each other's picket lines. The Teamsters union refused to haul the Ford cars coming off the final assembly lines in solidarity with the UAW union drive. The strike caught the attention of the city of Detroit and all eyes were focused on the drama, with its innovative strike techniques, being fought out in the press and on the radio. It was one of the few occasions where the union was able to match the corporation in delivering its message to the public.

Ford turned to the court for injunctive relief on the second day of the strike. A UAW attorney heard of this court action and rushed to the federal court house to request a few hours' postponement. Judge Arthur J. Tuttle refused the union request on the grounds that a barricade had been erected and that any attempt to pass had been met with violence by the pickets. Ford then appealed to Governor Van Wagoner for state troops.

After five days the mediator issued a statement indicating that significant progress had been made toward an agreement. However, a day later acrimonious statements by both the union and Ford counsel I. A. Capizzi refuted the published report. The union responded, asking the company to abolish the Ford Service Department, to establish parity of wage rates with General Motors and Chrysler, to create a system of employment security based on seniority, and to devise a recognized grievance procedure. Capizzi duly replied for Ford:

> Typical of all U.A.W.–C.I.O. statements, this is another attempt of the Communist leaders behind the local strike movement to attain the first great objective of all Communist party tactics, to create confusion and bewilderment in the masses and break down public confidence in major American institutions.[12]

UAW Victory

Demagogic press comments notwithstanding, the Ford negotiators agreed for the first time in thirty-eight years to meet an official union delegation, which was led by Philip Murray. The change in attitude came following three separate blows to the Ford corporation. First, the bid for a government truck contract was lost when the union protested its award to the company. Second, both the state and the federal government refused Ford's appeal for military intervention in the strike. Third, injunctive relief was postponed by union concessions, such as the removal of barricades and allowing traffic to flow freely (the Ford workers and their sympathizers had been circling the plant in all three lanes at a very low speed).

Thus, after ten days of the strike, the Ford Motor Company entered into an agreement with the UAW. The agreement included the following: a return to the pre-existing bargaining procedure; the return to work of fired employees, except for three whose cases were referred to arbitration; an election of union representatives in forty-five days. Issues outstanding would be submitted to arbitration. The board would include Harry Bennett and another unnamed Ford representative; R. J. Thomas and Allan Haywood of the CIO union; as well as Governor Van Wagoner, and Federal Conciliator James F. Dewey.[13]

On May 21, 1941, the NLRB conducted the election for union representation at the Ford River Rouge plant. Ballots in favor of union representation were cast by 78,000 workers. The UAW emerged with 51,868 votes cast; the AFL received 26,132—a considerable proportion of which were cast by Black workers, according to the press. Less than 3 percent of those balloted voted for no union.[14]

A contract was signed a month later. It was the best contract achieved by the UAW from any of the big three auto companies. Ford had agreed to union recognition without qualification. They wrote into the contract that all employees were covered. Dues and other deductions or assessments would be deducted and transmitted to the union. The union leaders were elated by its winning of this check-off clause, the first it had obtained. It was agreed, furthermore, that the Ford Service Department men would henceforth wear badges, hats, and uniforms to eliminate spying. Wage rates rose to equal those of Ford's competitors—a raise of at least 10 cents an hour. For its part, the union agreed to drop all cases filed with the NLRB. It acceded to Ford's request that a union label be placed on all cars, to demonstrate the company's concord with the union and mark the opening of a new chapter in industrial relations.[15]

The UAW victory resulted from a strike that had brought to the fore all the problems of a society rooted in racial and ethnic prejudices. To bridge the gulf separating whites and Blacks the union improvised, and for the first time began to grapple with issues that went beyond the building of a union. The Ford strike taught the fundamental lesson that a union could be built and, furthermore, could bring some sense of equality in shop conditions; nevertheless, it failed to address successfully the larger issue of racial equality. Union leaders in effect retreated from the most volatile of societal pressures, and thereby failed to confront a capitalism that practiced division and deception by pitting one group against another on grounds of race or politics.

Chapter 8

Equality of Sacrifice?

I can hear some of you saying, "Yes, we know we are in a war, Yes, we are ready to make sacrifices to win the war." And, I know you have also asked the question: "Why should we, who fight the war, also carry its full burden at home."

R. J. Thomas, War Emergency Conference, 1942

With the ink barely dry on the Ford contract, the UAW found itself involved in a new imbroglio. The union's leaders must have felt they were on a roller-coaster ride. The problems arose from events immediately following the Japanese attack at Pearl Harbor on December 7, 1941. Factional differences at the top were muted by the drive to war: Thomas, Addes, Frankensteen, and Reuther united in patriotic support of the war effort. At the grassroots, however, contrary forces were at work. UAW local leaders, scarred by years of bitter struggle, distrusted the corporate world and its political control of government institutions.

John McGill typified this union stratum. The official newspaper of Buick Local No. 599, *Headlight*, reported in its October 21, 1941, issue the election of John McGill as president of the local. McGill came from a small coal-mining town in Illinois, and was formerly a member of the miners' union. In Chicago he had worked as a metal worker and was an AFL union member. In 1934 he found work in Flint Chevrolet and joined the Chevrolet Federal Auto Workers Union, an affiliate of the AFL. Union activity led to his subsequent discharge. A year later he was employed by Buick and joined the Buick federal local in 1936. Buick retirees James Kalemis and Al Federico report that McGill was a frequent visitor to the Pengelly Building during the Flint sitdown strikes.[1] He was an active participant in union discussions. They describe McGill as an eloquent speaker, on a par with the very best of those leading the strike in 1937.

McGill was elected to the first bargaining committee of the Buick local, a position he was to hold until his appointment as an organizer for the UAW International. He subseqently resigned this position to return to work in Buick, where he was again elected a committeeman. From the time of McGill's election as president of Local No. 599 in 1941, he was an elected delegate to UAW conventions except for the time spent in the Navy. After the war he was again elected president of the local. McGill was a typical auto-worker leader: class-conscious, militant, politically experienced, even though he had no affiliation to any of the radical political parties that proliferated during the Depression. He supported the Thomas–Addes faction until the four-month General Motors strike of 1945. McGill's first loyalty was to his local. As we will see, he objected vociferously to giving up the right to strike, to which the union leaders were to agree following the attack on Pearl Harbor.

Roosevelt's Demands of Labor

Seventeen days after Pearl Harbor Roosevelt asked the labor movement to convoke an emergency conference. The conference would be asked to forgo the right to strike for the duration of the war. Roosevelt informed the union leaders that all must make sacrifices. To this end, he indicated, there would be a limit placed on the corporations' profits; moreover, he decreed that no one should receive a salary of more than $25,000 a year. Furthermore, Roosevelt informed the union leaders that he intended to keep production in the major industries operating around the clock, seven days a week. Workers were requested to forgo overtime and premium pay.[2]

The record was later to reveal that serious consultations had taken place between some of the national union leaders and Roosevelt in advance of the scheduled emergency conference. CIO monitor Philip Murray disclosed subsequently, in a speech to the 1944 UAW convention, that in fact he had volunteered to surrender the right to strike a week before Roosevelt requested it. At times, Murray could act in a dictatorial manner; nevertheless even he knew it was necessary to call an emergency conference of labor to gain broad approval for the pledged abdication of labor's most powerful weapon—the right to strike. The UAW leaders were faced with a formidable task: to confront a democratic union that treasured its rights and believed that only a convention of delegates could effect such a radical change in policy.

The problem was that the power of the UAW leaders was voted to them in convention by delegates. And of course those leaders wished to be re-elected at future conventions. They thus had to devise a sweetener to accompany a program of surrender so that the bitter pill would be more palatable. They had no illusions that this would be an easy or popular task, even in an atmosphere of rising patriotic ardor.

(The one exception to the agreement between labor leaders and the government was the Mechanics Education Society of America (MESA), whose president was Matthew Smith. The union had a wartime membership of fewer than 100,000. The MESA rejected the government demand that it relinquish the right to strike, whereupon Smith was called to Washington by the War Labor Board. However, the government backed off when Smith disclosed that his union constitution forbade a no-strike pledge.[3])

On March 28, 1942, the UAW's International Executive Board met in Cleveland to promote the Equality of Sacrifice program. They voted to take advertisements in the leading auto center newspapers and to arrange a War Emergency Conference of the officers and committeemen from UAW locals on April 8–9 in Detroit. At this meeting Thomas announced his appointment of a Defense Committee consisting of George Addes, Richard Frankensteen, Walter Reuther, and Richard Reisinger. Thomas further announced that the conference had been called under the auspicies of the Defense Committee and not by the entire IEB. They distributed to the delegates copies of a pamphlet called *Victory through Equality of Sacrifice*. This strange procedure for calling the conference was not explained by R. J. Thomas. However, the opposition to the union ceding the right to strike and giving up overtime and premium pay made it necessary to call the Seventh Constitutional Convention five months later, August 3–9, in Chicago.

The convoluted procedure followed by the IEB at its March 28 meeting, where it adopted the recommendations of Donald Nelson, chairman of the War Labor Board asking the unions to give up its right to strike and to overtime pay, was in anticipation of sharp resistance by the local union leaders who came of age in the sitdown strikes that had convulsed the nation just a few years earlier. This may partially account for the need to take out full-page advertisements in the newspapers, as an attempt to explain to the public and auto workers that corporations would be called upon to sacrifice in equal measure with the unions. These maneuvers amounted to a blatant charade, the purpose of which was to shroud the existence of class struggle.

George Addes reported to the Board that "the CIO's position was not totally favorable and acceptable to the rank and file." In his view the rank and file did not understand the country's predicament. He then suggested that industry should share the sacrifices of labor. Before the adoption of the resolution, Addes recommended against sending out information in advance of the special meeting. The union spoke of shared sacrifice with industry in the Equality of Sacrifice Program:[4]

1. End of premium and overtime pay.
2. No-strike pledge.
3. Increase production by all available means.
4. War plants should operate on a 24-hour, seven-day week.
5. End of war profiteering, rigid control of profits. Taxation on all profits above 3 percent.
6. No luxuries in wartime. No war millionaires. Limit of $25,000 on salaries.
7. Prevent inflation—stop rising costs.
8. Rationing of food, clothes, housing, and other necessities.
9. Adjustment of wages to meet increased living costs.
10. Security for dependants in the armed services.

"A major flaw in the Equality of Sacrifice program," according to Nelson Lichtenstein, "was that the concessions called for by industry were made merely in the form of recommendations to the President and Congress, whereas labor's sacrifices were to be put into effect without preconditions."[5] The Program seemed egalitarian, with the leaders of labor wanting to graft planning, wage equality, and profit-sharing—identified with the Soviet system—onto the carcass of the foremost capitalist country in the world. In fact, the absurdity of this effort was so obvious that hardly a whisper of protest or criticism was uttered by the supporters of capitalism, who normally would be outraged by any suggestion that threatened to restrict capitalism.

Betrayal of Labor's Self-interest

The patently fraudulent nature of the Program was attested to in R. J. Thomas's report to the War Emergency Conference, which had as a prime exhibit the net income, after taxes, of 825 manufacturing corporations for 1941 as compared to 1940. The figures were compiled by the National City Bank. Some representative examples will prove the point: Allegheny Ludlum Steel, increased 36 percent; Baltimore and Ohio Railroad, 280 percent; Remington Rand, 125 percent; Lima Locomotive, 1,360 percent; Youngstown Sheet and Tube, 49 percent.[6] What union man in his right mind would believe that Roosevelt's proposal to limit salaries to $25,000 a year would be put into practice? Indeed, no sooner were the words uttered by FDR than he made modifications: the salary figure would not include the cost of insurance and income from stocks and bonds, and, if the restriction turned out to be too onerous, other exceptions could be made. When Roosevelt was president, $25,000 was still a tidy sum, of course—ten to fifteen times an auto worker's annual salary. It would therefore have been a handsome salary in those years. Nonetheless, the notion of such a salary ceiling was unacceptable to Congress—where it was dismissed as a "socialistic proposal"—and to their masters, the chief executive officers of industry.

Thomas's report to the War Emergency Conference also aired the fact that Charles Wilson of General Electric had his salary raised from $135,000 in 1940 to $175,000 in 1941; in the same period, that of T. M. Girdler of Republic Steel Corp. rose from $176,000 to $275,000; these raises were modest, however, compared with E. H. Little of Colgate-Palmolive, whose income rose in the same period from $131,463 to $306,193—a 233 percent increase.[7]

Thomas, further, called attention to the following significant fact: "In 1913, all corporations having an annual net income of $1,000,000,000 or more made $438,000,000 net profits ... while in 1917 war orders had swollen the profits of the same corporations to $1,234,000,000, or 24% of net worth."[8] And what conclusion did Thomas draw from the impressive array of statistics showing that capitalists had not changed their spots? In war or peace, the nature of the entrepreneurial system meant that the rich would get richer!

Thomas's statistics bombarded the delegates. What was out of kilter was the conclusion that it was the responsibility of labor to disarm. Nevertheless, the field marshals of labor launched their ongoing war with capital by surrendering their tanks, howitzers, and torpedo planes, and entered the fray armed with pebbles and slingshots. They gave up their weapons without getting anything in return from the secret negotiations. The same process had occurred in the First World War. One might think that these leaders would have learned something from that experience, but they were either fools or conscious betrayers of labor's interest.[9]

The radical rhetoric and phraseology of the Executive Board of the UAW, designed to obfuscate the betrayal of labor's self-interest, did not deceive many delegates. Among the leaders in opposition was the Buick Local No. 599 with twenty-one elected delegates, led by John McGill. They voted unanimously to oppose the Equality of Sacrifice Program. Following the conference, McGill wrote in the local's newspaper *Headlight*:

> The records will prove that by labor giving up these overtime provisions it will not increase production, but will only add to the enormous profits of the corporation. Records will prove that high-ranking officials of the corporation receive thousands of dollars each in salaries, bonuses, and dividends every year, and they get higher year by year.[10]

There was apparently sufficient opposition for the International Board to schedule a convention four months later to gain constitutional approval for their decisions.

Buick workers witnessed the company drag its feet on the process of conversion to war production. Buick in the meantime persuaded the government to build a huge plant in Chicago cost-free. Furthermore, General Motors was splitting a surplus of $16 million between its top officials. The union responded with a suggestion that the company turn this money over to the government. The editors of the Buick union paper wrote: "Our opposition [to the Equality of Sacrifice Program] was based on the fact that labor is giving all, but the industrialists have not agreed to sacrifice, nor is there a very great demand on Congress to have industry share in the sacrifices."[11]

Seventh Annual UAW Convention, August 1942

Four months after the April 7–8 conference to consider the union's Equality of Sacrifice Program, the UAW held its Seventh Annual Convention. It was unusual for the union to hold two gatherings in such a short span of time. However, protests at the War Emergency Conference had persuaded the International officers to seek official sanction for a program that did not attract wholesale support.

Resistance began with the opening bell of the convention, when John McGill tried unsuccessfully to amend the rules to bar International representatives from the floor unless they were elected delegates. McGill's amendment was peremptorily ruled out of order by Thomas.

This ruling was in fact illegal: Thomas based the decision on precedent despite the rule that each convention sets its own standing orders. The chairman got away with violating the rules only because the opposition was not organized.

Soon after the opening of the convention, R. J. Thomas introduced George Addes, secretary-treasurer of the UAW, whom he had appointed, as chairman of the union's War Policy Committee. On the committee with Addes were Frankensteen, Reisinger, Leonard, and Walter Reuther. Addes read a detailed resolution with nineteen "whereas" clauses that summarized the situation, from Roosevelt's appeal to the union to forgo the strike clause in contracts, to the request to surrender premium pay for overtime. The subsequent report showed how the union negotiators had worked to satisfy the president by entering into negotiations with the Big Three of auto to rewrite the contracts. They bragged that "such arrangements were effected with dispatch."

However, the War Policy Committee had to concede in their resolution that all had not gone according to the pattern they had been determined to set for the labor movement. AFL unions, and in particular the unions competing with the UAW to organize the aircraft industries, refused to give up premium pay and used the UAW's contracts as a valuable propaganda weapon in elections conducted by the National Labor Relations Board. In the Curtiss–Wright aircraft election, for example, this tactic led to a rejection of the UAW in favor of the International Association of Machinists.

The resolution concluded that the UAW could not continue to give up overtime pay unless such action was universally accepted by all divisions of the house of labor. Addes, on behalf of the officers, duly urged the adoption of all measures set forth by Roosevelt, including restrictions on corporation profits.

Addes continued to report that other independent unions (such as the MESA) had refused to revise their contracts. Nevertheless he failed to call attention to those local unions in the UAW that had also refused to alter their contracts to give up premium pay. He justified the UAW position in giving up premium pay as the union's effort to ward off seventeen pieces of threatened anti-union legislation in Congress.[12] Erwin Baur, a former president of Budd Wheel Local No. 306, remembers the uproar over the giving up of premium pay: "In my local we never gave it up." Baur claims that the leaders of the opposition came from a network of former coal miners who had found work in auto and brought many of the miners' traditions with them.[13]

Mazey Brothers Force Partial Retreat

The first delegate to rise in opposition to the resolution was Emil Mazey, president of Briggs Local No. 212. He categorically rejected the claim of Roosevelt and the unions' top officers that premium pay had to be given up at any time, citing the huge profits of the corporations, their plush cost-plus contracts, as well as the new plants and reconditioned plants that the government was building for privately owned companies at public expense. Furthermore, Mazey took direct aim at the resolution's claim that the union had to retreat under the threat of anti-union legislation in Congress. His main attack, however, was aimed at what he saw as the heart of the resolution:

> [It] implies that we are asking President Roosevelt and the Congress to pass anti-labor legislation that will abolish time and one-half for Saturday as such, and double time for Sunday as such. I think that is a dangerous precedent, and I am unalterably opposed to that provision of this resolution.

He concluded by demanding a wage adjustment to take account of the enormous rise that had occurred in the cost of living, and expressed his dissatisfaction with wage increases that did not keep abreast of these changes. (The War Labor Board used January 1, 1941, as the base rate. By the time of the convention in August it had risen 15 percent.)

It was rare in a convention of more than 1,500 delegates for a speaker to be followed on the platform by his brother. By an extraordinary coincidence, this happened when R. J. Thomas recognized Bill Mazey, a delegate from Hudson Local No. 154 and the brother of Emil. Formerly employed at Briggs, he had been a delegate of Local No. 212 to the Fifth Annual UAW Convention. Bill Mazey had left when the plant closed to transfer to war production, and gone to work at the Hudson Sterling Heights Plant. His election as a delegate after only three months on the job was eloquent testimony to the power of the Mazey name on the East Side of Detroit.

Bill Mazey's speech to the conference exposed the propaganda of the leaders, whose pseudo-radical speeches were intended to cover up their betrayal of the auto workers' interests. He declared his opposition to the resolution with his first words, then cut through the smokescreen the leaders had used to confuse the delegates:

> When this so-called War Emergency Conference was called, it was unconstitutional. There was no provision for such a meeting to be called. They were hand-picked people who attended that conference, and they gave away

the rights of the workers. The officers of this union have paraded up and down this International Union trying to sell this program to the workers of this country. They came to the Hudson Local just a few weeks ago trying to sell this program to them, and the Hudson workers unanimously rejected it. The officers of this union sent a letter to the membership of this Local condemning them for being a disorderly element who would not take their rightful place with 500,000 other workers.

The rank and file of Hudson Local demonstrated the opposition of the rank and file of all our unions. They are unalterably opposed to giving away time and a half and double time.

Bill Mazey scoffed at the exaggerated fears of the leaders, who thought they had to capitulate to Congress or face the introduction of anti-union legislation:

They tried to sell this program on the basis that the Fascists, the Smiths, the Coxes, etc., of our nation are going to take away these things. We are so damned weak we don't need to fight them to keep them from taking it for nothing. The only way to defeat the Fascists is by fighting them on these issues, and let us demonstrate to the workers of this country that we are interested in our welfare and we want to defeat Fascism here in America.[14]

The Mazey brothers' participation in the debate clearly had a salutary effect on the UAW War Policy Committee. It proceeded to withdraw the resolution, submitting one more militant in tone—a major concession to those opposed to sacrificing premium pay. The rewritten resolution asked Philip Murray to convene an Executive Board Meeting of the CIO to adopt a resolution in conformity with the new position of the UAW. The Board wanted to re-establish premium pay in the union contracts.

On the third day of the Convention, the War Policy Committee submitted a new resolution, calling on Roosevelt to set up regional labor boards. These were to consist of representatives of labor, management, and the government, with the purpose of settling disputes rapidly. The resolution claimed there was a large backlog of unsettled grievances, as management was now successfully manipulating the process to ignore labor. Bill Mazey of the Hudson local was still not satisfied and again challenged the new resolution. He objected to the unions begging for the establishment of boards. Mazey insisted that unions should have the right to take effective action when the government boards stalled in rendering decisions. He contended that the union had built-in safeguards against strikes on incidental issues, and, furthermore, that the union must be able to exert its economic power if it was to control its own fate. "I think," Mazey continued, "we should send this resolution back and let them come out and tell the officials in Washington that if our grievances are not settled, we intend to take our right to strike back and shut down every plant where the employers are trying to smash our union."

The intervention of the Mazeys in the convention discussion was too provocative for the Communist Party to ignore. In the first days of the convention the hard work was done by the leaders of the union, who had the same policies as those of the Communist Party. The CP had sat back and let the top officers speak on their behalf. However, this turn in the debate proved to be too much for Lindahl of the Packard local. He beseeched the delegates not to be betrayed by Trotskyites:

> Is it coincidental, my friends, that the arguments used to strike down the resolution yesterday on the "Victory Through Equality of Sacrifice," were contained in a Trotskyite sheet passed out at the gates of the hall? Is it coincidental? Trotskyites have been indicted by the Department of Justice, and yet upon this floor yesterday, the press of this country stated the UAW, representing seven hundred thousand workers, echoed subversive sentiments of the Trotskyites. Someone is evidently being taken in.

Lindahl's intervention did not go unanswered. William H. Hill of Dodge Local No. 3 responded and dealt with the broader issues of the convention:

> I recall the St. Louis Convention quite well. Some of these speakers that are speaking in favor of the resolution today did not speak that way in St. Louis.
> We were not at war then.[15] And for some reason or other I cannot support this resolution because I don't think it is necessary to waste thirty days to see what managements are going to do....
> At the conference that was held in April, I happened to be at that conference. I took the floor and made a motion to table these rules until such time as all of our unemployed people were back to work. I was ruled out of order....
> I would have asked these government officials just exactly how far they were going to go in forcing the manufacturers to tighten their belts, and why should we pledge before they pledge.

Hill was part of a large group who fought against the CP. He recalled that at the St. Louis convention the CP advanced the slogan "The Yanks are not coming." Hill ascribed the party's change in tune in 1942 to social patriotism.

It is clear from the transcript of the proceedings that the War Policy Committee and its spokesman, George Addes, had to retreat from their hardline position established at the UAW April Conference in Detroit. Though they had the majority of the convention behind them, they could ill afford a fight with the more militant and politically independent section of the union, centered primarily in Detroit and Flint. Addes told the delegates that unless industry accepted the Roosevelt program as set forth in Equality of Sacrifice, then in thirty days the union would be free to reinstate the premium-pay provisions. Hill and others didn't want to wait and set the stage for another battle at the 1943 convention.

Reuther and Addes, along with the other members of the War Policy Committee, retreated tactically but held firm to the no-strike pledge. They were more fearful of a break with Roosevelt than with their own unorganized union militants.

In the official report to the convention of August 1942, R. J. Thomas claimed that the Equality of Sacrifice Program was "overwhelmingly adopted." What was in fact remarkable about the Seventh UAW Constitutional Convention, held so soon after the United States declared war on Germany and Japan, was the victory of the unsung militants who forced the UAW administration to retreat on premium pay. This marked the beginning of the struggle to retain labor's right to strike during the war, as concrete events demonstrated that the class struggle had not ceased. The militants were led by Emil and Bill Mazey, John McGill, William H. Hill of the Dodge local, and many others, who made their voices heard in the highest tribune of the UAW, refusing to bend before the pressure exerted by Washington and the UAW administration.

Chapter 9

Anti-union Forces Take Revenge

> I read the papers avidly. It is my one form of continuous fiction.
>
> Aneurin Bevan

Briggs Manufacturing Company, the largest independent auto body builder in the industry, supplied bodies to Chrysler before being retooled in 1942 for war production of airplanes. It had eight plants in Detroit, employing 18,000 workers. The heart of the Briggs enterprise, with the world's largest press room under one roof, was situated between Mack and Warren avenues, employing 7,500 workers. The corporation had a long history of anti-union practices. Several attempts to organize before 1937 had been rebuffed. Not until the wave of sitdown strikes did the Briggs workers succeed in establishing a union, under the militant leadership of Emil Mazey.

Tough corporations produce tough unions. Such was the case at Briggs. The core leadership had waged many battles. They earned a prestigious reputation in union ranks by aggressively aiding the organization of many other factories on the heavily industrialized East Side: Hudson, Budd Wheel, Chrysler, and Motor Products, employing in total 75,000 workers. This area of Detroit was like the Vyborg district of St. Petersburg in tsarist Russia: in this industrial heartland were some of the finest class-conscious workers.

The Flying Squad of Briggs Local No. 212

The key unit leading the drive to unionize the city was the famous flying squad of UAW Briggs Local No. 212, an amalgam of Irish, Italians, Greeks, Hungarians, and Poles. They fought in every major battle in the city and across the state. Squad members would pile into cars and drive into battle after the day shift. In the wake of the successful

1937 sitdowns in Flint General Motors came a firestorm of strikes in Michigan. The squad joined the picket lines in all the auto centers. Members of the squad were unpaid volunteers who risked life and limb to establish unions. They were admired and respected by the workers in the plants, who recognized that membership was a price that only a few were prepared to pay. The squad members wore leather jackets with the UAW local name on the back, a symbol and means of identification in a fight.

The armed security forces of the corporations were paid assailants. They expected and received fat pay packets. Hired Pinkertons, ex-felons, associates of the Mafia, they wielded blackjacks, lead pipes, knuckle-dusters, and guns. Before the founding of the CIO, corporation influence in the major auto cities of Detroit, Flint, Pontiac, Saginaw, Lansing, and Grand Rapids extended to every sector of the city, county, and state—including the press, the courts, and the police. The police, for their part, in turn ruled these cities with an iron fist. In past anarchic union eruptions, they had mercilessly put down the strikers. After 1937 union members set out to even the score, no longer prepared to lick their wounds in silence. The Briggs militants gave no quarter in a picket-line fight; after each battle, their reputation as a formidable group of picket-line fighters soared.

In 1936, Robert La Follette's Senate Committee on Labor and Education conducted hearings to investigate the nefarious labor practices of General Motors. The hearings revealed that the corporation had employed the Pinkerton Detective Agency along with fourteen other agencies to spy on unions, spending millions of dollars to prevent union organization. Most auto corporations duplicated this pattern, as is documented in the series of reports by the Senate committee. The one major exception was Ford, which, as we have seen, employed its own spy and policing force.[1]

Capital ruthlessly opposed the union movement. The La Follette committee's exposure of anti-union practices—spying on labor and the employment of felons to beat union organizers and union adherents—inevitably created a body of unionists determined to mete out the force necessary to establish unions. It was fist against fist, club against club. B. J. Widick wrote:

> On Detroit's East Side, Emil Mazey, later secretary-treasurer of the UAW, directed the most popular of all flying squadrons, the young militants from Briggs Local No. 212. Their appearance on any picket line signified two

things: first, that the police would have more than they could handle if they used force, and second, that the union was going to win.[2]

Flying squad members were leaders in their union departments. Roy Snowden, one of the chief stewards in the press room, was captain of the Briggs squad. Other members of the squad came from different parts of the plant—ordinary young men in terms of size and appearance, but in a scrap they fought like tigers. Snowden was a veteran unionist from the coalfields of Pennsylvania and brawler against the infamous coal and iron police. His activities in Briggs were the stuff of heroic myths. The UAW produced many militant union activists but few comparable to Snowden. He was a shade less than six feet tall and weighed probably no more than 180 pounds. He was in his mid-forties, older than most members of the squad. Normally he was a smiling Irishman, with a shock of pepper-grey hair and missing his front teeth— lost to the coal and iron police in the strikes of Western Pennsylvania. Yet in battle Roy Snowden became Jack Dempsey, striking out with both fists, to devastating effect.

Before the union came to Briggs, the corporation had hired foremen on the basis of their size in order to intimidate the workforce. One foreman in particular created fear in the men. The union therefore needed to neutralize this company man. Roy volunteered for the job. Informed that the foreman used the Briggs Mack Avenue exit, Roy waited for him. The broad-shouldered foreman stood out a foot taller than those around him as he exited the plant. Roy walked up to him and delivered a combination of blows, knocking the foreman unconscious. The next day the news of this event spread through the plant from Mack Avenue to Warren Avenue: it was the main topic of conversation as the union spread the word that its members would no longer stand for company intimidation.

During the several weeks that Roy lived with Genora and me, he told us about the squad assisting the Ford organizing drive in 1941. The flying squad had been active from the beginning of the union campaign. Harry Bennett, director of the Ford Service Department, achieved notoriety by hiring ex-convicts; men who were, in the main, accustomed to breaking the bones of unionists, spying, and engaging in other forms of intimidation. A famous photograph shows the beating they gave to Walter Reuther and Richard Frankensteen, who had been attempting, quite legally, to hand out leaflets at the Ford gate. Both men were bloodied and bruised. Walter had been tossed down a flight of stairs. The union, consequently, had no illusions when it encountered Ford Servicemen.

Roy chuckled as he described going into battle armed with a baseball bat. Jess Ferrazza and Roy confronted one of Bennett's hired thugs and set about beating him. Roy swung the bat down in the direction of the hunched-over strikebreaker, who was dressed in a heavy overcoat and hat. Unfortunately he moved just as Jess Ferrazza was hitting him with an uppercut. Roy missed his target, hitting Jess instead. The moment of action was caught on film. The photographer who snapped the picture won a Pulitzer prize for the best photograph of the year. The picture was to have serious consequences for Roy, however: he was obliged to disappear for a time, as the city prosecutors tried to bring charges against him for attempted murder of the Ford Serviceman.

Snowden and the other leaders of the squad were members of the Mazey caucus that ran the local union. When, in due course, Emil Mazey was drafted into the Army, his followers were determined not to allow the union to be undermined in his absence. Yet the unrelenting drive by Briggs for greater profits made it difficult for them to keep to their pledge. During these war years, management took advantage of the no-strike agreement. Furthermore, women were hired in large numbers to replace the men drafted into the army; most had never worked in a factory before and had no experience of the union procedures so recently established by the UAW. Foremen attempted to erode the conditions established by the union in 1937 and tried to take advantage of the women's inexperience.

Genora Takes a Leadership Role in Local No. 212

In 1943 Genora found employment in Briggs. The blacklist had caught up with her at Budd Wheel, where she had hired as Genora Johnson. At Briggs she applied as Genora Dollinger. She intended to observe the rules quietly for ninety days, the minimum requirement to obtain seniority, after which time she would have union protection. A few days before this period was up, many of her co-workers pleaded with her to attend a union meeting to select a chief steward. Though reluctant to do anything until she had obtained seniority, she decided to go and sit unobtrusively at the back of the hall, not knowing that Emil Mazey would address the meeting. Mazey was attending all department meetings prior to his departure for Army service.

Genora slid down in her seat, fearing that Mazey would recognize her. She described the event thus:

> He kept looking in my direction. Now, one attribute of that guy is that he has a memory of an elephant, and he kept looking in my direction. Now remember, I was in Flint, he was in Detroit. I don't think we met too many times. Finally at a part in the speech he stopped and said "Wait just a minute. I don't know what you need me for up here. Sitting back there is one of the original organizers of the UAW. She was in Flint! ... I don't know her name now, but back then she was Genora Johnson."[3]

When the formalities had ended, Genora was elected chief steward. She told Emil that his exposure of her in the meeting probably assured that she would never get seniority. Emil called over Jess Ferrazza and introduced him to Genora. (Jess was to succeed Emil as president.) Emil instructed Jess to shut down Briggs if any attempt was made to fire Genora. This was Genora's auspicious introduction into the close-knit caucus that Mazey had built.

Genora worked in an inspection department of 580 women who inspected airplane parts for the military services. Military security required the separation of the department from the rest of the plant. Until Genora's election, the union didn't have full access to the department; it was therefore elated to find an experienced union leader in this segment of the plant.

Genora was catapulted into a leadership role. They elected her to the education committee. The Briggs militants could fight, but they were dreadful public speakers. Genora therefore organized a speakers' class, where they learned by doing—practicing speeches to deliver at the public membership meetings. She also edited *On Guard*, a special bulletin the local union distributed to the chief and line stewards. It carried shop news and detailed problems encountered with particular superintendents and foremen as well as news of contract negotiations. Frank Marquardt, educational director of the local, commented on Genora's activity in Briggs:

> Genora (then the wife of Sol Dollinger) was a chief steward in the Briggs Mack Avenue plant and the editor of *On Guard*, a monthly steward bulletin that exposed supervision's violations of the union contract and bristled with pointed attacks against foremen whom Genora accused of union-busting tactics. A worker in her department told me: "The foremen hate Genora's guts; she's not afraid to tell them off when they stall on grievances."[4]

Genora was subsequently elected vice chair of the stewards' body—a rise to prominence in such a short time was rare for a unionist and especially for a woman in a union local of this size. This prominence would eventually have dire consequences.

During the war years, Local No. 212 militants had two enemies: the most powerful was the Briggs corporation; the other was the top leaders of the International Union, which had banned strikes for the duration. The Briggs corporation took advantage of the delays in settling disputes—it took months to get answers from the War Labor Board. The union fought against the stalling tactics with wildcat strikes—30 in 1943, 115 in 1944. Nelson Lichtenstein corroborates the role of UAW Local No. 212 as "the most oppositional and politically sophisticated in the entire UAW, posing a constant irritation to the international's top leadership."[5]

The second enemy, a more insidious opponent, was union regional director Melvin Bishop, the nemesis of this East Side local. Bishop fought the Mazey group out of political principle and personal pique. He believed in the enforcement of the no-strike pledge policy. At several meetings, Bishop asked for approval of the new contract he had negotiated with Briggs management; in a deliberate affront to his leadership, the local rejected it each time. Genora's public-speaking classes and her own denunciation of the proposed contract were proving effective. Nevertheless, Bishop refused to accept the membership decision as final, and repeatedly brought the same contract back for a new vote. This stalemate seemed to have no end.

The Beatings Begin

Shocking news was then received: the indomitable Roy Snowden had been severely beaten. He had returned to his home late one night, approached the door on the alley side of the house, and tried to put his key into the lock. When it would not enter, he bent down and saw that a piece of metal had been inserted into the keyhole. Suddenly, two men appeared out of the darkness and slugged Roy repeatedly with blackjacks or metal pipes. He was badly hurt. Roy was taken to the emergency room of a hospital, where many stitches were needed to sew the wounds in his scalp. It was assumed in the union that one of Roy's enemies had caught up with him; little further attention was paid to the episode.

Soon after the Snowden assault, however, more violence occurred. Art Vega was beaten while walking home with his wife. Art's wife had tried to drive off the assailants with the high heel of a shoe, but not before they had broken Vega's arm. Again, the local did not give this attack much consideration.

Later that summer, Roy Snowden and Frank Silver, the latter the captain of the Motor Products Flying Squad, and others were strolling on Mack Avenue after dinner. Frank Silver, over six feet tall, was walking a little ahead of Roy. Suddenly, two men emerged from the doorway of an adjoining wood-frame three-story apartment building and clubbed Roy to the ground. Before Frank Silver and the others knew what had happened, the assailants had fled through the entrance of the building and out the back alley.

It was decided that these three beatings called for investigation. Local union leaders mooted the existence of a conspiracy to frighten the leaders; a committee was therefore set up to discover what was behind the assaults. Gordon MacDonald (a vice president of the local) was elected chairman. Genora Dollinger was elected secretary. Also on the committee were Ernest Mazey (brother of Emil and Bill), Tom Gallery, and Gene Morosco.[6]

At the early meetings of the committee, witnesses appeared. For some it was a chance to settle old scores with enemies. A number of members suggested that Melvin Bishop, the regional director, had instigated the attacks. For the first few days he was a prime suspect. There was ample reason to suspect Bishop, especially because of his numerous efforts, referred to earlier, to ram the contract down the throats of the Briggs workers. Local newspapers fuelled the speculation, suggesting that the beatings were instigated in reprisal for the local's long-standing opposition to its regional director. Melvin Bishop immediately denounced the investigation committee. In a letter to the UAW president, R. J. Thomas, he declared:

> Since these "detectives" of the local union 212 Investigating Committee have publicly charged me with responsibility for so serious a crime, I am therefore requesting you appoint a committee composed of International Board members ... [to check] the validity of any statements implicating me with said crime.

It is hard to appreciate, more than fifty years after these events, how successful the criminal forces behind the assaults were in instilling fear into the local union. For example, members of the caucus held meetings behind barred doors. Visitors were welcomed into the house by a host armed with a revolver, rifle, or shotgun. In Michigan, a great hunting state, almost all workers were armed. Union militants made it a point not to walk singly when leaving a union meeting.

The investigating committee thought it advisable to approach the International Union for assistance. They wanted to see president R. J. Thomas and request that a reward be posted for information leading to the apprehension of those responsible for the beatings. As Thomas was out of town, the committee took the matter down the hall to Walter Reuther, the vice president. It was agreed that Genora would be the spokesperson because of her association with Reuther during the sitdown strikes. In Reuther's office, Genora gave the details of the three beatings and stressed the fear they were causing in the union. She suggested to Walter that he request the International Board of the union to establish a significant reward. Genora wrote in a later article:

> I can still recall the general tenor of my remarks to Reuther, which concluded as follows: They will step up their attacks. If they are successful in the Briggs local, Walter, it will very likely spread to the International and who knows, you might be the next victim.[7]

"Now, now," responded Walter, "let's not get dramatic. We can't be putting up a reward every time someone goes into a beer garden and gets knocked around." The investigating committee left empty-handed.

At about this time, Vincent R. Dunne, a founder of the American Trotskyist movement and the leader of the famous Minneapolis Teamsters' strike of 1934, flew to Detroit to consult with Ernest Mazey and Genora and give them the benefit of his experience in dealing with violence in the union movement. The Minneapolis strikes, which had lasted from February through July 1934, were bloody encounters between vigilante citizen groups allied with the police and the Teamsters. The union victory, which included a signed contract, heralded the end of the open-shop era. Based on his experience, which included being beaten himself more than once, Dunne suggested that the committee resist the efforts to handle this as an internal union affair. He advised them to focus their attention instead on the corporation, the beneficiary of the beatings. He said, "From my experience with the Teamsters and their bosses—gangsters and thugs can only exist when employers empty their purses and grease the palms of the Mafia or similar goons. Corporations can and do finance this kind of operation."

Genora Pays the Price

On October 16, 1945, before dawn, while sleeping in bed with me, Genora herself became a victim of the thugs. I was awakened by the thud of blows being delivered to the body of my wife. I kicked the blankets off and kicked across her body to force the assailant back. As my foot pushed the thug backward, I saw the silhouette of a second man standing against the wall. I jumped from the bed, the assailant raining blows across my thigh and lower leg; I collapsed on the floor. My right leg was numb; I couldn't stand. The two hoodlums turned and exited the house through the kitchen and rear door, leading to an alley.

I stumbled in an effort to turn on the light. It was five o'clock in the morning. Looking down at Genora, I saw one of her eyes filled with blood; blood ran down her check. She moaned, "Oh, my leg!" I shouted, "What have they done to your eye?" I called for an ambulance, then for Ernest Mazey. Ernie was on the investigating committee and a very close friend and comrade. The Detroit ambulance service took Genora to the old, dirty, cockroach-infested Receiving Hospital, the routine destination for emergency cases. The doctors said that Genora was completely paralyzed on her right side. She had suffered a broken collarbone, concussion, and damage to her facial nerves. The last condition would remain with her for the rest of her life: she lost the feeling on one side of her cheek and nose; as a consequence, her right lip drooped.

Given the seriousness of the paralysis, the UAW arranged for two famous neurologists, Doctors Gurjian and Webster, to treat her. Fortunately, after two weeks, the union arranged to have Genora transferred to the more modern Grace Hospital. It would be six weeks before she was released. Recovery was slow, and she had to walk in a cast and on crutches. For many months she experienced recurring pain in her head and ringing in her ears.

Genora's battering sent shockwaves throughout the city of Detroit. The newspapers took the opportunity to beat labor over the head. An editorial in the *Detroit Free Press* and other newspaper articles seized the opportunity to smear the union movement and UAW vice president Dick Frankensteen, who was a candidate for mayor of the city. Accompanying an article was a large picture of Genora in the hospital bed with a nurse hovering over her bloodied and bandaged head. The article failed to mention that Genora had joined the staff of Dick Frankensteen's mayoralty campaign a few days before the beating. In a hostile statement on the eve of the dirtiest race-dividing campaign ever witnessed in the city, the *Detroit Free Press* stated:

> Within the labor movement there are many bitter controversies between rival unions and factions. This was demonstrated just a few days ago when a

woman union worker was dragged out of her bed at midnight by a gang of hoodlums and beaten into insensibility.[8]

Briggs local responded to the beating by again asking the International Union to establish a reward for information on the beatings. It also demanded that the police allow every member of the investigating committee to carry a gun.

The head of the police investigative squad, Albert De Lamielleure, questioned Genora just as she was emerging from sedation. The detective later told the press that the victim "clammed up" when members of the committee came to visit her. This was the first of several attempts by the police and De Lamielleure to turn the beatings into an internal union affair. When Genora became more lucid, she informed the police that several days before the attack she had observed a man with a long scar on one cheek watching the front of the apartment house. When he became aware that Genora was watching him, he walked away, pretending to be drunk. The police asked if she could identify him, and she said that she thought she could; however, the police made no attempt to follow this lead.

For days the newspapers continued their attack on the UAW. The *Detroit Times* informed its readers that Genora was one of fifteen union officials whose dismissal by Briggs Manufacturing Company caused "a prolonged strike last spring. With seven others she was reinstated." Jack Crellin wrote: "She has been active in the UAW almost from its inception. In Flint, during the General Motors sitdown strike of 1937, she headed a women's 'emergency brigade' which helped picket the strike-bound plants."[9]

On her release from Grace Hospital, Genora returned to our apartment. She thought her appearance at the next union meeting would encourage the members to unite against the union busters who were intimidating and inflicting pain on the members. Though her body was still in a plaster cast and she had to use crutches, she duly went to the union meeting, assisted by two of her stewards, Cecile Bisaga and Mary Lynch. With their help she made it to the podium. The meeting was well attended as usual; the two strong caucuses vying for leadership guaranteed good turnouts. With gasoline rationing keeping workers close to home and their unions, these meetings provided better entertainment than that usually available in wartime Detroit.

Genora's appearance hardly inspired workers to keep to their course. Genora was an excellent orator, among the best in the local, and could sway an audience; yet many probably wondered at what price, when they saw this fiery union leader escorted to the platform on crutches. The words of encouragement from this battered union militant hit home with tremendous force. The audience generously applauded Genora's speech, recognizing her rare courage and unswerving devotion to the union—though many must have reflected on how dearly she had paid for that commitment.

Six months later Ken Morris became the fourth victim of assault and the fifth beating. Morris, who had just returned from military service, was a strong supporter of Emil Mazey (he would later become local union president and regional director). Morris, who was attacked in broad daylight, suffered a broken leg and concussion.

In an era of relatively tranquil labor relations, the violence in Briggs was a return to the days of the open-shop era, when assault against union leaders occurred frequently. Some of the International Union leaders considered the events in Briggs a mere aberration. Later events would prove them wrong. They paid the ultimate price for the belief that harmony had been achieved in industrial labor relations.

Chapter 10

Briggs and the Mafia

No endeavor is in vain;
Its reward is in the doing
and the rapture of pursuing
is the prize the vanquished gain.

Henry Wadsworth Longfellow

Genora recuperated slowly from the violent beating she received in October 1945. War had ended, first in Europe and then in Asia. Briggs and other auto plants were converting back to peacetime auto production. This was largely to the detriment of women in industry: men with high seniority were returning from their war service and would be hired first after reconversion. Genora and the other women in the inspection department were consequently laid off.

Genora was reluctant to concede that her brief career as a union activist had drawn to a close, considering that for a few years she had had the opportunity to work in the industrial union mass movement and prove her abilities as a union leader of men and women. She was also reluctant to move back to Flint from Detroit, though a month before the assault the Socialist Workers Party had asked me to help reorganize the dormant Flint chapter. After several months, Genora finally concluded that her union work in Detroit had ended. It was time to pull up stakes.

In Flint, housing was an enormous problem. We solved it by trading our apartment for a ramshackle wood-frame house on Fenton Road. We got the worst of the bargain. The house was rat-infested. The second floor had not been completed; nevertheless we succeeded in converting it into a primitive second bedroom. Once I returned home and heard a scratching noise coming through the papered ceiling, then saw small feet breaking through the paper. Could it be a rat? Suddenly, a bird broke through and flew out the door.

Some months later I found employment in the Chevrolet Assembly Plant on Van Slyke Road. In early 1946 Ernest Mazey called us to suggest we come back to Detroit for the state CIO convention. By this time, a grand jury had been established following insistent pressure by the union, with Judge Gerald T. Murphy presiding in the investigation of the Briggs beatings. Ernie thought he could arrange for us to see his brother Emil there and learn from him if any progress had been made. We duly met Emil and Ernie at the entrance to the Masonic Temple Auditorium, where the convention was being held. Emil told us what he had gleaned from the grand jury proceedings and that they were being kept secret from the public. Genora suggested, "Emil, why don't I publicly denounce the grand jury for keeping the information secret? What can they do to me? I was the victim; they'd find it difficult citing me for contempt." "I'm not so sure of that," Emil said. "We haven't got all of the information they've uncovered, and I think until we know more, it's premature to attack the grand jury."

While we were in Detroit, Ernie Mazey got us together with Walter Nelson, a prominent civil liberties attorney whose reputation in historic civil rights cases dated back to the famous July 1926 case of Doctor Ossian H. Sweet.[1]

We met in Walter Nelson's office to give him the facts about the five beatings and told him of the rumored grand jury information that pointed to the involvement of the Briggs Manufacturing Company. We also told him we lacked specific information that would lead to an indictment of the persons involved. Without any hesitation, Nelson declared, "I am prepared to take the case. I will indict the Briggs Corporation." "How can you indict the company without information and the identity of the felons who beat up the four Briggs workers?" Genora asked. "That is not an insuperable problem," Nelson said. "There's not a jury in Detroit that wouldn't find Briggs guilty after I get through with the case. However, there is one proviso: I insist, before I go through with an indictment, we must have the full support and cooperation of the United Automobile Workers Union."

Genora, Ernie and I concluded, over a cup of coffee, that Walter Reuther was not likely to accede to a trial of Briggs Manufacturing that involved prominent unionists identified with far-leftists of a Trotskyist persuasion. This view was confirmed a few days later, when Ernie telephoned and said that the UAW had vetoed Nelson's handling of the matter.

Face to Face with the Perrone Gang

Soon after the meeting with Nelson, we received a call from the office of attorney Nick Rothe, a friend of Emil Mazey who had represented Local No. 212 in many legal matters. Roy Snowden told us that Nick had used his influence to get the attempted murder charges brought against him by the Wayne County prosecutor—following publication of the photograph of him wielding a baseball bat against a Ford-hired Serviceman in 1941—dropped. The lawyers wanted me to go to Detroit because the members of the Perrone gang of strikebreakers were on trial for union-busting activities at the Michigan Stove Company, which employed a thousand workers in the Jefferson Avenue plant.

The attorneys were keen to know if I was able to identify one of the Perrone gang as involved in the brutal attack on Genora less than a year earlier. Information filtering out from the grand jury hearings had made it common knowledge in union ranks that Perrone had been the major mafioso behind the Briggs beatings, though this information was not yet public knowledge.

Nick Rothe's office was in the Barlum Towers, which also housed the municipal courtrooms, a short elevator ride away. I met Roy Snowden there. We were advised that Mafia chief Santo Perrone and several of his gang were slated to be sentenced. We went to the courtroom and sat in the first row behind the railing separating the audience from the court participants. Ken Morris and his wife were in the rear of the courtroom, three rows behind us. They had been asked to identify Ken's attackers.

The judge was on a dais directly in front of the spectators. To the judge's right a door led to his chamber and to a holding area for the defendants. Along the wall to the judge's right sat the defendants: Santo Perrone, Perrone's son-in-law, and several others. Perrone sat in the middle of the group. According to the leaked grand jury information, he had employed some of this gang to intimidate the Briggs workers.

In front of the railing several court officials were talking with Nick Rothe. Rothe had the physique of John L. Lewis, probably a few inches taller, and bushy eyebrows like Lewis's as well as a booming courtroom voice. When he spotted Roy Snowden, he came over. Roy made the introductions. Rothe exclaimed in a voice that could be heard all over the courtroom: "Are any of those sitting in the dock involved in your beatings?" In a moderate voice, I replied: "The one sitting to Perrone's left looks like he could be the one. It's hard to tell since he's seated."

Abruptly Nick gestured to Roy and me: "Come with me!" He ushered us past the railing and walked us into the court area; no more than three feet separated us from Santo Perrone. Rothe bellowed, gesturing to Perrone and his gang members: "Take a good look at them!" Perrone never blinked an eye, acting oblivious to the expostulating Rothe directly in front him.

When we returned to our seats, I told Rothe that the son-in-law to Perrone's right could have been Genora's attacker, but I needed to know how tall he was. "When he gets up," Rothe said, "he will walk past the judge through the door at his right. Measure his height against the molding that's several feet below the ceiling." Rothe then returned to the inner court area, and Roy and I watched the proceedings until the prisoners exited the courtroom. I was surprised to see that Santo Perrone was not much more than five feet tall. His son-in-law, Carl Renda, was much taller and broader. Walter Nelson's confident re-marks about his ability to take on Briggs crossed my mind as the trial worked its way to a climax.

Santo Perrone personified the evil criminal character. Union-busting tends to attract reprehensible members of society. The grand jury revealed this Mafia gang's record of union bashings, murder, extortion, immigrant smuggling, and other crimes. Knowing how to beat the system, many of them had escaped. That was in the past; now the union counterbalanced corporation influence with some political influence. The trial represented this partial shift. Armed with the knowledge that this gang had beaten Genora and the other Briggs workers, I was determined to be a witness against them, and through them get the Briggs corporation put on trial.

We retired to Rothe's office. I told Nick that in size and build, Carl Renda looked like Genora's assailant. Rothe picked up the phone and dialed Emil Mazey's private line and told him I had identified the son-in-law, Carl Renda. As he held the phone away from his ear, we could hear the expostulating Emil: "Impossible," he shouted. "The bastard was in the Army." Rothe, normally no shrinking violet, answered in a chastened voice. "It would provide Renda with a perfect alibi. He could have arranged a weekend pass." "That's ridiculous—forget it!" With that, Mazey concluded the conversation.

After a few moments of silence I said, "Perrone can have no doubt that I identified someone in his family. They have a reputation of doing away with witnesses. What do I do now, Nick?" Decidedly less ebullient, Rothe responded, "Why don't you go see Ken Morris? As president of

Local No. 212, and a close personal friend of Emil, maybe he can talk to Mazey." I immediately went to the East Side local to talk with Morris, who informed me that he hadn't recognized any of the men in the Mafia group. I explained to Morris the danger of my exposure to Perrone at the trial. He was sympathetic to my plight but had no advice to give; nor did he volunteer to talk to Emil. When I asked him how he was protecting himself these days, he opened a bottom desk drawer to reveal a small revolver. Morris said, "When I get ready to leave the office, I always check through the shuttered blinds overlooking Mack Avenue and make sure the street is clear before I go to my car."

Reuther Brothers' Shootings Force Senate Investigation

On April 20, 1948, Walter Reuther was shot with a 12-gauge shotgun while preparing a late-evening snack in his kitchen. The attackers just missed killing him. The International Union responded by posting a reward of $100,000 leading to information and conviction of whoever attempted the assassination of the UAW president. The union hired Ralph Winstead as an investigator. Winstead had a distinguished career working for the Senator La Follette labor subcommittee, which had exposed corporation employment of labor spies, gangsters, and goons during the 1930s. Less than a month later, Victor Reuther, Walter's youngest brother, was shot in the face, losing an eye and sustaining a smashed jaw. The UAW International increased the reward to $200,000. This unprecedented attack on labor compelled action from Congress in 1951.

The opening of the Senator Estis Kefauver crime investigating hearings in Detroit were preceded by the release of the findings of the Gerald T. Murphy Grand Jury hearings held in 1948. The latter testimony filled twenty-eight volumes. Kefauver was now in possession of the facts pertaining to the granting of a million-dollar scrap contract to Santo Perrone's son-in-law, Carl Renda. The testimony disclosed that a former industrial relations director of Briggs claimed the contract bought labor peace at the unrecovered loss of $14,000 dollars a month. Even more devastating was the revelation that a Briggs official protested the contract to the FBI and was fired by the company.[2]

The Kefauver investigations into gang operations in Detroit and the rest of the country focused on the Perrone scrap contract with the owner of the Michigan Stove Company. The hearings compelled Michigan Stove to terminate the contract. The court ruling on the mobsters' alleged strikebreaking, modest as it was, delivered the second blow. Perrone, Carl Renda, and four others were found guilty of bribing workers at Michigan Stove, were fined $1,000 each, and placed on probation. The ruling charged the defendants with illegally resisting UAW efforts at union organization. In the wake of these two Perrone scandals the UAW finally succeeded in obtaining a union contract with John A. Fry, president of Michigan Stove.[3]

One evening I returned home from work at the Chevrolet Assembly plant to find an elderly grey-haired man drinking a cup of coffee and chatting with Genora. It was Ralph Winstead. He asked if, after dark, Genora would be willing to try to identify the man with a large scar across his cheek whom she had seen two years earlier, apparently scouting our Detroit apartment house. After she agreed, Ralph brought us up to date on the progress of the investigations. He had no doubt about who was involved in the beatings and the shootings of the Reuther brothers. However, the union didn't know which person had participated in each act. This remained to be resolved.

Ralph gave us a short history of the Detroit Mafia. He told us about witnesses to murders who had been killed by the Mafia; some, under guard by the Detroit police in a high-rise hotel, were pushed or jumped out of a window. Other witnesses who had confessed to crimes recanted at the last moment. One story followed another for the next three hours as Ralph revealed the insidious influence of the Mafia over members of the police department. Ralph reminded us that Detective Albert De Lamielleure's wife and Santo Perrone secretly owned the Canton Bar across the street from Michigan Stove, whose owner had fought unionization for years.

We were particularly surprised to learn that Melvin Bishop, former regional director of the UAW on the East Side of Detroit and the arch nemesis of Local No. 212, enjoyed the hospitality of Santo Perrone's hunting lodge during the deer-hunting season. Members of the Mazey union caucus had always thought Bishop was involved in the Briggs beatings, but hard evidence had never been uncovered.

Winstead informed us that the Mafia used illegal Italian immigrants for criminal activities. He thought it very probable that one of these immigrant families lived on the block near us and, by looking across a vacant lot, could see our arrivals and departures. These illegal immigrants owed a debt to Perrone, which was repaid when he needed help in strikebreaking activities and other pursuits.

The Department of Immigration and Naturalization had long

suspected Perrone's employment at the Michigan Stove Company as the ideal cover for an immigrant-smuggling operation. The agency conducted a raid in January 1950 and arrested twenty illegal Sicilians. A close associate of Perrone, Clarence Jacobs, was arrested in 1928 in Mt. Clemens "on a charge of smuggling as many as 200 aliens a month into Michigan from Ontario."[4]

I asked Ralph, "You must be known to the Mafia. How do you protect yourself? Do you carry a gun?" "No, I don't carry a gun," he replied. "When we leave here tonight for this bar in Mt. Clemens, before we leave I'll call my wife and tell her where I'm going and how long I expect to be gone. If she doesn't hear from me in a reasonable period of time, she'll notify the police." At twilight, Winstead, Genora and I left in our respective cars for the Mt. Clemens bar, which was controlled, operated and owned by Perrone's friends and gang members. Having been told about the activities of the Mafia in Detroit over the last decade, we were not reassured by the news that Ralph did not carry a gun.

The bar jutted out over Lake St. Clair. Smugglers rowed aliens from Canada across the lake at night, and took them up a ladder to a storeroom in the rear of the bar. From there they were taken to a fish market in Mt. Clemens owned by Perrone and to other destinations. Ralph told us, "When we get to the bar talk about something innocuous like the Detroit Tigers." It was a coal-black night. The bar sat back several hundred feet from a two-lane highway. Low-wattage bulbs strung from an overhead wire lit the gravel road to the bar. The setting was like a scene out of Dashiell Hammett. Only two other customers were at the long bar. We walked to the rear and ordered beer. After we placed our order, another bartender came through the swinging rear door. We could see he instantly recognized Ralph Winstead as he passed. Regrettably, that was the only instance of recognition that evening. Neither bartender fitted the description of the person Genora had seen casing our home in Detroit. The evening had been useful only because of the illuminating information we had been given about our adversaries.

Kefauver Hearings Expose Mafia Influence

Six years after the Briggs beatings, five years after the investigation by the 1946 Detroit Grand Jury, and following continuous pressure on Congress from the International Union, the Estes Kefauver Special Senate Committee investigation of crime in Detroit began its hearings.

The Senate Committee was primarily concerned with the shotgun attacks on the Reuther brothers. All of the evidence originated from the five beatings of the four Briggs workers. Our fate and the shootings of Walter and Victor were inextricably linked.

Among those called to testify were Santo Perrone; his brother, Gaspar; his son-in-law, Carl Renda; the president and general manager of Briggs Manufacturing Company, Dean Robinson; the owner of the Woodmere Scrap Metal Co., Louis Freedman; and Emil Mazey, secretary-treasurer of the UAW International Union.[5]

The hearings, which lasted three days, revealed Santo Perrone's arrest record from 1920 through 1945:

1920   charge of murder;
1930   prohibition;
1932   arson;
1934   carrying concealed weapons;
1935   leaving the scene of an accident;
1936   six-year rap on prohibition charges;
1942   concealed weapons in a locker at Michigan Stove;
1945   arrested, woman killed left a note for police to talk to Perrone.

Perrone was described as "a pocket edition of Al Capone" by Jack Strohm, writing in the *Detroit Free Press*.[6]

Perrone had worked at Michigan Stove as a core worker. Core workers worked in the foundry and made molds into which molten iron was poured. The plant employed a thousand workers, but only sixty to seventy belonged to a union. John A. Fry, the president of Michigan Stove, had successfully resisted several efforts by the UAW to organize the Michigan Stove workers. Perrone's strikebreaking, head-busting technique, and the introduction of illegal aliens as strikebreakers destroyed union efforts. The Michigan Stove plant was an anti-union shop surrounded by tens of thousands of UAW workers.

Mr. Burling for the Senate Committee questioned Dean Robinson, a son-in-law of Briggs, founder of the company. Burling established that Briggs had signed a 25-year scrap contract with Louis Freedman of Woodmere Scrap Metal Co. In April 1945 the company had abruptly terminated this and awarded the contract to Carl Renda, Perrone's son-in-law:

> Burling: Did you know anything about Renda in 1945 when he got the contract?
>
> Robinson: No, sir. I met him shortly after he got the contract.

Burling: Did you ever ask Cleary [in charge of awarding contracts, but deceased before the hearing] why he would take a fellow one year out of college, without an office, without a telephone, without any technical training, with no capital, no trucks, no loading equipment, no yard, no siding, no processing equipment?

Robinson: No, sir.

Burling: You never asked him?

Robinson: No.

Renda's testimony revealed that he was twenty-eight when he was given the Briggs contract to haul scrap. He had worked at National Twist and Drill for $1.46 an hour, where he made $100 a week. It was incomprehensible that a major manufacturing corporation would bestow a scrap contract on an employee at another Detroit plant making $1.46 an hour, and who possessed none of the capital equipment necessary for hauling scrap metal. The trucks and other capital investment of Louis Freedman amounted to several hundred thousands of dollars.

Briggs officials suggested to the shocked Freedman that he talk to Perrone. He duly called Perrone and asked him to arrange an appointment with Renda. He met Perrone and Renda in the lobby of the Statler Hotel and begged them to let him continue hauling the Briggs scrap. An arrangement was made and accepted. Instead of paying Briggs for the scrap, Freedman paid Renda, and Renda in turn paid Briggs. This collusion netted Renda $46,000 in the first year and $100,000 in the second year.

Burling: [to Renda] Is it true that after 18 years or 20 years they [Freedman, Woodmere Scrap Metal] left their equipment there; they picked up the scrap with their loaders and their mechanical trains and they put the scrap on their trucks and drove their trucks to the yards and processed them and put them on railroad cars for shipping, and you did not touch the scrap at all; is that correct?

Renda: That is correct....

Burling: At any rate, the fact is that the physical handling of the scrap did not change when you came in with your contract. The only difference was that they paid you instead of paying Briggs.

Although the Kefauver hearings, conducted by a subcommittee, produced startling information, no charges were made by the committee. The hearings were the result of Reuther's pressure on members of the Senate and the House at a time when the UAW exercised great influence with the Democratic Party. Notwithstanding all the information obtained (much of which still remains concealed from the public), it was always highly unlikely that the captains of the Detroit auto industry would ever be prosecuted.[7]

While Reuther wanted to find the persons involved in the Reuther shotgun attacks, and demonstrated it by posting UAW reward money of over $200,000, he was less concerned about the Briggs victims of 1945. Mazey was intensely loyal to his caucus followers and needed little additional motivation when he learned that Melvin Bishop, the former East Side Director of the UAW, used the Santo Perrone hunting lodge in northern Michigan. Bishop negotiated contracts with Briggs that UAW Local No. 212 had rejected as inadequate on several occasions during the war. As we will see, Walter Reuther nevertheless submitted Bishop's name as his candidate for vice president of the UAW at the 1947 UAW International convention. (The locals on the East Side of Detroit, led by the Briggs local, exploded in anger, proceeding to vote into office R. J. Thomas as vice president and re-electing Addes as secretary-treasurer, thereby upsetting Reuther's plan to dominate the union.)

In 1951 Ralph Winstead met with the Michigan state police and reported on several meetings held by major Detroit automobile executives:

> In 1943 a series of meetings had been held by large employers, Messrs. Fry, Bennett [of Ford Motor Co.] Dean Robinson and others for the purpose of discussing ways and means to eliminate unions at the termination of World War II. These meetings were attended by Perrone ... and Tony Dana. Information indicates that Sam Perrone was likewise to get a scrap contract from Ford and Chrysler. A similar meeting was held May 12, 1950, at the Book Cadillac Hotel attended by Messrs. Bennett, Fry, Dean Robinson, Hutchinson and other persons.[8]

The questioning of Robinson and Fry by the Senate committee established that they enjoyed close relations for many years. Despite the great weight of circumstantial evidence, Perrone had successfully evaded jail, except for one or two rather brief stays. Such corporate violence would probably continue to go unpunished. It confirmed to us the truth of the observation by Vincent R. Dunne, leader of the Minneapolis truck drivers, that a symbiotic relation existed between corporations and the Mafia thugs.

In the summary report of the committee issued publicly in February 1951 the committee declared in a spectacular headline, "How Gangs Sap U.S. of Billions." The committee reported that a secret government within the existing institutions ruled the underworld. The report included the shocking information that this underworld had a budget of $20 billion a year to support its nefarious activities.[9]

Following the hearings, Genora wrote to Walter Reuther and to Local No. 212. Her letter was answered by Emil Mazey on February 27, 1951:

> I wish to advise you that we are taking many steps, including a number of legal steps, to bring about a complete solution to the Briggs beatings as well as the Reuther shootings.
>
> I am certain that the aggressive campaign that we have mapped out in this connection will ultimately lead to the solution of these crimes.

Victor Reuther states in *The Brothers Reuther* that the FBI closed the case years before the statute of limitations had run out.

In 1953 Joseph Ritchie, ex-convict and a nephew of Clarence Jacobs, a member of Perrone's Mafia group, was induced to cross over from Canada to Detroit and to give evidence. He met with Detroit's prosecutor, and the prosecutor made public the following statement by Ritchie:

> I was in a car the night Walter Reuther was shot.... The night of the shooting I was picked up at the gas station. I sat in the back seat. Jacobs drove and Peter Lombardo was in the front seat with Jacobs. I was there in case there was any trouble. If anything happened, I was to drive the car away. Jacobs did the shooting. He was the only one who got out of the car. I don't know how long he was gone.... I heard the report of a gun. Then Jacobs got back in the car and said, "Well, I knocked the bastard down."
>
> We took off in a hurry. After the job they dropped me back at the Helen Bar about 200 feet from the gas station. I don't know what they did with the car. I heard later it was demolished and junked. Haven't any idea what happened to the gun. I had some drinks and then went to see Carl Renda. Why? I always went in to see Renda. He said, "I have something for you." He got a bundle of cash and handed it to me.... It was exactly five grand.[10]

Foster Hailey of the *New York Times* reported:

> Ritchie, according to the story, said the shooting was ordered by Santo [Sam] Perrone, a wealthy former bootlegger, union buster and scrap iron dealer who is a fugitive from a warrant. Ritchie said he had been paid his share for the job—$5,000—by Carl Renda, Perrone's son-in-law.[11]

Ritchie was under guard at the Statler Hotel, where he was held as a material witness. While pretending to take a shower in his three-room suite, he slipped out a side door and fled to Windsor, Canada. The two policemen involved were found negligent and forfeited thirty days' pay.

The Kefauver Committee investigations into the activities of Perrone and his associates revealed a lucrative scrap contract with Michigan Stove Company, netting Perrone $65,000 a year since its inception in 1933. The Renda contract with Briggs rewarded him with a yearly payment of $100,000. The Senate committee concluded that the purpose of these contracts was to "have Perrone exert his and gangdom's influence" on the labor problems of Briggs and Michigan Stove.[12]

In December 1957 we read in the *Detroit Free Press* that Ralph Winstead's body had been recovered from Lake St. Clair. Ralph enjoyed the common practice of fishing by making a hole through the ice. He had been investigating the Briggs beatings and the Reuther shootings for eight years. When they found his body, he was wearing a fisherman's outfit.

Chapter 11

Reuther Slams the Door on Union Democracy, 1947–1948

Is it true that the leaders of our movement are to be the first of our mighty hosts of eight million members to put their tails between their legs and run like cravens before the threat of Taft–Hartley bill? I am reminded of the Biblical parable, "Lions led by asses."
John L. Lewis, San Francisco AFL Convention, 1947

At the UAW International Union convention in Atlantic City on November 9–14, 1947, Walter Reuther was re-elected president. An early casualty of Reuther's victory was Ray Tucker, a Trotskyist and a Fisher Body union leader, whom I wrote about under the nom de guerre Emmett Moore in the *Militant*.[1]

The articles reviewed the firing of Tucker, former vice president of UAW Fisher Body No. 1 local, who worked as a millwright. He was dismissed by the company for removing his work clothes three minutes before time. For this common infraction, the shop rules laid down a penalty ranging from as little as a reprimand to as much as a week's loss of pay. Union officers were consequently astonished to learn that Tucker, a member of the shop committee for four years, chairman of the same body for two, elected delegate to all the national conventions but one, would be the target for the enforcement of this rarely implemented rule.

At the 1947 UAW International Union convention, a year before Ray's dismissal, the Thomas–Addes caucus had appointed Ray Tucker to the important resolutions committee. The union caucuses expected that among the most important matters before the convention would be the struggle over the Taft–Hartley bill. Tucker joined with the majority of the committee in recommending to the convention that the union reject the proposed Taft–Hartley legislation.

Taft–Hartley required officers to sign a non-Communist affidavit. Its more egregious measures banned the closed shop, and provided for the president to establish a cooling-off period of sixty days before a strike that would affect the health and welfare of the nation, Furthermore, it granted the National Labor Relations Board the right to issue injunctions and made secondary boycotts illegal. The passage of the bill into law set back unionization for the next five decades.[2]

The arbitrator's decision on Ray Tucker, following the convention, was to uphold his firing. How could a violation of the contract that provided for a maximum penalty of a week's wages result in termination of employment? We will never know how the Reuther-dominated department handled the presentation, but to those experienced in these arcane proceedings the following scenario could be imagined: the UAW bargaining representatives attended the hearing with a batch of grievances. Trades were made, and in the shuffle the union bartered away Tucker, a Trotskyist, in favor of a machine-caucus supporter. It had more to do with union politics than with union justice.

Targeting the Left

Ten months before the UAW convention that would consolidate Reuther's control and eliminate the Thomas–Addes caucus, the Mazey–Reuther caucus of the Briggs local had met to decide on candidates for local union office. Tom Clampitt, a supporter of Emil Mazey and a member of the Socialist Party, planned to run for president of the local. Ernest Mazey, a member of the Socialist Workers Party, planned to run for the post of vice president. Ken Morris, recording secretary of the local and a point man for Emil, brought in a motion designed to knock Ernest from the slate. "We support CIO policy," Morris declared. "We will oppose the attempt of any minority political party or group to interfere or control the local or the international."[3]

The statement, though innocuous on paper, was understood to mean that the Reds were taking their orders from Moscow. This outside political force had to be fought. Ken Morris, Emil Mazey, and Walter Reuther had no scruples about lumping Trotskyists with Stalinists, even though they knew of the historic division between the two groups. Trotskyists were *persona non grata* to Reuther. Yet he welcomed the support of the priest-ridden, Vatican-influenced Association of Catholic Trade Unionists—an acceptable outside force. Their newspaper, the *Wage Earner*, reached into every local union. Many priests worked as unpaid staff on behalf of Reuther slates. Outside the confessional, they canvassed members of the opposition caucus to woo them to Reuther's side.[4]

From the beginning of his administration, Reuther had made his intentions clear: to root out opposition or buy out former leading opponents with positions after they had taken an oath of loyalty. Many of his former opponents surrendered without a backward glance. Among the more notable of those who crossed over were Shelton Tappes, former leader of the Blacks in Ford Local No. 600, and Douglas Fraser, a former leader in the Thomas–Addes group. Loyalty to Reuther and his beliefs would eventually deliver Fraser the presidency of the UAW.

Reuther had an administrative staff of more than seven hundred to handle in-house chores and service the local unions. For the first time, the Detroit headquarters exercised its right to intervene actively in the life of the locals. Such intervention had occurred rarely during the Thomas regime, and Homer Martin's effort in this regard was rejected by the actions of the Cleveland convention in 1939.

Porkchoppers (the common term for administration hired hands) were like the Jesuits in the Catholic Church, who took orders only from the Pope. They answered only to that higher authority located in the offices of the new UAW Vatican leader. They poked their noses into every nook and cranny of union activity. The one-party regime was swiftly transformed into a one-man authoritarian administration. "We need teamwork in the leadership," Reuther told the delegates to the eleventh convention of the union, "and we need unity in the ranks."[5] In a few years that unity was to produce the silence of the mausoleum.

Walter Reuther was sensitive to criticism, but he carefully controlled his reactions to it. We heard critical observations from more than one staff member chafing at the strict rules for continued employment at Solidarity House. Many years later, Genora and I were party to a demonstration of the thinness of Reuther's skin when we visited professors Joyce and Hy Kornbluh in Ann Arbor after an annual celebration of the sitdown strikes by Flint Chevrolet Local No. 659. There we met B. J. Widick, coauthor with Irving Howe of a book on Reuther. We had not seen him for many years. Genora remembered that he had come to Flint during the sitdown strike to work on the *Flint Auto Worker*, the union newspaper during the strike. I had not seen Widick since the 1939–1940 conflict in the SWP over the nature of the Soviet state. Widick and Howe left the Socialist Workers Party; they were staunch adherents of Max Shachtman, who had broken with Trotsky on his characterization of the Soviet Union as a deformed workers' state.

When the conversation drifted around to his book on Reuther, Widick, even after four decades, still couldn't understand why the UAW and Reuther boycotted the sale of the book. Reuther had taken umbrage at some critical remarks in the book, despite the fact that Widick was a loyal supporter. This didn't make sense to Widick, but came as no surprise to those who knew Reuther's character.[6]

Whereas Widick had always been loyal to Reuther, our group, the SWP, only gave him critical support in 1946. Most of our auto union delegates voted to support Walter Reuther's run for president for his militant conduct of the four-month General Motors strike. Until the 1945–1946 strike, we perceived the two groups, Thomas–Addes and the Reuther camp, as factional cliques without a particle of major difference. In a matter of a few hours, we knew our support for Reuther was a serious blunder.

Reuther's victory speech following his re-election at the 1947 convention occurred at a meeting of the Reuther caucus. We sat in stunned silence, along with the entire audience, as Reuther announced his intention actively to attack members of left-wing political groups who disagreed with his policies. The pregnant silence was broken by an inebriated delegate in the front row. John McGill broke through the stifling atmosphere to ask Reuther to spell out if by outsiders he meant Socialists and Trotskyists as well as Communists. Reuther's answer amounted to a declaration of war against the radical left: his target was both the large Communist Party contingent in auto and the Trotskyists with influence in a number of key UAW locals.

Immediately after his victory speech, Reuther told a large caucus meeting he intended to run Melvin Bishop for vice president against R. J. Thomas. Until the announcement, Bishop had been an active supporter of the Thomas–Addes group. Reuther made his choice without caucus consultation; the Briggs delegation interpreted his action as a crass betrayal. Bishop, after all, had fought the local over the no-strike pledge during the war and had been a suspect in the Briggs beatings. In response, the Briggs delegates, having voted for Reuther for president, switched their votes and joined with delegates from the East Side locals, soundly defeating Reuther's handpicked nominee for vice president.

This was not the first demonstration of Reuther's contempt for the collegial rule of the union. As the eightieth Congress mounted its campaign for anti-union legislation under the leadership of Hartley in the House of Representatives and Taft in the Senate, Reuther shamelessly manifested the unprincipled nature of his union leadership by his failure to mobilize labor to fight against a bill that was to hang around the neck of labor for the next fifty years.

Locals Rally against Taft–Hartley Bill

Alarmed by the stringent laws proposed by the Republicans to curb the power of the labor movement, and to restrict many aspects of union activity, the lower echelons of the union erupted in opposition. Trotskyists took the lead in key UAW locals to oppose the congressional legislation. The role of the Trotskyists in UAW history has not been properly assessed by labor historians. In their efforts to understand the role of partisan political groups, they have tended to concentrate instead on the main power groupings in the UAW. It was thus easy for them to slight the contribution of the far-left Socialists, who were far more than fringe players in that history. Although small in comparison with the major political forces at work, they nonetheless exerted an influence far beyond their size.

In March 1947, Ernest Mazey introduced a resolution in Briggs Local No. 212 in Detroit, calling for a demonstration in Cadillac Square to protest against the Taft–Hartley Bill then passing through Congress. It urged the union to lead in sponsoring the demonstration. The local submitted the resolution to the Wayne County CIO Council, which concurred with the call for a protest action by the union movement. On April 15, the International Executive Board of the UAW met and approved the call for a demonstration and asked all workers to take time off work from 2 p.m. to 7 p.m. They called on the AFL and independent unions to participate in the demonstration. A few days later, on April 24, Detroit witnessed the largest demonstration in its history as 500,000 workers walked out of the plants. Over 250,000 marched into Cadillac Square. Among the Detroit General Motors plants that walked out were Cadillac, Fleetwood, and Chevrolet Drop Forge. Plants with pro-Reuther leadership in the General Motors locals remained at work. This gave rise to reports that Reuther had opposed the walkouts of the GM workers.[7]

John Anderson, president of GM Fleetwood Local No. 15, chronicles these crucial events in his book *Fifty Years of the UAW: From Sitdowns to Concessions*. His version of events is as follows. As a member of the GM sub-council, Anderson submitted a resolution for a Cadillac Square demonstration, which was passed despite the opposition of Reuther supporters. The resolution was forwarded to the UAW International Board meeting in Buffalo. The Board voted for the demonstration, and Reuther duly sent telegrams to the locals informing the officers to close the plants two hours earlier for a march into Cadillac Square on April

24. A short time later Anderson and the other officers of the General Motors locals were called to a meeting by Art Johnstone, director of the GM department. He told them that an early walkout would be in violation of the contract. Anderson informed Johnstone that his orders came from a higher authority: Reuther and the International Executive Board. The plants closed and the auto workers marched to Cadillac Square to hear speeches from Thomas, Addes, George Edwards (chairman of the Common Council), and Victor Reuther. Those GM locals led by Reuther supporters, for their part, left the plants at the regular time and came to the square later.

Officers of GM locals Fleetwood No. 15, Cadillac No. 22 and Chevrolet No. 735 were penalized or fired, with John Anderson among those receiving the maximum penalty. The presidents from 150 UAW locals then met and instructed the officers to negotiate the reinstatement of those fired. The reported settlement provided for penalties of up to seventy days' lost time. An effort to refer the agreement to the officers of the locals was rejected by Reuther. He told the aggrieved workers to accept the settlement or negotiate with GM themselves. Reuther finally informed the locals that the union would observe the no-strike clause during the life of the contract.[8]

Labor historian David Brody, having observed the cast of union leaders for several decades, concludes:

> While he might exploit rank-and-file militancy on the road to power as Reuther skillfully did over the no-strike pledge during World War Two— ultimately the test of any union leader consisted of his ability at managing the pressure from below. In this endeavor, he needed the help of management and it, in turn, needed him.[9]

Every UAW leader—Thomas, Addes, and Reuther—had wanted the power to restrict strikes, but not until the Reuther era did that power become an unchallengeable fact. It was Reuther's way of punishing union militants who went beyond his guidelines, and thus of regimenting the ranks. Violations of the no-strike clause in union contracts would no longer be tolerated.

Reuther Heeds Washington's Call

Reuther downplayed his criticism of Taft–Hartley in his opening address to the November 1947 convention, devoting only a few sentences to this draconian anti-union measure. This brief statement followed a long list of strikes in which the union was currently engaged, as observation regarding the rising profits of the corporations and criticism of the ads of the National Association of Manufacturers railing against price controls. Reuther's action contrasted sharply with that of John L. Lewis, who fought against the bill in the October AFL San Francisco convention. William Green and his counterparts at first tried to assuage Lewis but in the end voted for the non-Communist affidavits. In response, and with no formal notice, Lewis took his miners out of the American Federation of Labor.

Reuther did not find the provision of Taft–Hartley, which required every officer to sign a non-Communist affidavit, particularly advantageous; nevertheless, once it had been introduced, he was quite willing to use it as a weapon when it suited him. Red-baiters in the era of McCarthy didn't use stilettoes when pickaxes worked as well.

With regard to the Communist Party, Walter Reuther ran the gamut from close collaborator to hostile political opponent. No one ever questioned the political instincts of this former Socialist. Nevertheless, he did miss the change in thinking that came to America by way of the former prime minister and wartime leader of Great Britain. Winston Churchill's 1946 "Iron Curtain" speech at Fulton, Missouri, signaled the beginning of the Cold War. Reuther missed its original significance. In fact the speech was made three weeks before the UAW convention that elected Reuther to the presidency. Reuther denounced Churchill's speech. Much later, however, he quietly altered his position. The national media were slow to recognize this change and its significance: Walter's new political stance was now in consonance with Washington. The politicians, for their part, also failed initially to see him as a reliable ally in its campaign to rid labor of its left wing. By the end of the 1947 convention, the media had corrected their stance and shifted their support from Thomas–Addes to Reuther.

The first months of 1947 had seen the anti-labor legislation pass through Congress. At the beginning, the bill was loaded with anti-union provisions; these were later moderated in the face of mounting labor opposition and some of the largest demonstrations the country had ever seen. Political representatives in Washington recognized that the unions were uniting around labor's left wing, thereby producing the opposite effect to that sought by the reactionary legislators. Concentrating on that part of the law that would require every union leader to sign a non-Communist affidavit, Congress came up with a workable strategy: it would separate the militant leftwing leaders from the broad ranks.

At the 1946 convention Reuther, even though he had won the presidency, nevertheless did not gain control of the majority of the Board. The Thomas–Addes group, holding a majority of the Board, therefore appointed the chairmen for all the standing committees at the eleventh International convention of November 1947. Reuther, however, controlled a majority of the convention delegates. Reuther could act like Bonaparte, standing above the fray, but in truth he remained in full control of the debate.

Leo Fenster from Cleveland introduced the resolution against Taft–Hartley. His omnibus "whereas" clauses (subordinate clauses appended to a resolution) attacking the anti-labor legislation sidestepped the thrust of the issue of non-Communist affidavits. Only the last "whereas" brought the matter to a head. In support of the Thomas–Addes resolution, Fenster referred to Philip Murray, who on another occasion had said the following:

> I was unwilling to file an affidavit that I was not a Communist. That is a matter of principle. I do not know why the Congress of the United States should require me to do that, as a citizen. I think the Congress is very presumptuous, because I think if they could do that to me about the question of Communism, they could do it about any other kind of issue.... It is reasonable to assume that if a man is required to file an affidavit of this description, the Congress that enacts legislation of that kind can readily enact a law which says to a labor leader, 'What are you? A Catholic, Protestant or Jew?[10]

Willoughby Abner, representing Walter Reuther, presented the minority position. The core of his contribution came down to a declaration that if the affidavits were not signed, "our organizational work will bog down considerably.... Without complying with the affidavits, we do not have the right of appeal for these workers. The NLRB machinery would not be available to us."

Johnny McGill of Buick Local No. 599 made one of the more cogent speeches in the debate. He reminded the delegates of the trickery used to get the union to give up overtime pay after the bombing of Pearl Harbor. The union leaders had promised that the sacrifices made by union members would be matched by equal sacrifices by the corporations. It had instead turned into a one-sided deal, said McGill: Labor made the sacrifices and the corporations piled up the profits. McGill charged that the proposed Taft–Hartley legislation would enslave labor. He resented the UAW leaders condemning the bill and then telling the delegates that the union was compelled to use its provisions.

Emil Mazey joined the debate to say that although Taft–Hartley was unconstitutional, the union had to comply so that it could use the facilities of the NLRB in a few contested union elections. Thomas entered the fray and issued a challenge for a debate, which was accepted by Mazey. All the while, Walter Reuther stayed aloof from the fracas, meting out democratic rulings as set forth by the rules committee. Why not? His re-election was preordained, along with control of the Board. Principles be damned; getting re-elected was what it was all about.[11]

After the convention, all of the UAW locals received instructions to comply with the provisions of the Taft–Hartley legislation when it became law.[12] The Buick local, led by John McGill, had fought against Taft–Hartley at the convention, protesting at the clause requiring the signing of a non-Communist affidavit. At the previous convention, McGill had voted for Reuther as president, in appreciation of his aggressive leadership in the 113-day General Motors strike. A sea-change had occurred in the few months since the convention. Reluctantly, the Buick local complied with the Taft–Hartley law and signed the non-Communist affidavits.

Although Ernest Mazey's effort to stop the drift of labor before the onslaught in Congress had succeeded on one level, ultimately the tidal wave of political reaction had rolled on. The ranks of the UAW had changed in terms of age, character, and union experience since 1937. Barely union-conscious, the new recruits returning from the war lacked class consciousness. They had not been hardened by the Depression; hunger was a distant memory. As Army recruits, they were taught to obey authority; with shelter, clothes, and meals provided, they believed and obeyed government propaganda. Class-conscious union leaders could rouse the mass to defend unionism, but the larger political questions, brought on by the Cold War, were too complicated for the membership.

The eleventh convention would be the last at which a modicum of opposition was mounted against Reuther. The media spurred on the campaign to oust radicals from union ranks. A symbiotic relationship between the press and Reuther enabled the president to pose in public as an opponent of the law. Reuther's defense of the left-wingers hauled before government committees was merely a token theatrical gesture.

The three-tiered struggle going on in the country—Reuther's subtle Red-baiting, Taft–Hartley, and the *coup de grâce*, McCarthyism—wiped out the militant unionists from labor's ranks. No succeeding generation would have the opportunity to learn from practical union experience like those who had built the union from the bottom up.

Flint's Last Hurrah

Before Walter Reuther was in a position to exercise full hegemony over his domain, an obstruction occurred in Flint, Michigan. In 1947 Jack Palmer advanced to the presidency of Chevrolet Local No. 659 to succeed Donnel Chapman, who became director of Region 1-C.

Palmer had migrated from Sioux Falls, South Dakota, to Flint, where he found employment at Fisher Body 1. He participated in the 1930 strike, which had broken out spontaneously and then come under the leadership of the Communist Party. Mounted police drove the mass meeting of strikers across the county line, breaking the strike. Though young at this time and with little formal schooling, Palmer never forgot this object lesson of the class struggle. Palmer was hired by Chevrolet to work in Plant 3. In 1937 he was a strike supporter, but at no time was his plant engaged in any strike action. During the 113-day General Motors strike, Jack submitted a membership application to join the Socialist Workers Party.

The Chevrolet local had two caucuses. Before Reuther became president, these comprised hard-line followers of Reuther and a large contingent of Trotskyists. A third group of militant class-conscious workers always supported the Trotskyist group. This latter group had IWW tendencies. When Reuther denounced the left and speciously promised to rid the union of outside political control, the Trotskyists and their supporters joined the Thomas–Addes group. The latter had fallen on hard times and accepted SWP leadership of the caucus even though several of their members were in the Communist Party.

Jack Palmer and I met to plan a course of action for the first months of his presidency. We knew that his administration would quickly come under attack from Reuther, who would put every possible obstacle in his path. We worked out a three-point program, with appropriate accompanying resolutions to introduce at the first meeting following his assumption of the post of president.

By 1947 inflation had wiped out the wage gains made in the previous contract. The US economy could scarcely supply the postwar demand for consumer products. Many economists predicted higher inflation, which in a few months would again negate the raises negotiated in a new UAW contract. During the past year some locals, mainly under the influence of Trotskyists, had been proposing tying wages to the cost of living. Frank Marquardt recounted:

> Ernest Mazey and Erwin Baur debated Tom Clampitt and myself on the proposition "Should the UAW bargain for a cost-of-living or wage escalator?" At that time, the Trotskyists were the strongest advocates of wage escalation. I learned later that Leon Trotsky first raised this issue as a "transitional demand"; he theorized that the employers would not grant it, but in the course of fighting for it workers would become more radicalized. When we debated the subject in Town Hall, the UAW was opposed to the escalation principle on the ground that "what goes up, must come down." Accordingly, the local officers were opposed to our holding the debate because "it's against UAW policy!" I consulted the education committee and they agreed that "the show must go on!" Ernest Mazey and Erwin Baur are formidable debaters. Clampitt and I got trounced.[13]

In Flint Chevrolet, more mundane problems confronted us. Jack Palmer and I had to establish a base rate that would make up for the inflationary loss of the previous year. Though not economists, we knew the rise in the cost of living rendered obsolete the unions' proposal of a $0.15-an-hour increase. We settled for $0.25-an-hour for the base rate and the sliding scale of wages; this program obtained through industry-wide bargaining.

Having experienced a four-month strike in 1945–1946, General Motors workers were worried about the possibility of another long strike. Reuther's one-at-a-time strike policy catapulted him to national prominence. Its consequence was to exhaust the wartime workers' savings. During the GM strike the Trotskyists were in favor of industry-wide bargaining to shorten the strike. The steel, glass, and rubber industries were faced with the same problem as auto. A unified strike policy involving all CIO unions made sense: it would exert maximum economic and political pressure to hasten a settlement for all unions.

The sliding-scale-of-wages program was submitted to the Chevrolet caucus and then taken into a Chevrolet meeting. After Jack Palmer's installation as president, he addressed the membership meeting and followed it with a statement to the press dealing with the economic crisis, citing government reports showing that "the next three months will find prices soaring even further into the stratosphere." He continued:

> From all this I conclude that it is urgent and necessary that the UAW request a hearing for a substantial immediate cost of living wage increase. We must find a solution to price jumps at every juncture of the economic cycle which wipes out wage increases.[14]

Later in the meeting, a resolution was proposed to empower the president to publish articles in the local union paper (now in the hands of the Reuther forces). The resolution also enabled Palmer to print handbills for general distribution and to speak on the radio. The resolution was adopted.

Following the meeting, Jack Palmer convoked a meeting of the five Flint UAW local union presidents, representing forty thousand GM workers. They were Joe Berry of Buick, Bob Carter of A.C. Sparkplug,[15] Bill Connolly of Fisher Body 2 and Larry Finnan of Fisher Body 1. The five presidents duly adopted the program submitted by Jack. Of the five, two were supporters of the SWP. Bill Connolly had joined during the 1945–1946 strike; Bob Carter had belonged before the war and, though not now a member, had maintained friendly relations during the years Genora and I were in Flint. Larry Finnan and Joe Berry, for their part, were in the Thomas–Addes caucus.

I drafted a press release and leaked the story to Jack Crellin of the *Detroit Times* to make sure that at least one of the three newspapers carried the release. In fact it made headlines in all three Detroit papers. The Detroit papers apparently thought Reuther was using the Flint unions as a trial balloon. They assumed Reuther was launching his new wage program for the upcoming negotiations. Never before had the five Flint presidents united on an issue. This fact alone made it newsworthy to savvy labor reporters. Many other local unions made the same interpretations and passed supporting resolutions. Solidarity resolutions followed from locals representing a quarter of a million workers. Reuther had been outflanked, and he didn't like it.

We prepared for the expected counterattack, taking advantage of the disarray in the Reuther camp. After the January meeting of Chevrolet Local No. 659, I wrote to the *Militant* (January 14, 1948):

> At the largest meeting of Chevrolet Local #659 UAW–CIO since the 1946 strike, the membership by a 10-to-1 majority voted to support the wage program of the (five) Flint presidents and commended them for their leadership in the wage drive.
>
> Prior to the meeting, the local Reuther group campaigned to block action on the sliding scale-of-wages clause. They deleted all references to the wage program in the local union paper. This was followed by an attempt to gag the local president from issuing press statements on the wage issue.

Coburn Walker, financial secretary of the local, told the *Flint Journal* that the Chevrolet leaders were Communists and Trotskyists. While he was whipping up a minor-key Red scare, it remained for Reuther to do the same on a major scale at a hastily called meeting of the executive boards, shop committees, and officers from Flint and Lansing. Reuther launched into a specious and calculated Red smear of Jack Palmer. Of the several hundred officers present, fewer than a handful read the *Daily Worker* or the *Peoples's World*: only this small group knew that the Communist Party shared Reuther's position in attacking the notion of a sliding scale of wages. The CP identified the idea with Trotskyism; Reuther identified it with pie in the sky.

The most despicable part of Reuther's speech was an attack on the sliding scale proposed, asserting that wages, as well as going up, could also go down. Reuther and Weinberg, his staff economist, had created a nonissue; they knew from Palmer's articles, his speech on the radio, and handbills that he was insisting on a negotiated base rate below which wages could not fall. Other unions had such a clause in their contracts. Reuther's use of this argument showed his deceit, in what was a one-sided debate.

Walter Reuther insinuated that the criticisms of his wage policy were inspired by the Stalinist press. He held up the *Daily Worker* while quoting from Jack Palmer's radio speech, leaving the impression that Palmer took orders from the Communist Party. Reuther charged that it was easy for his critics to find fault with his policies, but they didn't have leadership responsibility. Reuther's wage program called for a $0.15-an-hour increase in wages. He declared that he was bound by the GM conference decision of half a year earlier. Had the conference voted for $0.25-an-hour, he would have been duty bound to fight for it, he insisted. Then he said that those who didn't obey the decisions agreed by the majority would have to be dealt with. The meeting of local committeemen, officers, and executive boards from Flint and Lansing then ended without questions or discussion.

Walter Reuther's attacks on Flint Chevrolet continued at every meeting, delivered by his proxy representatives. Grand debates took place at meetings of the local. Reuther assigned as many as seven porkchoppers to every meeting. To one of the meetings came Roy Reuther, an honorary member of the local for his leadership role in the sitdown strikes. Under ordinary circumstances he would have been shown respect. On this occasion he was met with an unrelenting barrage from talented speakers like Kermit Johnson, Larry Jones, Everett Sides, Bert Boone, Harrison Johnson, and a score of others. He never attended another Chevrolet meeting.

Evidently, Walter Reuther's first visit to Flint had not accomplished its purpose. So another public meeting was arranged in the Flint armory. The five presidents, Marlon Butler, and I met to make plans for the meeting. We considered the problem of the hour-long speech that Reuther would make before anyone could get the floor in rebuttal. We agreed to attack from the floor and not to allow the meeting to adjourn without our participation.

At the armory meeting of seven hundred auto workers Reuther began with his usual hour-long, fist-pumping speech—some delicate Red-baiting larded with fallacious argumentation, misstatement of facts, and obvious distortions of the position of his opponents. At the conclusion of his speech there was total silence: not a single question; no one raised a hand to join in the discussion. How was it possible that in an audience of several hundred no one was prepared to challenge Reuther?

Astounded by the silence, I resolved not to let his speech go un-challenged. I stood in the center aisle and waved my hand in a wide arc so that the audience could see that I was asking for the floor. Don Chapman, regional director and chairman of the meeting, kept scan-ning the audience for a friendlier supporter. But no one else wanted to speak. All the while, I was waving my hand for recognition and taunting Reuther, "Are you afraid to let me speak?" Reuther jumped up from his seat and told Chapman, "Don't recognize him until he is at a seat." I retreated to the first open seat on the aisle and was finally recognized.

I walked up the aisle, leaped onto the platform and spoke to the issue, for perhaps no more than a minute. I could hear Reuther behind me instructing Chapman, "Tell him his time is up." It was the end of the discussion period. Reuther rose to answer. He said he would debate Marxism with me any time, and then, realizing he was giving me more attention than intended, continued by saying he had some young mem-bers on his staff who could debate Marxism with me. With that, the meeting ended. Why hadn't others tried to speak? Probably because these were ordinary auto workers not given to this unusual situation of a debate with their president. Perhaps there was nothing to gain from a debate that opened them to a Red-baiting attack from Reuther. Accord-ing to Ronald Edsforth, "Reuther branded Jack Palmer and the escalator clause Red, adding, "these people are trying to destroy our union."[16]

Giving Credit Where It's Due

In 1980 Kathy Groehn El-Messidi extended a doctoral thesis on the Escalator Clause into a book, *The Bargain: The Story Behind the 30-Year*

Honeymoon of GM and the UAW. Her father was a former public relations director of General Motors. He had given her access to GM files, with the proviso that they could be used only as background information. In the book, El-Messidi offers a straightforward rationale for Reuther's behavior in attacking the five Flint presidents: "Reuther undermined the five presidents in order to keep his power secure, and to maintain a fragmented leadership at a very crucial time. He also opposed escalation out of legitimate fears expressed by many union members that it would freeze real wages." These fears were in fact generated by UAW headquarters. They emerged from Reuther's factional bag to confuse the real issues. "Palmer claimed," writes El-Messidi, "that Reuther only opposed the wage escalation because he wanted to crush political opposition. The people, not the program, were at issue."

Palmer's suggestion was substantiated in a later review of the fight for the escalator clause. Ronald Edsforth said this of Walter Reuther's motives:

> Yet as many Americans found out during this period, truth was irrelevant in a red-baiting campaign like the one Reuther launched against the Five Presidents' program. The accusation of Communist party connections alone, coming from an authority figure such as the U.A.W. president, was enough to discredit the rank-and-file revolt and it led in a few months time to Palmer's defeat in the local union elections.[17]

On April 20, 1948, Walter Reuther was shot. While he was lying in a hospital bed, General Motors proposed a sliding scale of wages, similar to that originally put forward by the five Flint UAW presidents, to the UAW bargaining committee. With a few changes it became known as the cost-of-living clause.

Twenty years later Victor Reuther would brag that the escalator clause had added $18,000 to the paycheck of the GM worker. The UAW contract set a pattern for many other workers in the glass, steel, rubber, and associated industries. It profoundly transformed the economic status of the industrial working class. Reuther never acknowledged that the credit for this program that benefits millions of workers rightfully belongs to five Flint UAW presidents who had the foresight and courage to advance an idea whose time had come.[18]

It took ten years for Walter Reuther to gain control of the UAW. There were several attempts to challenge him during the years of his presidency. Those who succeeded Reuther as president inherited the Reuther machine. Along with the bureaucracy, they espoused his philosophy and program. The UAW today looks old and acts older. The clogged veins of the union indicate a patient in urgent need of medical attention. Humans today have the option of transplant surgery. The annals of labor history do not record the resuscitation of a union organization ill and in decline. The current leadership of the UAW gives no indication that it knows the union has a problem; if it does know, it keeps to itself the cure that could save the patient.

Electric Auto-Lite strike, Toledo 1934: Troops lead the charge behind a
tear-gas barrage.

The National Guard returns fire against strikers with stones from the street.

Electric Auto-Lite Strike: a strikebreaker, stripped of clothes,
is marched down the street.

Picket line at Toledo Chevrolet Transmission strike 1935.

Left: A. J. Muste, National Secretary of the American Workers Party.
Right: John McGill, president of the Buick local 1940, 1945, 1946.

Left: Roy Snowden, Genora and Sol Dollinger in 1944.
Roy and Genora were chief stewards in Mack Avenue Briggs Plant, members of the famous chief stewards' aisle-way caucus; Sol worked at Motor Products.

Right: John Anderson, President of Fleetwood UAW Local No. 15, standing in front of the factory.

Roy Snowden wielding bat at the Ford 1940–1941 organizing campaign;
Jess Ferrazza facing camera, delivering a blow to a bent-over Ford-hired Serviceman.
The photograph, by Milton Brooks, won a Pulitzer prize.

Left to right: Emil, William, Ernest, and Emil Mazey,
in a photograph taken in 1943 on Bill's visit home from boot camp.

Genora Johnson and son Jarvis at the 1937 children's picket line.

Genora and some of the five hundred women inspectors in Mack Avenue Briggs in 1944. Genora is in the second row, center.

Flint, 1937: Car blockade of Fisher Body 2, site of the Battle of Bull's Run.

Strikers at Fisher Body 2 repulsing tear-gas attack at the Battle of Bull's Run.

Women's Emergency Brigade marching in front of Chevrolet Plant 9
after breaking the windows to release the tear gas.

Chevrolet Avenue after the capture of Plant 4.
In the distance is the overpass, the site of the Battle of Bull's Run.

Genora Johnson (seated) with members of the Women's Auxiliary.

John Lamesfield, recording secretary,
and Kermit Johnson, president,
Chevrolet Division UAW Local No.
156. Photo taken at the national
Milwaukee Convention 1937.

Part II

Oral History

Chapter 12

Striking Flint

Genora Dollinger Remembers the 1937 Sitdown

It is quite true that there are no limits to masculine egotism in ordinary life. In order to change the conditions of life we must learn to see them through the eyes of women.

Leon Trotsky, *Problems of Life*

The following account of the Flint sitdown strike is taken from an oral history interview with Genora conducted by Susan Rosenthal in February 1995, and published as a pamphlet the following year.[1] I believe that Genora's contribution to the strike has not been fully acknowledged for a number of reasons, including the fact that she never wrote her own account of it.[2] This narrative goes some way toward setting the record straight. In the words of Victor and Sophie Reuther: "Genora is of the great tradition of Mother Jones who in an earlier generation was to the mine workers what Genora became to the auto workers. A living legend in her own time!"[3]

Conditions Before the Strike

We hire Chevrolet workers from the neck down.

Arnold Lenz, Chevrolet–Flint Plant Manager, 1936

Conditions in Flint before the strike were very, very depressing for working people. We had a large influx of workers come into the city from the deep South. They came north to find jobs, because there was no work back home. They came with their furniture strapped on old jalopies and they'd move into the cheapest housing that they could find. Usually these were just little one- or two-room structures with no inside plumbing and no inside heating arrangements. They just had kerosene heaters to heat their wash water, their bath water, and their homes. You could smell kerosene all over their clothing. They were very poor.

One woman came from a small section of Flint around Fenton Road, where many of these poor southerners settled. She would walk the picket line in the snow in tennis shoes with no gloves. She was a wonderful person. She was there every day, and we'd have to make sure she got warmed up in the union headquarters before she went out on the picket line again.

Before the strike, the women didn't have the opportunity to participate in any activities. The small neighborhood churches were the only places they had to go to. They knew some of their neighbors and they would go to some of these little churches, but that's all. The men frequented the beer gardens and talked to other men about shop problems or whatever. They got to be shop buddies.

When you worked in the factory in those days, no one cared what your name was. You became "Whitey" if you happened to be blonde. Or you might be "Blacky" if you had black hair. If you asked, "Well, who is he?" you'd get, "I don't know, he works in department so-and-so, Plant 4, on the line half way down." It was just "Blacky" or "Shorty" or some nickname. They were wage slaves with a complete loss of identity and rights inside the plant.

At first, when these workers were approached to join the union, they were afraid they might lose this job that was so very valuable to them. At that time, men working in the auto plants were getting paid around forty-five cents an hour. The younger girls that worked in the A.C. Sparkplug division of General Motors were being paid twelve-and-a-half cents an hour to make minor car instruments. That was the only plant that employed women.

I'll tell you about the conditions of these young women. After the strike, a Senate investigating committee found that in one department of A.C. alone, the girls had all been forced to go to the county hospital and be treated for venereal disease traced to one foreman. Those were the conditions that young women had to accept in order to support their families. Sometimes they earned just enough to provide food for the family and they couldn't lose their jobs because nobody else in the family had a job.

Flint was a General Motors town—lock, stock, and barrel! If you drove past one of the huge GM plants in Flint, you could see workers sitting on the front lawns along the side of the plant just waiting for a foreman to come to the door and call them in. And maybe they'd work them for an hour or maybe for a day, and that was it. But workers were so desperate that they would come and sit every day on that lawn in the hopes of being called in and possibly getting a permanent job. That's how poor these General Motors workers really were, at least the ones in hopes of getting a job at GM.

I had a most wonderful father-in-law, a very fine union man who had a little college education in South Dakota, then moved to Flint to work in the auto factories where the big money was supposed to be. Big money then was nothing when you stop to think of it today. But compared to jobs in the rest of the country and considering there was a national depression, it was big money. And if you were a tool and die maker, you made a little more. But the tool-and-die men were not in favor of organizing the plain, ordinary industrial workers. They wanted their skilled unions kept separate. And, of course, they wanted their wages to be kept higher.

Conditions were terrible inside the plants, which were notorious for their speed-up systems. They had men with stopwatches timing the workers to see if they could squeeze one or two more operations in. You saw Charlie Chaplin in *Modern Times*? Well, this is exactly what happened. They did everything but tie a broom to their tail. It was so oppressive that there were several cases of men just cracking up completely and taking a wrench and striking their foreman. When that happened, the worker was sentenced to what was then called an insane asylum in Pontiac, Michigan. The speed-up was the biggest issue. The men just couldn't take it. They would come home at night and they couldn't hold their forks in their swollen fingers. They would just lie down on the floor. Many of them wound up in beer gardens to try to forget their problems and their aches and pains.

They had many medical problems, too, because you couldn't go to the rest room whenever you felt like you had to. When "Mother Nature" called, that was just too bad. You had to wait for the foreman to summon a relief man to come and take your place on the assembly line. Sometimes that took a while. In one plant a worker brought a chamber pot and put it on top of the assembly line. All the workers got a big bang out of that, but he was fired. He lost his job just for that kind of protest.

They used to say, "Once you pass the gates of General Motors, forget about the United States Constitution." Workers had no rights when they entered that plant. If a foreman didn't like the way you parted your hair—or whatever he didn't like about you—you may have looked at him the wrong way, or said something that rubbed him the wrong way—he could fire you. No recourse, no nothing. And practically all foremen expected workers to bring them turkeys on Thanksgiving and gifts for Christmas and repair their motor cars and even paint their houses. The workers were kept intimidated because if they didn't comply with what the foreman told them to do, they would lose their jobs and their families would starve. You can see what a feeling of slavery and domination workers felt inside the GM plants.

Not only that, but when workers started talking about organizing, management hired lip-readers to watch the men talk to each other, even when they were right close to each other, so they could tell if they were talking union. One of our friends who was a member of the Socialist Party wore the first UAW button into the Chevrolet plant. He was fired immediately. He didn't even get to his job. They spotted the button and that was it. If you went into a beer garden or other place like that and began to talk about unions, very often you didn't get home without getting an awful beating by GM-hired thugs.

That was the condition inside the plants. Combined with the bad conditions on the outside—poor living conditions, lack of proper food, lack of proper medical attention and everything else—the auto workers came to the conclusion that there was no way they could ever escape any of this injustice without joining a union. But they didn't all decide at one time.

Preparing for Battle

> General Motors Corp. spent $994,000 for labor spies between January and June, 1936. GM also had more tear gas and other riot-control equipment in its possession than the combined supply available to all cities nationwide.
>
> UAW Local No. 659 *Searchlight*, February 3, 1995

A considerable amount of preparatory work was done before the strike by radical parties. We had several very active organizations in Flint and Detroit: the Communist Party, the Proletarian Party, the Socialist Labor Party, the Socialist Party, and the Industrial Workers of the World. And, with the exception of the Communist Party, we all had our headquarters in the Pengelly Building, a very old building that became the major strike headquarters of the whole United Automobile Workers Union of Flint. Even as the strike was going on, we still had our rooms on the second floor, while the main activities in the auditorium were on the third floor. Two years before the strike broke out, the Socialist Party in Flint organized the League for Industrial Democracy (LID). We held meetings in garages and in basements, secret meetings, so the people wouldn't get caught and beaten up.

As we got bigger, the Socialist Party started sending us their speakers from New York. Many of them were from the Brookwood Labor

College. We put out leaflets and sold tickets for these meetings, which were held in the basement of the biggest Methodist church and in the Masonic Temple. We held lectures in socialism mainly, plus labor history and current events, focusing on what was happening politically. Those were very popular meetings. We would get three and four hundred people at some of our meetings.

This was all before the strike, in preparation for when the struggle actually broke out, when the workers couldn't take any more and rebelled. A core of socialists understood that this would eventually happen. I was busy organizing the LID and the Socialist Party during this time before the strike. I was well known in Flint.

Our Socialist Party was the next biggest organization to the Communist Party. The Socialist Party held ongoing classes in labor history, public speaking, and parliamentary procedure. These classes were very important and produced many capable people.

One of the Reuther brothers, Roy, was a member of the Socialist Party. Roy had organized several workers' education projects and was sent into Flint to organize the UAW in 1934 and again in 1936.

Our newspaper, the *Socialist Call*, was distributed widely as an aid to our recruitment of GM workers into the Socialist Party. We laid a solid groundwork so that some of the first people who took the initial brave actions in the shop were Socialist Party workers.

The Communist Party met at the north end of Flint because that's where most of the immigrants from Russia, Poland, and Hungary lived. They were mainly Buick workers. They had a lot of social activities, dances, and political meetings. They also had an insurance organization, the International Workers Order. Robert Travis, the top UAW organizer in Flint, was in the Communist Party, and he selected Roy Reuther to work as his second-in-command during the strike. But, in my opinion, the main leaders of that strike, the ones who were able to organize, to speak in public meetings and so on, came out of the Socialist Party.

Workers were receptive to the idea of a union, but so much fear came along with it. When we started signing people up to be in the union, General Motors organized a huge rival organization called the Flint Alliance that cost nothing to join, but you signed a card so that they had a record of you. A great deal of anti-union propaganda was disseminated into the homes of workers through the Flint Alliance. The workers knew conditions were horrible, but they were in fear of losing their jobs if they refused to join the Alliance. They also saw what happened to some of their buddies who would go to a union meeting and get beaten up and come to work the next day with black eyes or a busted head.

So workers didn't all rush to join the union. In fact, if General Motors had known the real number of union members at the time those plants went down, a successful strike wouldn't have been possible. We had to keep the actual membership figures as secret as we could.

As I said, a fermentation was taking place for a couple of years before the first sitdown. No question about it. Many revolutionaries, so-called, talk about "spontaneous combustion of the workers." I can't see that at all, because it took time for the organizers in various plants of this whole General Motors empire to talk to the workers and to bring them to classes—to make some contact, create a bond. You had to trust your fellow worker if you were going to be an active union member because we had an awful lot of spies in there, a lot of people who would get special favor for squealing on somebody else.

I should add that the one big daily newspaper, the *Flint Journal*, was controlled completely by General Motors. They wrote things like, "You don't bite the hand that feeds you," and "These people coming in are all imports from Soviet Russia, and they want communism." So everybody was labeled a Communist who joined the union. The radio stations (we didn't have television then) and every avenue of information was controlled by GM.

The only thing the union had at first was mimeographed sheets. Finally, we were able to put out a weekly, the *Flint Auto Worker*, with reports of what the union was doing and what we were working for— what kind of a society we wanted. We handed these out at the plant gates after work. And the distributors often got beaten up by the company's paid agents. They had Pinkerton men in there, two or three different spy agencies, plus the people that they would pull out of their own ranks, General Motors protection police. It was a dangerous period—no question about it.

And we had our sound car, an ordinary car fitted with loudspeakers on top with large batteries. During the strike we would send it around to the various plants that were still operating—A.C. Sparkplug and Buick. As the workers were going in, we would taunt them with the conditions that they had to face, and we'd give them a little pep talk: "As an individual you are only one, but the union gives us strength." Many of the workers in those plants came down and walked the picket lines in sympathy, but there was not enough preparation done in those plants and not enough leadership for them to take the chance to shut their plants down.

Sit Down!

They have taken untold millions that they never toiled to earn.
But without our brain and muscle not a single wheel can turn.
We can break their haughty power, gain our freedom when we learn,
That the union makes us strong.

Ralph Chaplin, "Solidarity Forever"

The first sitdown was on December 30 in the small Fisher Body Plant 2 over a particularly big grievance that had occurred. The workers were at the point where they had just had enough, and, under a militant leadership, they sat down. When the UAW leaders in the big Fisher Body Plant 1 heard about the sitdown in Fisher 2, they sat down also. That took real guts, and it took political leadership. The leaders of the political parties knew what they had to do because they'd studied labor history and the ruthlessness of the corporations.

Picket lines were established and also a big kitchen in the south end of Flint, across from the large Fisher 1 plant. Every day, gallons and gallons of food were prepared, and anybody who was on the picket lines would get a ticket with notification that they had served on the line so they'd be able to get a good hot meal. The strike kitchen was primarily organized by the Communist Party women. They brought a restaurant man from Detroit to help organize this huge kitchen. They were the ones who made all of those good meals.

We also had what we called scavengers, groups of people who would go to the local farmers and ask for donations of food for the strikers. Many people in these small towns surrounding Flint were factory workers who would also raise potatoes, cabbages, tomatoes, corn or whatever. So great quantities of food were sent down to be made into dishes for the strikers. People were very generous.

John L. Lewis and the United Mine Workers helped us financially so that if there was somebody in serious difficulty we could help them out a little bit. Later on, the garment workers sent money. But with thousands of workers, you couldn't help everybody, so many families were taken care of by committees forming in plants, whether they were on strike or not. Committees in Buick, Chevrolet, and Fisher Body took care of some of the urgent cases so nobody starved or got into really major medical difficulties.

After the first sitdown started, I went down to see what I could do to help. I was either on the picket lines or up at the Pengelly Building all the time, but some of the strike leaders didn't know who I was and didn't know that I had been teaching classes in unionism and so on. So they said, "Go to the kitchen. We need a lot of help out there." They didn't know what else to tell a woman to do. I said, "You've got a lot of little, skinny men around here who can't stand to be out on the cold picket lines for very long. They can peel potatoes as well as women can." I turned down the idea of kitchen duty.

Instead, I organized a children's picket line. I got Bristol board and paints, and I was painting signs for this children's picket line. One of my socialist comrades came up and said, "Hey, Genora, what are you doing here?" I said, "I'm doing your job." Since he was a professional sign painter, I turned the sign-painting project over to him and that was the beginning of the sign-painting department.

We could only do the children's picket line once because it was too dangerous, but we got an awful lot of favorable publicity from it, much of it international. The picture of my two-year-old son, Jarvis, holding a picket sign saying, "My daddy strikes for us little tykes," went all over the nation, and people sent me articles from French newspapers and from Germany and from other European countries. I thought it was remarkable that the news traveled so far.

Women Come Forward

The women of Flint have made their fame and are known throughout the world for their heroic stand during the great General Motors
strike.

Robert C. Travis, strike organizer, 1937

I should tell you how the Women's Auxiliary was formed. The last days of December 1936 were when the sitdowns began. Following that came New Year's Eve. Among working-class families, everybody celebrates New Year's Eve. I was amazed at the number of wives that came down to the picket line and threatened their husbands, "If you don't cut out this foolishness and get out of that plant right now, you'll be a divorced man!" They threatened divorce loudly and openly, yelling and shouting at their husbands. I knew I couldn't go and grab each one of them to talk to them privately. So I could only watch as some of the men climbed out of the plant window up on the second floor, down the ladder to go home with their wives. These were good union members, but they were hooted and hollered at by their comrades in the plant who were holding the fort in the sitdown. This was a very dangerous turn of events because I knew how few men were inside holding that plant, and it worried many of us.

The next day, we decided to organize the women. We thought that if women can be that effective in breaking a strike, they could be just as effective in helping to win it. So we organized the Women's Auxiliary and we laid out what we were going to do.

Now remember, the UAW was still in the process of getting organized. It didn't have elected officers, or by-laws, or any of the rest of it. So we were free to organize our Women's Auxiliary, to elect our president, vice president, recording secretary and heads of committees, all on our own.

We couldn't have women sitting down in the plants because the newspapers were antagonizing the wives at home by saying that women were sleeping over in the plant. In fact, GM sent anonymous messages to the wives of some of the strikers alleging that there were prostitutes in those embattled plants. But we knew we could get women on the picket lines.

We organized a child-care center at the union headquarters, so children would have some place to go when their mothers marched on the picket line. Wilma McCartney, who had nine children and was going to have her tenth, took charge of that. At first, the women were scared to death to come down to the union, and some may have been against the union for taking away their pay check so they couldn't feed their children who were hungry or crying for milk. Then this wonderful woman, this mother of nine children who was pregnant with another, would talk to them about how it would benefit them for their husbands to participate actively. And if they won the strike, it would make all the difference in the world in their living conditions. We recruited a lot of women just through the child-care center.

We also set up a first-aid station with a registered nurse in a white uniform and red union armband. She was a member of the Women's Auxiliary. The women in the Auxiliary also made house calls to make sure every family had enough to eat, and they gave advice on how to deal with creditors.

But that wasn't enough as far as I was concerned. Women had more to offer than just these services. So we set up public-speaking classes for women. Most of the women had never even been to a union meeting. In those days, many of the men would go to union meetings and say to the women, "It's none of your damn business. Don't you mix into our affairs." So the women didn't express any of their ideas about what could be done to better their conditions.

One of our Socialist Party women, Tekla Roy, took over the public-speaking classes and was very popular. She was a very tall woman with a low and resonant voice. She seemed like a person who could handle any man or any opposition. She also taught labor history: what had happened in America in the early days when child labor was elimi-nated, and how the women garment workers in New York were the first to organize unions in the United States. Women came out of those classes thinking, "Well, women did play a role in the unions. We have got a right to say something." We trained them in how to get up in union meetings and what appeals to make. We gave them an outline of a speech and they practiced in the classes.

Some of the men were very opposed to having their wives at the union headquarters and a few of them never gave up their sexist atti-tudes. But most of the men encouraged their wives. They thought we were doing a wonderful job, making things better for them at home because their wives understood why their husbands had to be on the picket line all day long and do a lot of extra things for the union. They could talk and work together as companions. And the children were learning from their parents' discussions about the strike.

A few men still opposed women becoming active or walking the picket lines. I was often called a "dyke." Some men said that women who came down to the picket line were prostitutes or loose women looking for men. But as more married men with families became active in the strike, they kept those elements quiet. We eventually won respect and were praised highly by the leaders of the strike after victory was declared.

Organizing the women in the strike was the most wonderful expe-rience of my whole life. I was not as tall as Tekla but I had experience organizing. I was interested in building the Socialist Party and in build-ing socialist society, so I had a great deal of influence with these women.

The Women's Emergency Brigade

"Greetings and congratulations to the new officers and to the members of the Women's Auxiliary and the Women's Emergency Brigade. The automobile workers of Flint and America owe you a debt of gratitude for the part you played in the winning of The Big

Strike and in building our International Union. You are truly crusaders in this new American Labor Movement, and your fighting spirit an inspiration to all workers!"

Roy Reuther, strike organizer, 1937

The company decided they had to break the strike. On January 11 they attacked the smaller Fisher Body Plant 2. I happened to be on the picket line that day, and I was amazed to see what was happening. The plant guards prevented the men from getting any food for about twenty-four hours. It was very cold, and they turned off the heat in the building. The men inside were very angry.

Then the company police and the city police started shooting. At first they were shooting tear gas inside the plant, but that was too difficult, so they decided to tear-gas and shoot this huge mass of picketers that had formed in front of the plant. The police were using rifles, buckshot, firebombs, and tear-gas canisters. It was a shock to a lot of people. We had thought that General Motors would try to freeze us out or do something in the plants, but never open fire on us right in the middle of the city.

The union picketers took their own cars and barricaded off a section so that the police couldn't get us from both ends. Then, over the radio came the equivalent of saying that there was a revolution starting in Flint. With all the propaganda saying, "The communists are coming into the city to take over the union," people gathered in vast numbers on both sides of this battle. When the police misfired, tear-gas and bullets went over our heads into the crowds which had come out to watch. It was very frightening. People would run away and dart into restaurants up the street.

The battle continued for quite some time. Workers overturned police cars to make barricades. They ran to pick up the fire bombs thrown at them and hurl them back at the police. It was very, very cold. The men in the plant were using fire hoses against the police, and when the water ran down, it would quickly ice over.

I saw one of our Socialist Party members, Fred Stevens, jump over a gutter where there was icy water flowing down. A little stream of blood spurted down his leg into the water. I couldn't get my wits together for a moment.

The men wanted to get me out of the way. You know that old "protect the women and children" business. If there are any women or children around, usher them right out, protect them. I told them, "Get away from me. I've got as many weapons as you have." I was the only woman who stayed.

The battle went on for hours. Throughout the whole time, the sound car was giving instructions and trying to bolster the courage of the men inside the plant as well as the picketers on the outside. Victor Reuther spoke for a while and then other men substituted for him, giving him relief. But there were only the voices of men. At one point, Victor came over and told us that the batteries in the sound car were running down.

Lights went on in my head. I thought, "I've never used a loud-speaker to address a large crowd of people, but I've got to tell them that there are women down here." So I asked him, "Victor, can I take the loudspeaker?" He said, "We've got nothing to lose." The first thing I did was attack the police. I called to them, "Cowards! Cowards! Shooting into the bellies of unarmed men and firing at the mothers of children." Then everything became quiet. There was silence on both sides of the line. I thought, "The women can break this up." So I appealed to the women in the crowd, "Break through those police lines and come down here and stand beside your husbands and your brothers and your uncles and your sweethearts."

In the dusk, I could barely see one woman struggling to come forward. A cop had grabbed her by the back of her coat. She just pulled out of that coat and started walking down to the battle zone. As soon as that happened there were other women and men who followed. The police wouldn't shoot people in the back as they were coming down, so that was the end of the battle. When those spectators came into the center of the battle and the police retreated, there was a big roar of victory. That battle became known as the Battle of Bull's Run because we made the cops run.

By this time, General Motors was going crazy and got Governor Frank Murphy involved. The next day, the National Guard was sent in because it was a very explosive situation. At first, eleven hundred troops were sent, followed by more than two thousand later. By the end of the strike, almost four thousand National Guardsmen were stationed in Flint.

I decided that women could do more than just the duties of the Women's Auxiliary. We could form an Emergency Brigade, and every time there was a threatened battle, we could mobilize. We might make a difference. We didn't know that nothing like that had ever been organized before, at least not in this country. We didn't know we were making history. We didn't have time to think about it. The day after the

Battle of Bull's Run, just from the people we notified the night before, fifty women joined up right away.

When we held our big Auxiliary meeting, I got up and asked who would like to join the Women's Emergency Brigade. I said, "It can't be somebody who's weak of heart. You can't go hysterical if your sister beside you drops down in a pool of blood." Oh, I made it a bloody sounding thing! After all, sixteen workers and eleven police had been injured in that battle. Anyone who wanted to join had to stand up, announce publicly that they wanted to join, walk over and sign their names in front of everybody. It wasn't a secret organization and we didn't pressure anyone to join. We made it very difficult.

One old woman in her early seventies stood up. I said, "This is going to be too difficult for you." She said, "You can't keep me out. My sons work in that factory. My husband worked in that factory before he died and I have grandsons in there." She went on and gave a speech. She got applause, then she walked over and signed her name. Then a young girl, I think she was sixteen or seventeen, stood up and said, "My father works in that factory. My brothers work in that factory. I've got a right to join, too." She walked over and signed, and all the women applauded. We recruited about four hundred women for the Brigade out of about a thousand women in the Women's Auxiliary.

I organized the Emergency Brigade on a military basis. I knew a captain gave orders, so I was the captain. Then I picked five lieutenants. We organized groups under each lieutenant. We'd give out an assignment and that lieutenant would find a car, round up her people, and off they'd go to wherever they were needed. Three of my five lieutenants were factory girls. One of them was an A.C. worker who was nineteen years old.

Ruth Pitts was from Fisher Body and "Teeter" Walker was from Redmans, a supplier plant for GM cars. Those two lieutenants wore jodhpurs, pants that come out on the side like a military or riding habit. They wore big boots that laced up to the knees, short Eisenhower-type jackets, red berets, and arm bands. The workers in Fisher Body 1 made blackjacks for them. They laced them up with car leather on the outside and wristlets to go around the arm. They looked pretty jaunty and they meant business. Those two were always on the front lines.

We decided that we would use red berets as our insignia. They were very cheap at the time, something like fifty cents for a good felt beret. The Women's Auxiliary sewed red armbands with a white E.B. on them for Emergency Brigade. I have one still. We carried heavy wooden clubs with handles carved to fit a woman's grip. Whenever you saw one of those women, you knew that she was ready for action at any time, morning, night, or anytime.

News about the Women's Emergency Brigade made the front page of the *New York Times* and other papers across the nation. In France when they heard about women organizing and doing it seriously, not just carrying mops and brooms as the newspapers liked to put it, but carrying clubs, they called me the "Joan of Arc" of organized labor— of women warriors. They thought it was very dramatic.

After we sat down in Flint, fifteen GM plants across the country went on strike. And the news went out about the role women could play. Women in Detroit organized and wore green berets and armbands; Lansing, blue; Pontiac, orange. These were all cities right around Flint and Detroit, the heart of the GM empire.

The Emergency Brigade responded whenever any emergency arose. Saginaw was just a few miles from Flint and that was where the union was having the hardest time. After workers won the Chevrolet strike of 1935, General Motors moved its Chevrolet Parts and Service plants to Saginaw and established a vigilante organization called the Loyalty League to prevent any unionization of those plants.

The union organized a car of men to go from Flint to Saginaw to hold a meeting and help in any way that we could. The meeting went off all right and the local men escaped from the meeting hall, but when our organizers were driving back, vigilantes in big, black Buick cars followed them down the highway into Flint and ran them into a telephone pole. They sent our people to the hospital.

That was a challenge for us after we had gone up there and encouraged them to meet and given them such visions of success. The union organizer was out in the hall as one of our meetings was ending, asking for volunteers to send a second car up to Saginaw right away before despair set in. Two Socialist Party men and three women volunteered to go. They were Mary Donovan Hapgood, who was a writer at the time, and Fania Fish, who later became Fania Reuther, and me. I got the two women to volunteer to go. The UAW organizers were amazed that we were taking such a chance. I noticed that they weren't too quick to volunteer to get their butts up there.

We drove up to Saginaw and met in the basement of a building that had big, high windows. The hall was packed with men and women who spoke about their determination to build the union. We got up and spoke, and we got them to sing "Solidarity." That pepped the whole meeting up. Toward the end of the meeting, we noticed that there were eyes looking at us through those basement windows. We knew we were surrounded by Loyalty League vigilantes, so we gave emergency instructions: "As you're leaving the building, be sure you leave in twos and threes, and be prepared." A group of people were organized to protect the union hall, to get us to our car, and to escort us to the highway.

We were driving a new Pontiac, and we felt safe because we knew that it had a lot of power. As we drove out to the main highway, one of the little cars that was ahead of us was cut off by a big, black, Buick sedan that got in front of us. We turned the corner and another one got in back of us. We were boxed in. It was a fearsome thing, expecting to wind up dead or maybe injured for life by being rammed into a telephone pole.

Fortunately for us, our Saginaw brothers were determined to protect us. Two little out-of-date cars pulled up behind us, turned sideways into the road, smashed into the oncoming vehicles, and completely blocked the road. The driver of our car, seeing his chance, stepped on the gas, shot out around the other car, and sped straight ahead at ninety miles an hour. He opened the car up as fast as it would go. We were frozen. Driving ninety miles an hour then was like speeding through heaven and hell, and it scared the wits out of us. Now it means nothing, but those days cars didn't go that fast.

Finally when we saw the lights of A.C. Sparkplug on the left side of the highway, Mary Donovan Hapgood, who was sent in from New York to write about the strike, started to sing a union song, "When a scab dies, he goes to hell." We all joined in and our voices were shaking.

We got back safely and a UAW local was established up in Saginaw. They had enough people join the union to become a force that could protect itself. This is the kind of thing that the women stepped in and helped build.

In Flint everybody in the city was dependent on the auto workers. If the workers didn't have money to buy groceries, clothes, or food, everybody suffered. So the strike affected everyone and everybody wanted to join the union. The milk drivers wanted to join but we didn't have any union of milk drivers. We didn't have any union of store clerks or retail clerks. So they all came down to the main headquarters where our amalgamated local took in all of them. They all became members of Local No. 156 of the UAW–CIO.

People were joining the union all over the city, whether they worked in an auto plant or wherever they were working. We would get calls all the time, like "J. C. Penney girls want to sit down. They want to strike." So we would send the Emergency Brigade women down there in case there was any trouble. Then we had the Women's Auxiliary members go down after we saw that it was going to be all right and talk to those workers about labor history and about what we were trying to achieve.

Those were the roles women played. There were also many altercations on the picket lines, where sometimes women would come out and help. We didn't always carry the clubs because they were heavy, clumsy things to walk around with on a cold picket line. But we all carried a hard-milled bar of soap in one pocket and a sock in the other. That way, we couldn't be charged with carrying a weapon. But if somebody was creating trouble on the picket line, we'd slip that bar of soap into the sock and swing that sock very fast and sharp. It was as good as a blackjack.

I've had wonderful experiences in working with people, and I have found that sometimes the people who talk the loudest and act the bravest are the ones you can expect the least from. Sometimes, when there was a fight on the picket line you'd see a big, healthy man dive under a car! Yet you'd see other small men or you'd see women take a stand.

Breaking the Stalemate

> General Motors will not be obligated by contract to a principle that the corporation does not approve even though that principle is now a federal law.
>
> GM corporate press release, February 8, 1937

Across the nation, fifteen plants of General Motors were on strike, but we were making no progress. GM and the union had begun negotiations a few days after the Battle of Bull's Run but GM was stalling and bargaining in bad faith. The company tried to start a back-to-work movement with their anti-union Flint Alliance, and they tried to use the courts to stop the picketing and evacuate the plants. This was the same strategy that they had used against the Toledo auto strike in 1934.

It became quite difficult for some people to keep going. Every day the union was getting out bulletins and organizing the picket lines, trying to encourage people, to inspire them. We knew that something drastic had to be done and soon. Everyone knew that if we could take Chevrolet Plant 4 we could win the strike. Plant 4 was the single largest unit in the whole GM complex. It produced engines for all Chevrolet automobiles across the country and for export, too. If we could stop production there, we'd hit General Motors right in the pocket-book. But no one knew how to do this because Plant 4 was very heavily guarded.

This next part has never been written up in history. My husband, Kermit Johnson, worked in Plant 4 and was the leader of the strike committee for Chevrolet. One night he came home from work with a greasy little piece of paper in his hand. He said, "You know, I've figured out how we can take Plant 4. Plant 8 is located here. Plant 6 is there." He pointed to the paper. Those plants were all around Plant 4. "If we pull a strike," he said, "We'll have workers from all these other plants march into Plant 4. The problem is that General Motors has recruited professional Pinkertons, plant protection and organized vigilantes. It will be one big slaughter unless we distract them from that area and give ourselves time to barricade the plant."

Plant 4 employed four thousand workers, two thousand on each shift. And if you've ever been inside one of those plants, you'll know the doorways are as big as the side of a house. They're huge, long structures. It would take some time to barricade the doors and to weld the openings shut to prevent an attack by the police. So they needed to create a distraction to buy time.

When Kermit took his plan to the Socialist Party to get support, Walter Reuther and his group in Detroit were opposed to it. They were afraid that we hadn't had enough experience to carry through a plan like that. So our Socialist Party was split and the plan was voted down. But that was only after Walter Reuther came in and talked against it. Walter had a little more experience in Detroit and he'd been over in Russia, so some of the Socialist Party members deferred to him. What did we know in a little backwater town like Flint? Reuther came in and hammered against it, real hard, and they voted it down.

After that, I didn't know what to do. I went home and wrote a two-page, single-spaced letter appealing to Norman Thomas to help us. Norman Thomas was a great speaker for socialism and a wonderful writer, but he didn't know anything about the day-to-day problems that went on in the Socialist Party. He sent the letter to Frank Trager, the Socialist Party labor secretary.

Trager came to Flint on January 21 and I got all of the militants that I could get to talk to him to convince him that we should adopt Kermit's plan. Trager saw the workers trudging up to the big auditorium on the third floor where they were being shown movies like Charlie Chaplin's *Modern Times,* with everybody laughing. Other workers would come up and say, "What the hell is this? What are our orders for today? Where are our plans? What are we going to do?" Trager talked to these people as they trudged up and down that big stairway.

When we had our meeting, Trager decided that Kermit had a valid plan and there was a valid reason why we should carry it out. Walter Reuther was still opposed but he had to defer to the labor secretary. But he told Kermit that if the strike was lost it would be his fault. The vote was taken again and this time it carried.

Kermit and Roy Reuther were assigned to take the plan into the general strike committee to be approved and developed there. The rest is written up in history.

We've tried so hard to trace that letter I wrote to Norman Thomas, but after the strike Frank Trager went to work for the United States government, I've forgotten in what capacity. I think he may have mislaid it or destroyed it. I was always very sorry about that because if it hadn't been for that letter I don't know which route the strike would have taken. I do know we wouldn't have had that dramatic, decisive victory in the General Motors strike.

Kermit's plan was adopted by the strike committee. We knew there were some informers in the union meetings so a "secret" meeting was held with people who were going to shut Plant 9 and a couple of the suspected informers. That's how we let the company think that Plant 9 was going to be struck. We wanted GM to put all its guards on Plant 9 and leave Plant 4 free to be taken.

Kermit's plan was scheduled to be put into action on February 1 during the afternoon shift change. I had the Brigade out there, marching up and down in front of Plant 9. When the police saw the Brigade, they came and formed a line. At one point, the police pulled their revolvers and threatened the union men on the outside because they knew the plant police were taking care of the men inside. There was a newsreel truck that happened to be there at the time, and I told the women, "Raise your clubs." They got a picture of the women with their clubs raised in back of the police and the police with their guns pulled at the union men. I think General Motors got hold of those pictures some way. I never knew what happened to them.

When Plant 9 started shutting off some of the machines, the police began to tear-gas and beat the men. Then we heard glass break, and we saw the head of Tom Klasey look out. Blood was streaming down his face and he was yelling, "They're gassing us in here! For God's sake, they're gassing us!" That's all we had to hear. We used our clubs to smash the windows out so the men inside could get some air. Those men took an awful beating and by the time the ambulances came to carry them out, General Motors thought that they had squashed that one.

But I knew what was happening at Plant 4 half a mile down the street, so I dismissed the Brigade and sent them back to headquarters. Then my five lieutenants and I sauntered down to Plant 4 gate to see what was going on. We didn't make it obvious in any way.

When we got there we saw some big fights. Union men were throwing out the scabs and some of the foremen, and they said, "Hold that gate. Hold it, don't let the police come through here!" We strung ourselves across that gate, and it was only a matter of a telephone call before the police were sent down. They wanted to push us aside. We said, "Over our dead bodies." We talked to them—remember in Flint the policemen had uncles or fathers or brothers who were factory workers, too. We asked them, "What would you think if your wife was out here with us and you were in that damn plant? What would you think? Wouldn't you expect your wife to defend you and fight for better conditions for you?" They would start to tell us, "Well, you know, if we didn't have General Motors, what would we do in Flint? This is what feeds the people of Flint." We got them to procrastinate in these discussions just long enough.

Just as it was beginning to look risky for us, we saw the Emergency Brigade marching towards us, singing "Solidarity Forever" and "Hold the Fort." When they arrived, I climbed into the sound car that came from the other direction and instructed the women to lock arms and set up an oval picket line to prevent the police from entering the plant until it could be secured.

The successful occupation of Plant 4, which joined the occupations at Fisher 1 and 2, broke the resistance of General Motors and negotiations began in Detroit. We still maintained the picket lines and the security of the plants. The areas that weren't controlled by the union were controlled by the National Guard. The National Guard kept everyone away from the Chevrolet embankment. If you came down Chevrolet Avenue and you looked up at the buildings there, you'd see Guardsmen with their machine guns pointed right down the street.

The Brigade went to help the women from the kitchen get food into Plant 4 the first night, but we couldn't get by those Guards. I started talking to one of these young boys and his finger was actually trembling on that trigger. We didn't fool around with them because they were all excited. They thought this was a big adventure—what the hell, shooting a couple of people. It was war. But the governor declared that the strikers were to be fed.

However, General Motors had turned off the heat in Plant 4 and they had no cushions. Fisher Body plants have cushions and materials for seating and so they were much easier to hold. Not only that, the huge motorized picket lines at Fisher Body 1 meant we were strong enough so that the picketers and sitdowners could get out if they wanted to and go across to the union restaurant to contact people. They could even have their families come into the plant for a little while and get them back out again through the big front windows, because they were guarded by the union.

At Chevrolet you couldn't get out. GM used all kinds of tactics to break that sitdown. They sent in notes that some members of the strikers' families were very sick. One man was told his father was dying, and so he left. They had doctors come in saying that some little cough was very dangerous—a contagious disease. But Kermit was a very strong leader and he managed to keep the men together.

This time it was General Motors that was stymied. On February 11 they signed a peace agreement recognizing the UAW as representative for the auto workers. And on March 12 the first labor contract was signed.

A Blow against Racism

An injury to one is an injury to all.

Black workers did not generally participate in organizing the union. They used to say at our Socialist Party headquarters, "It's bad enough being Black without being Red, too." You had to understand that they had nobody, not even any white union people, that would fight for them if they were fired. Racial prejudice was so pervasive. Many workers had come up recently from the Deep South thinking that Blacks should get off the sidewalk when they passed by. We couldn't eat in the same restaurants. Blacks just wouldn't be served in any restaurant in Flint.

Out of twelve thousand workers employed by Chevrolet, only four hundred were Black. Fisher 1, Fisher 2, Chevrolet, all ten plants of Chevrolet, hired only white men on production. Black men were allowed to work only in the foundry of Buick and as sanitation workers, cleaning up the men's toilets in the other plants. Black men had no hope of ever getting a raise or getting a job promotion.

The only Black sitdowner in the Flint strikes was Roscoe Van Zandt in Plant 4. At first, the southern white workers didn't know what to make of it. All they could say to him was, "What the hell are you doing here? You haven't got any job to protect." When the food came in, he took his share and went around the corner because Blacks and whites never ate together. This embarrassed the rest of the sitdowners.

The first night, when it came time to sleep, there was only one clear table and one blanket. Who was going to have the blanket and sleep up off the cold cement plant floor? The strikers voted that because Roscoe Van Zandt was an older man, he should have the blanket and sleep on the table. Then they began to talk to him. Before that, Black and white workers never got to know each other because it was a period of intense discrimination. Being a socialist, Kermit helped those workers get a good, anti-racist education in those fourteen days before the strike was settled. When it came time for the victory parade, the strikers voted for Roscoe Van Zandt to carry the flag out of the plant.

After the strike was over, there were some honorary meetings for Roscoe Van Zandt in the Black community, and I was a featured speaker. That was a different experience. You say a few sentences and then you have to wait for "Amen, Amen, you said it sister!" At first when I was interrupted, I didn't know what to make of it. Believe me, before that speech was over I knew how to say something and pause to let them express their feelings. These were the older generation that felt we had won a victory for them, even though they couldn't actively participate. Conditions for Black workers improved greatly after the strike. Oh, yes! They were now in the union, of course, and they could begin to afford to own their own homes, buying them at so much a month. They took great pride in what had been accomplished by the strikers. Their sympathies were with us all of the time.

The Sweet Fruit of Victory

Faintly, in the distance a mass of men was moving. A wisp of song caught all of us waiting there and it grew as the strikers marched forward. That song of victory drew everyone together as the Fisher 1 men marched through downtown and across to Chevrolet Avenue where they descended the hill and met the triumphant shouts of the Fisher 2 and Plant 4 men.

Shirley Olmsted Foster, "Open Letter from Sit-downer's Widow," UAW *Searchlight*, February 3, 1995

Following the strike, the auto worker became a different human being. The women that had participated actively became a different type of woman, a different type from any we had ever known anywhere in the labor movement and certainly not in the city of Flint. They carried themselves with a different walk, their heads were high, and they had confidence in themselves. They were not only mentally different, but physically different. If you saw one of those women in the beginning and then saw her just a short period after going through this experience, learning and feeling that she had things she could fit together in her life, it would be an entirely different woman.

Not only that, but relationships within the family became much stronger. The kids understood why their parents were leaving them so often and why they had to go through a period of deprivation. It was not easy on them. The teachers in the schools were not in favor of the strike, and they showed it in many ways. Of course, in that period of great upheaval, the union couldn't do anything about what the teachers were saying in the schools. You couldn't take care of all the problems that cropped up at the time. But after their parents had this great victory, the children knew that their dads had won. It was mainly dads because it was mainly men in the plants, but their mothers had helped. Among the working class, it was a lot better.

Conditions also changed inside the plants. The foremen were tiptoeing around, being very careful. Every time something came up that couldn't be settled, or the workers got a tough foreman who told them "Go to hell," they'd shut down the line. The men were so cocky, they'd say to the foremen, "You don't like it?" They'd push the button and shut down the line. It was very pleasurable to think that these men were not afraid of the boss any more. They got a raise in their wages, and they weren't always followed to the can where somebody would step in to check how many cigarette butts were in the toilet. They became human beings to a degree even though they were still under the jurisdiction of a big corporation which controlled their lives. There was still the speed-up and other problems like that.

But in the family itself, which interested me most, it used to be that when a young man or a young woman got to the age where they were to graduate from high school the whole family celebrated because that was the glorious end of their education.

As conditions and wages improved in the plants, workers were able to have a more settled home life and raise families. The children did better in school, and they got to the point where they could go to college. After a few years of saving, the parents had the money to send them to colleges and universities. That's the period, in the 1940s and 1950s, when the college system began to proliferate across the country because of workers being able to send their kids. There was so much pride in the family: "My son is studying to become a doctor" or a lawyer. Or "My daughter is studying to become a librarian." They had hopes that were outside the factory. And so the whole family was changed. I think that was the biggest change of all. For the first time the children became very proud of their fathers and their mothers. They had gone through this big struggle to make it better for everybody, to put enough food on the table, to have enough clothes, and to have pride in school and the possibility of going on to colleges and universities.

There is something else that has to be emphasized: the fringe benefits that workers got from winning the strike; hospitalization and medical care, and in some contracts dental and eye care. I have neighbors across the street who are Black retired auto workers and they get all that. All of these fringe benefits were something the workers never dreamed they could have when they first got recognition. Little by little, the strength of the union was able to get these benefits, and as a result many other employers had to give them. Unionists set the standard.

The victory of GM workers set off a wave of union organization across the country. This wave grew to encompass the entire auto industry, including Chrysler and Ford. Then steel workers organized, then rubber workers, glass workers, and finally even professional, commercial, and service workers. They gained confidence after our victory because if we could force the largest industrial giant in the whole world to its knees, then they could win, too. This was the realization of John L. Lewis's dream, the Congress of Industrial Organizations. By the way, the CIO was formed in 1935 as the Committee for Industrial Organization, but after the GM strike, after Plant 4 was taken, its name changed to the Congress of Industrial Organizations. The initials CIO stood for power. You'd see posters in homes and posters on cars proudly proclaiming, "I am the CIO." Those letters became almost like "I am the deity down from heaven." Those three letters, CIO, had great significance. I've never known of anything else as powerful, even govern-ment agencies that were set up to help people. The government's Works Project Administration program helped a lot of poor people, and those letters were well known. But the CIO was an especially magical set of letters.

What else changed? Workers felt that they had the right to run for political office if they wanted to and they did. Many of the later legis-lative people in the state of Michigan and other political posts were either strikers themselves, if they were young enough, or the sons of former strikers. The whole nature of the city changed.

The rich, of course, never forgave and never forgot. They blacklisted those that they could get away with blacklisting, and it was especially easy when it was a woman like me, a political organizer who was right at the center of things. And I was right in the middle of it, there's no question about that. After the strike was over, everybody in Flint knew who I was.

Fighting Racism

For white workers from the recent south, racism was something that was very strong. They had nasty attitudes like "You wouldn't want to get too close to them. Your daughter might marry one." You heard it all the time. We Socialists kept on educating and writing articles in the union paper and doing everything that we could to argue against racism. Certainly, all the Socialist auto workers had the right understanding. The success of the union eased things for Blacks but racism was still there. That was the hardest struggle of all.

The only viable anti-racist organization in Flint at the time was the National Association for the Advancement of Colored People, and that was not a militant organization nationally—ever. But we formed a NAACP chapter in Flint that became very militant.

We threw out the president, the one they called "the downtown man," because he would go and report everything downtown. We threw him out and elected Edgar Holt, a Black Buick worker who was a graduate of Wilberforce University, to be president. He was a good orator with a wonderful personality—a very inspiring man.

When the city council voted down the Fair Employment Practices Commission, we organized a mock funeral with a casket in a hearse. A black minister in his robe marched with casket bearers wearing white gloves. This funeral procession wound through the city of Flint to stop at the bridge of the Flint River. We took the casket out, proclaimed "The burial of FEPC," and tossed the casket over the bridge into the river. Then the minister gave a long sermon using a loudspeaker. It was something for people downtown shopping and going through the city to see a demonstration like that. When you throw a casket over the bridge into the river, people stop to see what is happening.

I became very active as a leader of the NAACP following the strike. We always dramatized the actions we organized so we'd get a lot of publicity. Otherwise, it was the policy of a company town like Flint to keep everything quiet. There was no news coverage of working-class people's lives, of what they were doing or thinking, and so you had to be dramatic to get attention.

Organizing the Unemployed

The people on the bottom of the economic ladder who had become so completely demoralized, the people who felt they had no hopes, no help, no one who gave a damn about them—you could see that person stand up straight. "We can fight, too. We've got fight in us."

Genora Johnson Dollinger

After the strike, the unemployed workers were also having great difficulties. We petitioned the International Union to give us the right to organize a WPA and Unemployed Local No. 12, UAW–CIO, under the International's name and their protection. They didn't give us any money. I guess they didn't know what we were going to do and if they couldn't control it all the way down, they didn't want to fund it. We did organize a very militant union. Many WPA projects were street repairs. They used to call it "digging holes" and ridicule the workers. These projects kept men and their families barely eating, just barely eating, because the wages were so little.

I was the secretary of Local No. 12 because at that time a woman wasn't supposed to be president, even though she may have all the ideas. We used the big name and the big, bright lights of the UAW–CIO. Because of the success of the strike, we got an awful lot of WPA workers to join our union. The main organizers were the men who were digging in the streets and the women who worked on the canning projects. We had regular meetings and we had all kinds of projects.

There wasn't office space in the main building for the library project I was working on at the time, so we were put in the building that housed the water department facilities of the city. The city officials were very worried about what we were doing. One day we picked up the local paper to read that a leading communist of Flint was in a position to poison the city's water supply. It was a big story about me! Once again we were facing that big Red scare. Fortunately I knew the head of the WPA. She was a feminist from Britain from the Labour Party. She knew who I was and she knew my record, so she immediately got the whole project transferred to another building. The other officials in the WPA wanted me off the job and out of their hair. They wanted to fire me. But she held firm and transferred the whole project.

Local No. 12 brought in the unemployed people that had almost lost hope. The politicians were taking away milk from the children instead of giving them more milk, which they should have been doing. And they wouldn't give any surplus food to the hungry people. Homes were being repossessed and they were taking the women and children and putting them into one big shelter with the men in another. They were actually splitting up families. They would set furniture out in the street, but we had crews that would set the furniture back in and try to protect it. That became a lot of hard labor without any results so we started organizing big demonstrations. We would burn an effigy of the relief manager, the head of the welfare department, and we'd give out statements.

We finally decided to let the whole city of Flint know what was happening. We had a demonstration and announced that we would hold a "Death Watch." If they were going to do these things to the poor people in Flint, then let everybody see it. Across from the welfare building there was a big park with a lot of beautiful trees. This park also happened to be across from one end of Buick Motor Car Company, which was rehiring workers to go into automobile production after the 1937 recession. We put big signs up on each corner of the park inviting the public to come out to see poor people with hungry, starving children—to watch people die. We had whole families down there in great big army tents that we had procured. And we tapped into the street wires so that they had electricity at night in their tents.

Mothers were down there washing out diapers in tubs and hanging them up on ropes we strung between the trees. They built fires in large oil drums to keep warm and to heat water. They would cook their meals out there and heat their water to wash clothes and bathe their babies. They were really living out in public.

People came down to see what was happening. Great big signs on each corner of the park said, "This is the Death Watch" and "If you want to see people in the city of Flint die, here they are." That shook up a lot of people. You'd see cars driving around slowly to view what was happening. This was very bad publicity for the city. It hit the state capital and finally it hit Washington. Washington opened up surplus food to the people in Flint who were on the relief rolls. And they stopped separating families when they repossessed their homes.

The police did threaten us. But many union people came to hang around the periphery of the park. We also had union men in the park putting up clotheslines and doing whatever they could to help. On top of that, in the Buick plant we had a lot of UAW members that had just gone back to work. They knew the power of the union. The windows of this plant came down fairly low so the men could look right out into the park. Pat Murray, the chief steward in there, issued a statement: "If any cops come up anywhere within the district, we're going to come out with our pipes and our hammers and our wrenches, and we'll take care of them." We settled the grievance before that happened.

It was an exciting period. It took a lot of work and a lot of time and a lot of militancy, but it achieved results. The people on the bottom of the economic ladder who had become so completely demoralized, the people who felt they had no hopes, no help, no one who gave a damn about them—you could see that person stand up straight. "We can fight, too. We've got fight in us."

Unemployed people were inspired by factory workers who had won a union, and they came down to the union meetings, which became quite exciting, quite dramatic. They would get up and speak for the first time. Unemployed people found their voice and their strength. It was a wonderful experience, not only for the people that helped, but for the people who were doing it—for everybody.

It is the hardest thing in the world to organize the unemployed. They need strong backing. The strongest backing comes from the established unions, especially those who've had success in a strike. They feel that they have power. Once you see that in a worker or a number of workers, it's something you don't forget. They've been changed from people who have been kept down constantly to people who feel they have strength. They have knowledge and the ability to make changes. Before that, they'd only see the overpowering bureaucracy of the union and the overpowering bureaucracy of the government over their heads constantly with police and badges all around them. But when they have a great victory in a labor struggle, then they begin to feel that they are just as powerful and strong as their opponents.

That's the way that socialism will come in this country. When workers realize that they do have the numbers and the strength and the talents and the abilities. All of the creative things that workers come up with in a strike are usually original, because it pertains to the situation you are in right at that moment. You'll have people offering one suggestion after another, and they will discuss it together. The organizing process is very inspirational.

Personally Speaking

> It's not that I was born a heroine. It was a question of growing up in a company town where people were going without food and children were going without health services. These families were in dire need. That wasn't the concern of General Motors. They just wanted to get their production out. If you were living in a company town, you would feel that, and you would do the same thing.
>
> Genora Johnson Dollinger, 1994

During the strike, I had tuberculosis in my right lung and I had to have treatments to collapse that lung. I was fortunate that the doctor who treated me was a socialist, or else I would have had great difficulty finding a doctor in Flint to treat me during the strike. It was a very serious problem, but when you live through a period of revolt like that, then you understand a person saying, "I'll give my life for this cause if I can make it easier on other people," and mean it—really mean it. So I didn't stop to be sick. I was willing to go through anything for the strike.

After the strike, the labor movement raised enough money for me to go east on a speaking tour. I spoke before a number of unions and I spoke before their big May Day celebration. Then I came home and collapsed with tuberculosis. The unions and two lawyers in Detroit and New York raised enough money to send me to a sanitorium for six months. By that time it was impossible to save my lung. The loss of that lung has caused me much difficulty over my life. But I never regretted it because I had so many wonderful experiences.

The strike was one of the best experiences of my life, but also the most painful. After the strike my younger son, Jarvis, was killed in a car accident. The older one, Dennis, died a few years later of multiple sclerosis. Kermit and I separated. That part is painful. I think that's why I never wanted to talk much about that time, and I never wanted to write about it.

You get enriching experiences in life, even if you struggle for something and you lose. It's the people that you get to know—that you work with. It's the real strength and nourishment that you get from somebody working beside you that you can call brother or sister. So, if my life has been shortened, it also has been highly enriched.

Class Struggle during the War

I was blacklisted so completely I don't think I could have gotten a job anywhere in Flint. When General Motors blacklists you, the blacklist extends to other auto factories and other corporations. All of the automobile plants including Chrysler and Ford cooperated on that. If you're well known, the blacklist is really effective. The unemployed union got a lot of publicity from the "Death Watch," so I was well known from that, in addition to the strike.

I had to get out of Flint if I wanted to get a job. It was 1941 and they were hiring for the war effort. I had just married Sol and we both moved to Detroit. During that time housing was so scarce, you had to take practically anything. We found a very small, depressing apartment that had black paint all over the floors and the woodwork. My husband Sol and his buddies in the movement stripped all the paint off and repainted it. At least we had a place to live.

We didn't have sitdown strikes during the war. We would have had a great deal of difficulty doing that. Many of the workers that came into the shops during the war were new, so we had to educate them to unionism. Secondly, there was so much patriotism that people would have endorsed any kind of military action to stop strikes in those plants.

During the war, the government had a national "cost plus" agreement with business which guaranteed them a fixed rate of profit in addition to their production costs. That was how the government got the corporations to convert their auto plants to war production. So you weren't hitting a corporation in the pocketbook during a strike but the United States government. In spite of that, we did shut plants down just by walking out and going home. And there were lots of grievances! When they opened up the plants to war production, they left the same old foremen and management forces in there. You had the same old speed-up artists and the ones who would harangue you.

First, I went to work at Budd Wheel Corporation in a plant that was producing shells for the war. In the beginning the men were really cruel. They resented women coming into the plants. Their attitude was, since women weren't the breadwinners, "What the hell are they doing in those plants, anyway?" It didn't matter even if the woman's husband had been drafted and removed from the family. They didn't want any women in there. So they left all the toughest jobs in these plants to women. No matter how small you were, or how delicate you were, or how old you were, or anything else, these men took all the good jobs and left all the rough ones for the women. They would even side with the bosses when they razzed us and made sordid remarks to us.

I couldn't open my mouth until I got seniority after ninety days. I got seniority, but then they found out who I was, and I was fired, summarily, just like that. I had carried my name, Genora Johnson, to Detroit and the blacklist had caught up with me. I thought if I used my new married name, Genora Dollinger, I would have a chance. I came home and I said, "Sol, I'm going to start using your name now. I've worn mine out."

I decided to apply for a job at Briggs Corporation. It used to be a plant that produced auto bodies for Chrysler. During the war it had the largest press room in the world. They were producing complete B-27 airplanes. It was a huge plant. The plant had a good union leadership and I think that's what I was looking for—a little protection. Local No. 212 had a reputation for being very, very militant. They were called the "dead-end kids" of the UAW. They had sent flying squads up to Flint to help us win our sitdown strike.

I practically had to beg the employment manager to give me a job in the plant instead of in the office at a higher salary. He said I didn't belong in a factory because I had good grammar and I wasn't a "shop girl." But I told him that I had gone through a WPA course and learned how to run lathes and milling machines and grinders, and I knew how to use vernier calipers and all the necessary tools. When you completed that course you could go into practically any department of an automobile plant and know how to handle the job. I had all the qualifications to be hired in the plant, and I told him with a straight face that I had come out for the war effort, so he hired me.

Briggs Manufacturing Company had several plants in Detroit and they put me in the plant on Vernor Avenue. I was on the drill press and, I'm telling you, those were the longest days of my life. All the workers were exhausted from the speed-up. We had a militant union, but so many people thought that if you struck during the war, you were striking against our boys on the front lines. Patriotism was running high.

The hiring manager had mentioned that he had a large inspection department in the main plant on Mack Avenue. That plant employed seven thousand workers. I left the Vernor plant one day and walked into his office. I said, "You promised me that you were going to transfer me to the inspection department." So he transferred me. The inspection department was divided into "cribs" or sections. Chicken-wire walls divided the cribs from each other, keeping the Navy parts separate from the Army parts, because they were working on two different airplanes. Workers could see over into the Navy crib, and they could see over into the Army crib, but no one was supposed to ever go from one crib to another. The whole department was restricted. But the union covered all the grievances from both cribs, and the stewards and I had to go back and forth. We could always see if the foremen were doing something in one crib when we were over in the other crib. It was an interesting arrangement all right.

The workers were primarily women with maybe a hundred or two hundred men who were injured veterans returned from the war. The women were treated in a disgraceful fashion by the foremen. They talked dirty to them, saying things like "Get the rag out of your ass." and "It's time to stop your screaming and your bleeding." Dirty, sick, awful stuff. They were resentful of women coming into the plants. They seemed especially to enjoy tormenting women fresh out of their homes or school classrooms.

The union was trying to organize the women there. They had an old man come up from an adjoining local, and he would take up a griev-ance here and there and pat the women on the back. But he didn't solve anything, really, because the foremen didn't change their ways and the male union rep was blind to the harassment.

For ninety days, women kept coming around saying, "We're going to have a meeting. We're going over to the Local hall, won't you come?" And I'd say, "No, I can't. No, I can't." I couldn't talk to anybody because I had to work ninety days to get seniority. Finally, I had about three or four days left. The women in our department were organizing a meeting to go over and talk to the people at the main union hall. They were taking their list of grievances to tell them that they weren't being resolved. So I went over and sat in the back of the hall.

Instead of having a committee man address this department meet-ing, they had Emil Mazey come in to give his last farewell speech. Emil was the organizer and president of Briggs Local No. 212, and he had been drafted because of his militancy. He wouldn't go along with the

UAW's no-strike pledge during the war, so he was drafted by the United States government. (He later became the secretary-treasurer of the International Union.)

When I saw Emil come in, I didn't know what the hell to do. I didn't want to get up and be noticed by walking out, so I just held my head down during his speech and tried to be as inconspicuous as possible. When they said they needed somebody to be their chief steward, which is the same as a committee man or committee woman in the General Motors plants, he recognized me. He told these women that I'd been working with for almost three months, "I don't know what you're coming over here and asking me for help for. You've got one of the original organizers of the union right there in your ranks." All the women looked back at me.

I was embarrassed and angry, because I knew I was going to get fired because of the blacklist. After the meeting, when Emil came down to greet me, I said, "Thanks, pal. You know what you did? You just blasted me out of being a member of your union." The women were all around me. Emil called over the man who was succeeding him as president, a young militant by the name of Jess Ferrazza. He introduced me and said, "Jess, if that woman is fired, you pull every Briggs plant in the city of Detroit, all eighteen thousand workers, and you keep them down until she's put back in again."

A couple of days after the meeting, I was fired. Eighteen thousand workers walked out in Detroit and I got my job back immediately. I was elected Chief Steward of Department 15 and I organized it very well. There were five hundred workers in my department, mainly Hungarian, Italian, and Polish. There were all kinds of things they didn't have experience with and there were many problems that had never been resolved.

The workers had only half-an-hour to rush up to the cafeteria, eat their lunches, and get back down again, so they brought their lunches instead. They cleared off a few long tables so they could sit around them and eat. Every day I ate lunch with a different group and discussed unionism and solidarity.

One day, one of the women left crying and I chewed the foreman out. The foreman denied having anything to do with it. I didn't believe the foreman, naturally. But what had happened was that another women found out that she had an illegitimate child and said something nasty to her. So we had a big discussion on that and on a number of other similar topics, day after day.

We had three gay couples in there, too. One of them didn't like me. Her partner was very friendly, very warm. But this woman was not cooperative at all with things that I was trying to do to build the union. One day she said something about me being interested in her partner. So I took her outside the gates of the department and I said, "Look, I want to tell you something. I don't want you to think that there's anything between your partner and me. I've got a husband, and I'm not personally interested in your friend. I understand what the relationship is and I want you on my side." And she was on my side from that time on. She was a good one.

In the early days, you know, no one talked about those things. There was so much prejudice. But we got those women to the point where they accepted an awful lot of things that even the men with all their experience wouldn't accept. And we organized all kinds of militant actions. There were more walkouts at Briggs than anywhere else in the city of Detroit. Even though the UAW had agreed not to strike during the war, we kept organizing walkouts because the company never stopped trying to smash Local No. 212. But every time we struck, somebody usually got fired.

At one point, there was a major grievance in the plant in some other department. The union stewards decided that we had to strike over this grievance. But one steward after another said, "Don't look at me. I led the last one, and I nearly got fired." So finally they turned to me. "You haven't led a strike out of here for the whole building." I said, "No, I haven't. But I've got it pretty well organized by now." And so they said, "It's up to Department 15 to lead this one."

First I told everybody, "Don't clock out—to make sure you get your pay. It shows that you were consciously leaving the department on strike at that time." That was how the company was able to identify the strike leaders: they were the first to clock out. But I didn't know what the hell I was going to manufacture in my department to get all the workers out without recriminations. Finally, I came up with a plan. Eddie, the Army foreman, had a nasty mouth on him. I went into the superintendent's office and I started charging Eddie with all kinds of contract violations. The superintendent said, "Wait just a minute, Genora. We'll get Eddie in here." "All right, you get him in here." Then I said, "Look, you and Frasier (the Navy foreman) both said this and you said this." I charged them with a lot of grievances that didn't really exist although they could have. The foremen were amazed and they were angry. I said, "You want me to prove it? You know where I got my information? Call the general foreman in." I got them all in that office, off the work floor, all the foremen, Navy crib, Army crib, and Marine crib. I was yelling and hollering as hard as I could—like you had to do with those kind of foremen, charging them with all kinds of things.

Then the Army foreman looked out the window and said, "My God, the department is all gone!" They had walked off. I turned to the superintendent, and I said, "You didn't believe me, did you. You see what you've done? What they've done?" Then I walked out. I had had my line stewards lead the women out without touching the time-clock. They had all gone, so I walked out, too. We won that strike and none of my stewards was fired, but there were casualties in other departments.

From my viewpoint now, I know that if they had organized women like that in every plant, we would have had a much stronger union. But that wasn't the policy of the men in the unions then. They didn't think too much about women. Most of them were resentful of "women working in factories and taking jobs away from men." But I was able to prove to all the rest of the men in the plant, some of whom had built the union from the beginning, what women could do and how much they could learn and how fast they could develop in a short time. I had a great deal of satisfaction out of that experience.

I was fired three times. The last time I went back, it was rough. If I went to the toilet, they had somebody follow me and very obviously watch the clock. Everything I did was watched. Every time a grievance was brought up or there was a discussion with one of the employees, the foreman would come up a little too close. I'd say, "Get the hell out of here. This is a private grievance and you have no business until we call you in on it." In my department, the workers wouldn't let the foremen come anywhere near anything that I was saying or doing, but I couldn't stop it when I was out of my department.

During this time the local needed an educational director because our director was drafted. The executive board voted that I take over the job. But some of our people in the Socialist Workers Party didn't think it would be a wise thing because of my reputation as a socialist. They thought it would be better if I didn't take it. But the union kept insisting. I heard that another very good educator from Ford local was being released, so I asked the union if they would release me from their request if I could get him to come over to Briggs local. They agreed and so I took over the public-speaking classes instead.

Many of the committee men were very effective in the shop on grievances and in speaking to people one-on-one. But when a union meeting came up, they just didn't know how to stand up and make a persuasive speech. A number of these committee men from different Briggs plants came to my classes regularly. We had a very effective method of encouraging them. We recorded what they said one time and played it back when they got much better.

When the contract came up for consideration, lo and behold, these committee men stood up and spoke in the meetings. They did a beautiful job persuading the workers to turn down this contract because it didn't meet any of the union demands. One meeting after another, the contract was turned down, primarily because of these popular committee men who had never before taken a position on the floor. That was another reason why management didn't like me very much.

Then came the end of the war. All of the people on war production were laid off because the plants were going back into regular industrial production.

The Employers Strike Back

In 1945, when the plant closed down for retooling after the war, I was asked to help the UAW run its first candidate for mayor of the city of Detroit, Richard Frankensteen. I worked one or two days when one night as I was sleeping in bed I was beaten with a lead pipe.

Two men broke in through the back door of our apartment from the alley and put a flashlight in my face. I went up on my elbow to see who it was. That's when I got beaten pretty badly.

At that time, my husband, Sol, was organizing the Socialist Workers Party chapter in Flint. He used to come home to Detroit every weekend at the same time. But this particular week, he called and said, "I can't make it on Saturday. Is it all right if I come home for Sunday and Monday instead?" So it was not the usual time he was home. Normally, I would have been alone on that night, but he was sleeping on the other side of the bed when I was attacked. If he hadn't put his arm over my head, I think I would have been injured permanently—beyond help. He tried to climb over me, and they clubbed him on the legs so bad that when he tried to stand up against them, he collapsed. The two thugs immediately rushed out into the back alley and sped away. I was badly injured and had to stay in the hospital for several weeks. I had a brain concussion and was paralyzed on my right side. I had a broken collarbone and nerve damage to my face, and I was in a cast for six weeks.

There had previously been three other beatings in the local. The first beating was of a popular member of the Briggs local, Roy Snowden, who was captain of the flying squad, a fighting military group, the most militant flying squad in the whole UAW. Roy was a most courageous union man and afraid of nothing. The assailants ambushed him in his rooming house. As Roy went to put his key in the door, he couldn't get it in. He bent over to find out why. They had deliberately broken off another piece of metal in there. When he was bent over, they came up and gave him a severe beating.

The next time they got another militant man of the squadron by the name of Art Vega. He had also been in an awful lot of scraps to build the union. Art Vega and his wife were out walking when thugs rushed out and started beating him. His wife took off her high-heeled shoe and hit one of them in the back of the head. She started screaming and they ran away. But it was a real, genuine threat.

Then Roy Snowden was beaten a second time when he was walking up the street with Frank Silver, president of the Motor Products local. Somebody he knew beckoned to him from the sideline and he went over. His companion got a little ahead of him, and when Roy went to catch up, thugs dashed out from the back of an apartment building and gave him another severe beating.

We decided to form an investigating committee to find out where these beatings were coming from because we did not want them to spread further in the local. In the meeting only a couple of people volunteered because it was a real intimidation for the rest of the membership to think that the great captain of the flying squad, this physically and mentally powerful man, had been beaten up twice. So I volunteered. Dumb-bell me!

We began investigating and interrogating people, holding meetings and going over the information we had collected. We learned that Briggs had given out an important scrap contract to a man by the name of Carl Renda. Carl Renda was the son-in-law of Santo Perrone, the head of the Mafia in the city of Detroit. Briggs had given the Mafia this highly lucrative scrap contract in exchange for attacking the militants in the union.

Later Walter Reuther was shot and Victor Reuther was shot and lost his eye. Then the International Union became very, very interested. Prior to that when our committee went up to see them, they just pooh-

poohed it. "These guys get into beer garden fights. They break up the place, and they can be stepping out with somebody else, and some husband can come in…" and so on. They gave us a lot of silly talk. When I asked Walter Reuther to set up a reward that would deter any further action, he said, "Come on, Genora. Let's not get dramatic." That was after I had been attacked.

I told Walter that if he didn't put up a reward at the local level, the violence would come up to the International. Then he could be facing it. By the way, my warning is published in an issue of the *American Socialist* magazine. Sadly, my prediction came true. They shot both Reuther brothers. Then the International Union put up a very big reward and brought in a man from Washington, who used to be on the La Folette investigating committee. This man, Ralph Winstead, was a real detective. He followed every lead, every rumor. He was paid twenty-four hours a day for doing this.

We had to investigate some very suspicious characters, and the detective had to inform his wife every hour where he was. Later on the police found his body in Lake St. Clair. We think it was foul play and so did the International Union. But there was nothing we could do about it.

Back to the Future

> Nothing is ever handed to the working people on a silver platter. Improved living conditions and greater freedom are won through organized struggles. This is how the common people in America got the right to vote, the right to send their children to public schools, and the right to form their own independent organizations.
>
> UAW Local No. 212, Educational Committee, March 18, 1945

I think our duty today is to educate all of those who do not understand that they got their present benefits and their present standard of living from organized labor. We have to tell the story of people who suffered and died for the cause of labor. We have to teach people the history of the labor movement, and we have to tell the story that women played, so that women can be encouraged to play more of a role today.

We have won some wonderful economic advantages for working people in this country. But they are slowly being legislated away from us. Now, we've got to fight on the political level. We have to organize politically with the same intensity that we had when we began to organize the unions.

Today, most unions have a bureaucratic leadership that does little for working people and keeps them in a state of apathy. As soon as Walter Reuther found the back door to the White House so he could go in and talk to the President, he was more concerned about what the big politicals and the corporation owners said than his own members—his own members!

Right after the strike, they did away with the stewards collecting union dues on the job. Walter Reuther wanted to have money coming in regularly through an automatic dues check-off system. It was supposed to be more efficient and guarantee that in case of a strike the International Union had the funds available to help in any part of the country. But as soon as they got the regular dues coming in, you know what the bureaucrats did? They were secure, so they made all the decisions and that made the union less democratic.

We fought against this change because we thought it was better to keep the union leadership accountable to the members. Under the old system workers had some power over their leaders. They could say, "I want this done and I want that done and here's my dues." So the leadership had to deliver if they wanted the dues to come in regularly.

At the beginning of the strike, Walter Reuther said that no labor leader should get paid more than the highest paid worker in the industry. But he soon forgot those words. He started living a very comfortable life, and he spent a lot of the union's money without talking to the members about it. He built a very beautiful camp at Black Lake with some of that money. That camp is supposed to be an educational facility, but they don't want radicals in there giving workers the real solution to the problems of people in general and working-class people especially. That is socialism, social ownership of the means of production. That is the way to stop the ruling class from dominating humanity, and for working people to achieve their liberation.

Part III

Putting the Record Straight

Chapter 13

Good Housekeeping
Seal of Approval

Ah, love! Could thou and I with Fate conspire
To grasp this sorry scheme of things entire,
Would we not shatter it to bits and then
Remold it closer to the heart's desire!

Rubaiyyat of Omar Khayyam,
trans. Edward Fitzgerald

In preparation for the 1976 bicentennial celebration of the Declaration of Independence of the United States from Great Britain, the famed BBC documentary series "Yesterday's Witness" sent a scout, Jenni Pozzi, to the United States to prepare several stories. When Pozzi came to the West Coast, she learned from a Stanford University professor of a promising story for the series. The professor suggested Pozzi call Genora Dollinger, a leader of the United Automobile Workers of America in 1937. Pozzi telephoned Genora and requested an interview on the subject of the 1936–1937 Flint sitdown strikes. "How did you find me?" Genora wanted to know. Pozzi replied: "Some years ago, you addressed a convention of historians. A professor at Stanford told me that you have a good story to tell and I would like to hear it." Genora inquired, "What party do you belong to?" To which Pozzi replied: "Labour Party!" "Then I'll be happy to see you," Genora responded. "I suppose you are on a modest per diem. You may stay at our home."

A few days later Jenni Pozzi came down from Palo Alto. We learned from her that the Stanford professor had attended a convention of historians at the Biltmore Hotel during the 1970 Los Angeles teachers' strike, in which Genora participated as a concerned parent. Our son attended the Los Angeles high school and our home became a center for the striking teachers. In the midst of strike activities Staughton Lynd visited Genora. Lynd led a significant faction of left historians and invited Genora to address his group at the convention. When

Genora accepted, she thought the group she would address would have no more than a score or two in the room. Much to her surprise, the left-wing historians filled a large room to capacity—numbering several hundred—among them the unknown professor at Stanford University.

After several days of talking and touring Southern California, Jenni Pozzi called the BBC director and producer of "Yesterday's Witness," Stephen Peet. (Peet was in charge of the series for fifteen years and had been a film-maker for over thirty years. In total he produced nearly eighty popular documentaries in the series.) Pozzi informed the director she had a great story on the sitdown strikes. The BBC made arrangements for Peet and a crew to film in Los Angeles for the documentary, which he titled *The Great Sitdown Strike*. Genora subsequently agreed to accompany Peet's crew back to Michigan and to arrange for interviews of other participants in the strike. While in Detroit, Genora arranged for Peet and his film crew to interview Emil Mazey, secretary-treasurer and a leader of the UAW International Union.

The journey of Emil, the son of militant Hungarian immigrants, from an auto worker to second in command of the million-member union, could provide the core of a great biography. In his youth, Emil joined the Proletarian Party, and later on the Socialist Party. He successfully brought union organization and a contract to the Briggs Corporation. The Briggs flying squad of UAW Local No. 212 assisted in the organization of many Detroit and Michigan auto plants. During the war years Emil led a campaign to build a Labor Party in Michigan.

Emil achieved worldwide fame for his leadership of the US soldier demonstrations at the end of the Second World War. Millions of GIs joined in the protests that swept across the Pacific Islands demanding that the Army release them from service and repatriate them. This heroic protest action resulted in the army brass exiling Emil to a remote island outpost. His election to the International Board, while in the Army, and the protest of the International Union UAW, brought his speedy dismissal from the service; not incidentally, there followed rapid demilitarization of the Pacific war zones.

The meeting between Emil and Peet was held in Mazey's spacious International Union office. The recorded meeting did not appear in the film, however. When later questioned by Genora, Stephen Peet confided his reasons for not using the Mazey material:

> Mazey reminded us at the BBC of our own British union fat cats. His big desk didn't have a scrap of paper on it and he wore a Brooks Brothers suit and he just didn't fit in with the other auto workers that we later filmed in Flint.

After the meeting, Genora took Peet to the Walter Reuther Library at Wayne State University so he could research the material he planned to film in Flint. While they were in the library a young woman, Lorraine Gray, approached Genora. She told her that she and two associates, Ann Bohlen and Lyn Goldfarb, planned to make a documentary on the Women's Emergency Brigade and wanted to know if Genora would help them. Genora assured her that as soon as she had finished work on the BBC project she would assist them in any manner possible.

Peet subsequently completed his interviews of sitdown strikers in Flint whom Larry Jones and Genora had assembled. Jones was a life-long friend who had collaborated with us in union activities for over five decades. He had a prominent role in the film as one of the main interlocutors.

In July of 1976, we traveled to London on our way to Israel. We stayed at a hotel in Kensington, and had lunch with Stephen Peet and his wife, Olive. Stephen arranged a tour of the BBC. To our most pleasant surprise, we previewed the documentary with James Cameron, the narrator of *The Great Sitdown Strike*. He seemed genuinely pleased with the many complimentary remarks we later made about the documentary.

Stephen arranged for Genora to give an interview with a woman reporter from the *Guardian*, to be published when the documentary appeared on October 4 the same year on British television. Following the film's showing, reviews appeared in all the main British papers. The critics were laudatory of Stephen Peet and the film, with only the *Financial Times* suggesting that the film was one-sided. Several critics referred to Genora as a Joan of Arc of labor. The *Sunday Mirror* captured the spice of the reviews:

> One of the most telling strikes in the history of labour relations is recalled by some of the battlers who took part in it....
>
> One of the witnesses is the remarkable Genora Johnson, wife of one of the strikers, who was then twenty-three. She formed her friends into a militant women's group to aid the besieged strikers.
>
> "We didn't actually carry mops and brooms, but we did have to carry clubs—and good sized ones," says this elderly lady smiling. "I wonder what present-day Ford and British Leyland wives will make of that!"

Janet Watts's review in the *Guardian*, informed by the July interview, observed:

> Genora Dollinger is full of vitality, in spite of the bashings and ill-health she has suffered. Yet sadly her lifetime's objective—the establishment of a Labor

Party in America—is still unfulfilled; and she views the future with some concern. "Being a Socialist in America has never been popular—they always think you're ready to blow up bridges—and we have two capitalistic parties. I think we are coming to another climax, with the accumulation of wealth on one hand and great deprivation on the other. But I'll not see it in my lifetime."

Supping with the Enemy

Genora's promise to help Lorraine Gray and her associates produce their documentary (to be titled *With Babies and Banners*) coincided with two invitations to speak at UAW events. One came from the five Flint local union presidents to address the special celebration of the fortieth anniversary of the General Motors and UAW contract, scheduled for the IMA auditorium in Flint on February 12, 1977. The other invitation—written on headed stationery bearing the signatures of Leonard Woodcock, President of the UAW International Union; Irving Bluestone, Vice President, Director, General Motors Department of the UAW; and George Morris Jr., Vice President of General Motors Corporation—invited Genora to a dinner celebration of the fortieth anniversary of the contract. The dinner was to be held on the day before the Flint meeting, on February 11, at the four-star St. Regis Hotel in Detroit.

The dinner invitation to Genora induced a shock of recognition that the UAW leadership had sunk to a new low. The barometer of union consciousness had fallen and only a dramatic act could shake up the union leadership. Genora called Victor Reuther and asked him to join with her in a public denunciation of the UAW leaders for breaking bread with the 'enemy' while they permitted General Motors to co-opt the victory of the birth of the auto workers' union. Genora's anger stemmed from the fact that General Motors were obstructing the organization of their new plants in the southern states. The dinner would send the wrong message to southern auto workers. The menu of the dinner provided UAW lambs, as the main course, for the GM lions. Victor Reuther, who had just finished his book *The Brothers Reuther*, expressed sympathy with Genora's position and said he needed time to think about it. He failed to get back to her. Genora decided that she would go to Detroit alone if necessary. This she did. A press conference was arranged by friends, at which Genora sharply denounced the union celebration of its victory with the corporation. This was accompanied by a press release.

Two days before the dinner Jack Crellin of the *Detroit News* wrote an extensive report of Genora's press conference:

> A fiery woman veteran of the sit-down strikes of the 1930's has lambasted UAW brass for participating with General Motors executives in a joint observation of 40 years of contractual relationship.
>
> "Tuxedo unionism," snapped Genora Dollinger, 64, in explaining why, even though invited, she won't attend the party Friday night at the posh St. Regis Hotel, across the street from GM's corporate headquarters in Detroit's New Center district....
>
> "This year I cannot in good conscience take part in a celebration under the hegemony of the very corporation which has fought us at every step down to the present day where new GM plants are reopened in the south with non-union labor," she said.
>
> "And with these plants go the company agents who are playing the same role as the GM agents of 1937."
>
> Her reference was to last fall's negotiations between the union and GM which resulted in the union demanding and getting assurances from GM that it would remain neutral in representation elections at GM plants in the South....
>
> Mrs. Dollinger acidly questioned why union officials like Woodcock and Bluestone needed "GM's good housekeeping seal of approval on organizing drives."...
>
> "In only 40 years we witness a return to tuxedo unionism and the celebrating of our union history jointly with GM officials and agents."
>
> "While each of us marches to the beat of a different drum, the beat of my march must remain with those men and women who are in the factories, making the profits and providing the sustenance of our rich country."

After the dinner in the St. Regis Hotel a reporter of the *Detroit News*, Mark Lett, questioned Emil Mazey, secretary-treasurer of the UAW. He wrote that Mazey "wanted no part of the merriment":

> At a recent meeting of the UAW executive board members where plans for the party were announced, Mazey was said to have railed against the gathering. He reportedly branded the event as an example of "class collaboration."

John R. Emshwiller of the *Wall Street Journal* reported on the day following the dinner:

> Mrs. Dollinger might have felt a little lonely if she had gone. Victor Reuther, brother of the late UAW president, was the only guest who took part in the sit-downs. Also, fewer than a dozen of the roughly 200 invited were women....
>
> After dinner guests were treated to some newsreels of the 1937 sit-down strike. One of the more memorable scenes showed pro-union women smashing the windows out of a GM plant. Perhaps Mrs. Dollinger did make an unknowing appearance.

Genora for her part had driven with our son Ronald directly to Flint following the press conference on the eve of the dinner.

The invitation to speak in Flint had come from Sam Duncan, president of Fisher Body 2, on behalf of the Flint presidents. Along with the invitation came a promise to pay travel costs. The Flint UAW meeting was held the day after the Detroit meeting so the top officers could attend the banquet and then go up to the IMA meeting in Flint. Don Ellis, a Red-baiter from years back, thought he would score points with the leader, Leonard Woodcock, by keeping Genora off the program. He didn't know that Woodcock and Genora had been members of the Socialist Party before the strike. Genora, anticipating trouble, had tried to confirm that she was addressing the meeting. When she learned that it was an all-male program she called on several women's groups for support.

At Genora's behest the women organized a solid group of protestors consisting of Coalition of Labor Union Women, News and Letters group, headed by Olga Domanski, and members of NOW to lead the protest effort. Many old retired UAW sitdowners participated, wearing red crêpe armbands to recall the red armbands and berets of the Women's Emergency Brigade of 1937. The UAW sitdowners joined the other women in creating a raucous clamor in the auditorium which prevented the meeting from proceeding. The chant by men and women in unison, that the UAW needed an ERA clearly embarrassed the leaders. Leonard Woodcock advised Ellis to allow a women's representative to speak. Genora addressed the meeting, giving no indication of the heart fibrillations for which she had recently received medical treatment. She concluded her talk swiftly, to avoid the physical symptoms that might have been brought on by the event. The audience, unaware of the medical problem, cheered her effort.

With Babies and Banners

Genora's commitment to the producers of *With Babies and Banners* was meanwhile occupying her attention. Lorraine Gray had arranged a meeting at the home of one of the members of the 1937 Women's Auxiliary. Sara Pillsbury, who was in later years a successful producer of major Hollywood films, picked up Genora and drove her to the home of Delia Parrish. The director, Lorraine Gray, had arranged for a dramatic entrance. She intended to film the look of surprise when Genora entered and met members of the Brigade she hadn't seen for forty years. Only two of the original five lieutenants of the Brigade survived the passage of time. Sybil "Teeter" Walker and Nellie Besson greeted Genora warmly. However, Genora was surprised when she became aware of some of the other women that the film-makers had invited to this gathering.

Later, she took Gray aside and protested the appearance of Catherine Gelles from Detroit and active with the Detroit women. Genora thought the appearance of Lillian Hatcher, a member of the UAW Women's Department who had not been in the strike, inappropriate. Gray defended Hatcher's participation as an effort to show that the strike involved Blacks. While Chevrolet employed four hundred Blacks on sanitation, only one, Roscoe Van Zandt, sat down in Plant 4. Blacks only became active in Chevrolet in the war period—1943–1945. Gray averred that Gelles's appearance showed that other brigades had been organized in Michigan cities. While they were copies of the Flint Brigade, no other brigade acted with the militant action of the Women's Emergency Brigade of Flint. Genora thought that Gelles's and Hatcher's participation gave a misleading and historically inaccurate picture of the Flint Emergency Brigade.

None of the male historians of the sitdown strikes gave women their proper place in the historical battle to establish unionism in the auto industry. This event had transformed labor in America, and yet the historians had trivialized women's role in the great struggle. Now, for the first time, women were using film to break new ground in interpreting history. However, at the very beginning, Gray was introducing distortions. Genora thought it the wrong way to begin the revision process. Genora transmitted her misgivings privately to Gray.

She later wrote to Gray (May 1979) spelling out her criticism:

> I was surprised by a *fait accompli* by you when I walked into the filming with women who were never involved in the Women's Emergency Brigade nor even participants in the UAW Women's Auxiliary of 1937. (For example, I have a copy of the April 25, 1979 *Guardian* which was sent to me for comment on their review of the film. In it the writer postulates, "It is also regrettable that the film does not clearly explain the position in the brigade's formation of the one Black woman interviewed. When this is set against the well-defined leadership roles of the other women interviewed, the film is left open to charges of tokenism." How can I answer that? By acceding to your plea I was made an accomplice to this forgery of historical documentation.)

Later that year Gray came to California to attend the film's preview showing in Santa Monica. Genora's friends enthusiastically praised the documentary. Only Genora remained critical, but again she expressed her disappointment privately to Gray. Genora's further objections pertained to the license the producers had taken in showing scenes of the strikes in Detroit. For example, police on horseback were shown, despite the fact that Flint had had no such force. Likewise, scenes of workers in shirtsleeves, when in fact the strike occurred in winter with the streets filled with snow and slush, jarred her sense of accuracy. Also, some women wore dresses that were popular a generation earlier. Gray fended off the criticism by citing the paucity of funds she had to work with in making the film.

Notwithstanding its faults, *With Babies and Banners* received a nomination by the Academy Award Committee as one of the best documentaries of the year. Furthermore it won several prizes in Europe. It had a profound impact on union and general audiences alike. The documentary emerged as a timely event, relating both to the present state of the women's movement and to the role of women forty years earlier.

One special preview in a filled theater in San Francisco we especially enjoyed. On entering the lobby, we were greeted by young women all wearing red berets. After the showing, Genora addressed the filmgoers, who responded by giving her a standing ovation. The next morning, as we walked from Hotel Chancellor on Union Square, I observed a young woman do a double take. I told Genora that someone had recognized her. The woman approached Genora and threw her arms around her, exclaiming, "What a terrific high you gave us yesterday!"

For the next several months Genora spoke at theater premieres, union meetings, colleges and to community groups. The Committee of Labor Union Women (CLUW) held a premiere in Chicago. There were also press conferences, an appearance on Studs Terkel's radio program, and a talk in the theater following the showing of the movie in Hollywood.

A Debt of Gratitude

When Genora had returned home she received a telephone call from Ellen Ogintz of the *Chicago Tribune*. She wanted Genora's comments on a statement made by Emil Mazey claiming that in fact *With Babies and Banners* overstated the role of women in the sitdown strike of 1937.

Genora responded to this unexpected attack by sending a letter to Mazey and copied to the twenty-eight members of the International Executive Board of the UAW. None of these members had seen action in the Flint strike. For his part, Mazey had brought his Briggs Flying Squad to Flint occasionally to give strikers visible evidence of support from his Detroit local. Genora's letter included the encomiums of Bob Travis and Roy Reuther, two of the leaders of the sitdown strikes, addressed to the Women's Emergency Brigade of 1937. Travis said at the strike's conclusion, "The women of Flint have made their fame and are known throughout the world for their heroic stand during the great General Motors strike." Roy Reuther added: "The automobile workers of Flint and America owe you a debt of gratitude for the part you played in the winning of the Big Strike and in building our International Union."

Genora appended to each letter a clipping of the front page of the *New York Times* which gave an account of the Emergency Brigade at the battle at Chevrolet Plant 9, and of the ruse that made it possible to capture the huge Chevrolet Engine Plant 4. The reporter gave special mention to Genora's role in this action. "The UAW should be proud of its history," concluded Genora in her letter to Mazey and the UAW International Board members, "What other International Union can claim such a historical precedence for equal rights for all human beings, including women? And who else can tell it better than the women who saw the action?"

In the *Chicago Tribune* article, Mazey had also addressed the issue of the withdrawal of the invitation to Genora to appear on the anniversary program. He denied that a request had been made for a women's representative to take part. Genora also set the record straight on this matter in her letter:

> The Anniversary Planning Committee, under a motion by Sam Duncan, President of Local 598, UAW, sent me a formal invitation, offering to pay my transportation from Los Angeles to Flint to appear as a speaker on their special program.
>
> Prior to the meeting itself I spoke to Regional Director Don Ellis regarding plans for the program and protested vigorously when he advised me there had been a change and I was not to speak, nor any other representative, on behalf of the women. This change was made without consulting the local union presidents....
>
> At the Anniversary meeting over half the audience, mainly those who participated in the '37 strike, were wearing red paper arm bands in honor of the Women's Emergency Brigade of 1937! My only regret—and that of several of the original sitdowners—is that I didn't publicly expose Ellis and explain why the demonstration was organized on short notice to obtain the recognition we deserved....

For these reasons I can only hope that your statements were misunderstood, and that you still adhere to the ideals and aspirations we mutually held over 40 years ago.

Genora never received a reply to her letter from Mazey. However, within a week she had heard from Douglas Fraser, who had succeeded Woodcock as president of the International Union:

In terms of the 40th anniversary celebration, I did have a conversation with Leonard Woodcock about the event, and I think you realize that he had absolutely no objections to your speaking to that assembly. I know nothing of any conversations that might have preceded the meeting.

I do not believe the contribution the women made during the Flint sit-down can be denied nor ignored, and the *New York Times* article, which you attached, testifies to the significant role they played.[1]

Chapter 14

Who Led the Flint Sitdown to Victory?
On the Rewriting of History

In our hands is placed a power greater than their hoarded gold,
Greater than the might of armies magnified a thousand fold
We can bring to birth a new world from the ashes of the old.
For the union makes us strong.

Ralph Chaplin, "Solidarity Forever"

The distortion of auto union history occurred for selfish and political reasons. Walter Reuther rewrote history for reasons of ego and to suit the organizational needs of the moment. William Serrin, author of *The Company and the Union*, tells of a conversation between Reuther and Emil Mazey as they reviewed the date for the upcoming celebration of the twentieth anniversary of the UAW. Mazey contended that the union was founded in August 1935 in Detroit, Michigan. Reuther, however, maintained that the charter convention dated from April 1936, with the convention held in South Bend, Indiana. Reuther insisted on the later date since it also marked his first appearance at a UAW convention. Mazey told Serrin of his comment to Reuther: "Goddammit, Walter, the Russians aren't the only ones who rewrite history."[1]

The history of the UAW remained as Reuther proclaimed while he lived. Five years after Walter's death, however, Mazey insisted on correcting the record. A union publication observed that the founding convention took place in Detroit in August 1935 under the auspices of the American Federation of Labor, with two hundred delegates in attendance from seventy-one locals. This nugget of information created no stir, however; auto workers have limited interest in the history of the union.

The writing of history reveals errors of omission and commission. Often the writer introduces a subjective view of events. The selection of material influences the conclusion of the writer. Thus, the biases of the writer must be examined by the reader for proper understanding of the text. This writer must be put to the same test as others in this book. In the end the subjective approach will fade from view in the face of objective evidence.

The 1937 sitdown strikes shattered minimal labor–management relations. The victory of the Flint auto workers heralded the most profound social cultural and political changes in the United States since the Civil War. These events, led by radical political parties, produced partisan views. The recorded history, it should be noted, was largely the province of Communist Party supporters. It is my aim here to counterbalance the biased claims of these writers, particularly those of Henry Kraus, author of *The Many and the Few: A Chronicle of the Dynamic Auto Workers* and *Heroes of Unwritten Story*.[2] Kraus's first book, appearing in 1947, inflated the role of the Communist Party and diminished that of the Socialist Party and other dedicated unionists.

Ben Hanford, vice-presidential candidate on the Socialist Party ticket in 1904, wrote about the fictional character Jimmie Higgins—the guy who swept the floor at party headquarters, who arranged the chairs at meetings, passed the collection hat, and was available for all the sundry tasks that made it possible for an organization to function. Ben Hanford showed respect and admiration for the small cogs that helped turn the big wheels. While Hanford honored the Jimmie Higginses, he didn't exaggerate their contributions. Kraus, on the other hand, makes paragons of any Tom, Dick, or Jimmie; he also edits history or gives an unbalanced view of his opponents and their contributions. He is even prepared to go so far as to smear an opponent. As a consequence, many writers using Kraus's book as a reference, even those opposed to the CP, have been misled. Others have used the book to slant history further in favor of the Communist Party.

When the strike ended, over half a century ago, Kraus carted off the union records. The union and its officers could not appreciate their potential value and importance. However, Kraus, from his first association with auto workers, wrote of his intention to write a book some day. Where others saw dross, Kraus saw gold.

The records in the Kraus collection contributed significantly to the writing of the history of the strike. A critical addition was the publication of Sidney Fine's *Sitdown: The General Motors Strike 1936–1937*, the most factual review of the strike and the personalities engaged in it.

It was not until two documentary films on the sitdown strikes were produced in 1976 and 1977 (see Chapter 13), with the special assistance of Genora Johnson Dollinger, that the process of correcting the historical record began. *With Babies and Banners* focused on the role of the women in the Women's Emergency Brigade, which Genora organized and led. A wider lens was used by the BBC production *The Great Sitdown Strike*.

The Need for Revision

In the interests of historical accuracy, I now propose to examine selective aspects of the Flint strike as represented in the main published accounts, contrasting this record with my own perspective and that of Genora. This will entail a partial, though more detailed, reprise of those historic events of 1936–1937.

The sitdown strike at Fisher Body 2 started on December 30, 1936. It was followed by a sitdown strike at Fisher Body 1. The former plant produced bodies for Chevrolet; the latter supplied bodies for Buick. While the strike was in progress, the corporation, working through individuals associated with General Motors, was organizing its anti-union forces into the Flint Alliance.

The Flint Alliance enrolled thousands of members from the plants and the public. Corporation foremen and supervisors were instructing their GM workers to join the Alliance if they wanted to keep their jobs. In other major strikes of that era, similar groups had been used as strikebreakers. It was feared that history would be repeated.[3] General Motors hired a huge army of Pinkerton goons; furthermore, all the city agencies were dominated by GM, including the police and sheriff's departments. The city's only daily paper kept up a steady barrage of anti-union propaganda.

On January 11 an attack was launched against the small force of workers occupying the second floor of Fisher Body Plant 2. Outside, the police tried to prevent food being delivered to the strikers. The heating in the plant was turned off. The strikers, led by Victor Reuther in the union sound car, advanced to the front doors of the plant to reinforce the picket line that had held strong since that morning.

The police attacked the union men with tear gas and more lethal weapons. In the plant the strikers repulsed the advancing police by hurling heavy car hinges from the second floor of the plant. Victor Reuther called on his forces to blockade and overturn cars on Chevrolet Avenue to prevent the police from approaching; this successfully obstructed the way on both north and south sides of the entrance.

While the fight raged, the radio described the battle as a revolution in the streets of Flint. Thousands of Flint citizens flocked to both barricaded ends of Chevrolet Avenue. They could see the police firing into the small embattled band of unionists in front of Plant 2.[4] The battle continued for several hours until Victor Reuther confided to Genora and Kermit Johnson, and Jarvis Albro (Genora's brother) that the batteries on the sound truck were giving out. In front of Victor were a score of unionists bleeding from rifle and buckshot wounds. It was a desperate situation with defeat facing the strikers.

The Many or the Few?

Now let us consider how the historians relate the story of the conflict's outcome. First, Kraus's description of events, in *The Many and the Few*:

> Another time a queer enormous thing-on-wheels began to rumble down the hill toward the plant. What was that? To the pickets it looked like some monstrous new instrument of attack…. Then suddenly some torch flares on the truck bursting into flame and the monstrosity could be recognized as the ambulating apparatus of a newsreel photographer.
> As things quieted down everybody got busy making preparations for an all-night vigil, … certain that the police would attack again as soon as they received a new supply of gas.[5]

It is clear from this account that Kraus was not with the pickets. Instead, he was apparently behind the police line. His was a panoramic view of the battle scene down below—witness his description of the mounted camera on wheels approaching. In short, he is out of the action. This explains his wandering account.

In 1980 Roger Keeran published *The Communist Party and the Auto Workers Union*.[6] His research is notable for confirming the long-held suspicion that Wyndham Mortimer, Kraus, and Bob Travis were members of the Party long before the Flint strike. Keeran exaggerates the role of the Communist Party in the 1934 and 1935 strikes. His account of the 1937 strike are colored by his reliance on interviews with CP sources and are not supported by the historical material. Let us see how Keeran brings the battle at Plant 2 to a conclusion:

> In the afternoon of January 11, the guards locked the plant gates, turned off the heat and prevented the delivery of food to the strikers. Apprised of this situation, Travis rushed to the scene. Over the union's sound car, he ordered the men to seize the gates. The small band of guards 'phoned the police and then locked themselves in a nearby ladies' room. Under the pretext that the

strikers had kidnaped the guards, the Flint police attacked the plant with tear gas. Workers from Fisher #1, men from Travis's local in Toledo and a group of unemployed workers organized by Communist Charles Killinger, fought the police with bottles and rocks.

From inside their fortress, the sit-down strikers pelted the police with hinges and soaked them with fire hoses. Victor and Roy Reuther yelled encouragement and directions over the sound car loudspeaker, and Travis directed operations in the front lines. In the course of several hours fighting the workers successfully repelled several police assaults and demolished the sheriff's squad car. Seven workers received gunshot wounds, and Travis required brief hospitalization for gas burns.[7]

Victor Reuther's recollection is quite different from the description provided by Keeran. He reports seeing Bob Travis and his brother Roy on the outer fringe of the crowd unable to get through the police perimeter. After the battle, according to Reuther, Travis and Roy Reuther celebrated the victory over the company and the police at Fisher Body 2, which they thought was the most vulnerable outpost of the strike.[8]

The most searching examination of the Battle of Bull's Run can be found in Sidney Fine's *Sitdown*.[9] The same diligence evidenced in Fine's writing in *The Automobile Under the Blue Eagle* is practiced in this work, the successor volume. Fine exhibits a broader scope in his work than Kraus and Keeran, who are constricted by their efforts to portray the strike under the leadership of the Communist Party. Fine's examination of fifty participant interviews by the Senate La Follette subcommittee of Congress immediately following the battle seems to shed valuable new light.

Fine's account of the battle begins with the police moving south on Chevrolet Avenue past a row of restaurants on both sides of the street. The forty-five police officers are augmented as the engagement takes place. The strikers retaliate from the roof of the Fisher Body 2 plant. At one stage of the conflict, the citizens who gathered behind the police retreat when tear-gas canisters are hurled back at the police.

> In the midst of this new phase of the battle, twenty-three-year-old Genora Johnson, the wife of a union man who worked in the Chevrolet No. 4 plant, asked permission to speak from the sound car to the spectators beyond the police lines at both ends of Chevrolet Avenue. Mrs. Johnson had been rehearsing a play at union headquarters that afternoon when she heard that trouble was brewing at Fisher No. 2. She drove to the plant but finding the scene peaceful did not remain. She returned, however, later in the day to take a turn on the picket line, and soon found herself a combatant on the

battlefield. "During this time," she later declared in an affidavit, "I did not know fear. I knew only surprise, anguish, and anger." Taking the microphone in the sound car, she addressed herself first to the police. "Cowards! Cowards!" she shouted, "Shooting unarmed and defenseless men." Then she spoke to the women in the crowd beyond the police lines, telling them that it was their fight also and urging them to join the picket line but warning them at the same time that if the police were cowardly enough to shoot unarmed men they would no doubt fire at women also.[10]

Fine continues the account of the battle with the police firing at the strikers until the early hours of the morning. Like Kraus, Fine concludes that the conflict ended when the police ran out of tear-gas.[11]

While Fine's version is more accurate, it does not relate how the battle was concluded. The police may have run out of tear gas, but they were nevertheless armed with pistols, shotguns, and rifles. And the wounded gave graphic testimony to these being used. Fine reports that fourteen were wounded, all but one by gunshot.

In 1976 Genora was interviewed with Sherna Gluck as part of an oral history. Her account details the events that brought the battle to a final conclusion. In doing so, it raises the question of the failure of Victor Reuther and Henry Kraus to report this stage in their books.[12] While, for his part, Victor admitted that rewriting was called for,[13] Kraus's more recent book, *Heroes of Unwritten Story* (1993), repeats the inaccurate account contained in *The Many and the Few*.

The following extensive quotation from Genora's account completes the story of the historic battle, which ended in victory for the auto workers. She responds first to the question as to whether the strikers had any means to defend themselves.

Oh yes, but we didn't have any body contact. This was all shooting, you know. We had the water hoses from the plant and the hinges and the stones, that's all. Those hinges were kind of heavy hinges, you know; the old car-door hinge was a different thing. And they got box-loads of them and they got down so they could fire them downstairs, and they were upstairs on the roof firing them, too. No, we didn't have any [weapons].... The blackjacks would do no good; there was no hand-to-hand combat. Those cops had rifle shot and buckshot; there [were] firebombs and there were tear-gas canisters. We would run out and grab—the men were faster at that, they were better pitchers, I didn't try anything like that—the tear-gas canisters and hurl them back. And the fire bombs, they usually got those things—I mean they attempted to; the timing on those were very important.

So this went on. This was all we had, that was all there was that goddamn night. Looking back on it, there were a couple of humorous incidents that occurred right in the midst of all this danger. Fisher 2 had swinging doors—

one person's come out and you'd go in—double doors. Habits are so in-grained that at one point when I was going through and a man was going out, he tipped his hat at me [laughter] I never forgot that. I thought, "Of all things," you know, "tipping his hat"—in the midst of a bloody battle! And so anyway, the battle raged. The sound car was down there and Victor Reuther was the primary speaker, and then he would pull in other men to make their appeals, and this went on and on. It never dawned on me to speak. In the first place, this was primarily a man's operation and I was down there to help out. Although I never thought too much about men and women when we were right there in the heart of the battle, come to think about it. But it never dawned on me— I'd never made any kind of a public speech over a microphone—until Victor came back and told us that the battery on the sound car was running down and we couldn't get our message across, [much] longer, to the crowds that had gathered at both ends of the battle area.

He said, "Well, we may have lost the battle. The war is not lost but we may have lost the battle." And I said to him, "Well, Victor why don't I talk to them over the loudspeaker?" And he replied, "Well, we've got nothing to lose." He had no great confidence that this would help; men really didn't feel that women could do too much—although we were good and wonderful women for wanting to help them.

So that's when I got to take the mike, and again, under such circum-stances you lose yourself; you go beyond yourself and think of the cause. I was able to make my voice really ring out on that night because I knew the battery was going down and we had only a few minutes left. That's when I appealed to the women of Flint. I bypassed everybody else then and went to the women, and told them what was happening. That's when I said, There are women down here, mothers of children,—I made [it] sound plural be-cause I knew there was this gallantry that's always present in the hearts of men and other women [who might] come down here and stand by women in such a situation—There are women down here, mothers of children, and I beg of you to come down here and stand with your husbands, your loved ones, your brothers, your sweethearts.

And when I made that appeal, it was a strange thing. It was dark, too, but I could almost hear a hush. There was a general buzzing of the growing crowd at both ends. A hush came over that crowd the minute a woman's voice came over the mike. It was startling! All night long they [hadn't real-ized] that there was even a woman down there. Then I saw—I don't know, there were car lights or whatever it was in this darkness that we could see the action going on up there; probably, maybe they were factory headlights or spotlights on us or something, police lights. But then I saw the first woman struggling, and I noticed when she started to break through and come down, that a cop grabbed her by the coat. But she pulled out of her coat—and this was in freezing weather, freezing weather, there were icy pavements and everything was frozen—and she just kept on coming. And as soon as that happened, other women broke through, and then we had a situation where the cops didn't want to fire into the backs of women. When the women did that, the men came, naturally, and that was the end of the battle.[14]

General Motors Reneges

Following the events of the battle, Governor Murphy invited the representatives of the company and the union to a meeting in the state capitol, which took place on January 14. The company was represented by William Knudsen, John Thomas Smith (son-in-law of a Dupont), and Donaldson Brown (treasurer of General Motors), and the union by Wyndham Mortimer, John Brophy and Homer Martin. After a long session, it was agreed to evacuate the plants in return for GM's continuing the negotiations and not attempting to resume production in the struck plants. Implicit was the understanding that the negotiations would be confined to the UAW.

Mystery clouds this accord to the present day. The union committee agreed to give up its most powerful weapon, the strike, in exchange for GM's flimsy promise, despite the fact that the company had already shown in the 1935 Chevrolet strike that its promise was not worth the paper it was written on! The union's partial victory in 1935 was the first over GM in the National Recovery Act (NRA) era. Immediately following the strike victory, though, GM cut production of transmissions in the plant by half and sent the work to other GM plants. It is puzzling that Travis and Mortimer were not on guard against a repeat of such perfidious behavior.

The three union UAW leaders were counseled by a core of SP and CP leaders. They included Adolph Germer, Len De Caux, and Leo Krzycki. The blame for this colossal error can be spread equally; it could have had catastrophic results. The leaders began to execute the agreement without further consultation. John L. Lewis received frequent reports from his chief aide, John Brophy, in the negotiations with GM. While Lewis controlled the miners' union and kept it that way by appointing his own man, he knew those methods would not work with the maverick auto union, most of whose top leaders came from the ranks of left-wing parties. Lewis thus gave them free rein to organize the largest auto giant. While Lewis had views on the negotiations, he permitted his lieutenants the final decision. According to Fine, Lewis opposed any settlement without a signed contract with GM.[15]

The Communist Party had just entered the period of its Popular Front strategy. It was a heady advance for this hounded organization to have one of its leaders invited to the bargaining sessions at the governor's executive offices. Mortimer was the one committee member who had the ability to frustrate the evacuation of the plants, yet we know that he agreed to it in principle.

The union leaders were looking to the governor of the state for salvation, a sharp departure from the earlier union declarations that only the independent action of the GM workers could bring victory.

Two days later, Walter Reuther, Dick Frankensteen, and Homer Martin led the sitdowners out of Fleetwood and the Cadillac plants in Detroit and the Guide Lamp plant in Indiana. Plans were under way to end the sitdown in Flint. Victor Reuther asserts that the evacuation plans had the prior approval of Bob Travis. However, one must bear in mind that in the spring of 1935 Travis was on the strike committee of the Toledo Chevrolet plant. He knew from the 1935 Chevrolet strike that GM could not be trusted.

After the completed evacuation of the three GM plants, the union learned that the company had no intention of recognizing the UAW as the sole bargaining agent. Bill Lawrence, a reporter for the United Press, read a press statement issued by the Flint Alliance that had not yet been released. It confirmed that GM was not excluding the Alliance as a factor in the bargaining process. In Detroit, furthermore, GM sent telegrams calling employees back to work, thereby violating the accord reached in Lansing. The company's actions blew the agreement apart. Plans to evacuate the Flint Fisher Body plants were rescinded.

Deadlock

The strike had been in a state of stalemate even before the proposed evacuation of the plants. By their chicanery General Motors' representatives had confirmed the view of some of the militants that only further drastic measures could break the impasse. It was common knowledge that a shutdown of Chevrolet Plant 4 would bring production in all of the Chevrolet plants nationwide to a halt. How to accomplish this herculean task was the nut that had to be cracked. In such a rare situation the role of the individual assumes cardinal importance.

The actual strategy for shutting down Plant 4 originated with Kermit Johnson, the 24-year-old chairman of the citywide strike committee and a leading Flint Socialist Party member. Plant 4 was the largest of the ten plants in the Flint Chevrolet complex. Four thousand workers were employed on two shifts turning out Chevrolet motors. The plant faces Chevrolet Avenue opposite Plant 5; its back end leads to Plants 6 and 10. Kermit took home an oil-smeared diagram on a small piece of shop paper showing all of the entrances to the plant and the proximity of the other nearby plants. It was possible for workers to come to the aid of a strike in Plant 4.

Kermit discussed with his wife Genora, head of the Women's Emergency Brigade and also a leading member of the Flint Socialist Party, the feasibility of his plan: a diversionary attack on one of the other plants could make it possible to shut down Plant 4. The Johnsons submitted their proposal to a meeting of SP members, which included Walter Reuther in from Detroit. Walter opposed the plan as too risky, and it was narrowly voted down when he told the Flint SPers: "The union has to learn how to crawl before it walks."

That night Genora typed a two-page letter to Norman Thomas, appealing for help in overturning the decision taken in the local SP meeting. Thomas, a novice in union matters, referred the matter to the National Labor Secretary, Frank Trager, a university professor from the University of Chicago. He responded to the local grievance and came to Flint, where the matter was reviewed.[16]

Genora had arranged for Bill Roy and other party members to take Trager to all the strike centers. He witnessed hundreds of strikers going and coming from the Pengelly Building union headquarters, looking for some action. He talked with dozens of workers on the picket lines or involved in other strike duties. The lull in the strike was evidenced by the union's showing of the Charlie Chaplin film *Modern Times*. The dour mood of the workers wanting action contrasted with the comedy of the film. Meanwhile the Flint Alliance was intensifying its drive to sign up members.

Trager, imbued with the spirit of the strikers he encountered, intervened in support of the Johnson plan. Walter Reuther, annoyed with the decision, threatened Kermit: "If this fails, the responsibility will fall on your head!" Roy Reuther and Kermit were instructed to take the plan to the strike committee. The rest is history; though not according to Henry Kraus, the alter ego of Bob Travis and Wyndham Mortimer. His version of events is as follows:

> What chance would the union group, inexperienced, none too big yet, have against this mustering? With Ed Cronk, Howard Foster and Kermit Johnson, three Chevy workers, Travis retired to his Dresden Hotel room, with stringent orders not to be disturbed, to discuss these questions of strength and weakness and to work out a plan, if possible, of outwitting the Chevrolet guards.[17]

Kraus then devotes considerable attention to Travis's techniques of putting the plan into operation. This is justified: Travis indeed deserves much credit for the implementation of the ingenious strike strategy, part of which included deployment of the three leading Lovestoneites— Ted LaDuke, Tom Klasey and Melvin Center—who were in Plant 9 and would bear the brunt of the plant guards' gas and club attacks. For GM had prepared for the planned capture by mobilizing all of the Plant police and the Pinkerton agents in the basement of the nearby personnel building, whom it proceeded to turn loose on the sitdowners in Plant 9.

The Taking of Chevrolet Plant 4

While Plant 9 was the battleground inside the plant, the Women's Emergency Brigade, acting independently, engaged the Flint police outside. The Brigade, armed with clubs, were behind the police in Kearsley Street with their backs to Plant 9. Pickets lined the sidewalk across from the factory—the police more concerned with them than with the women at their backs. Suddenly a window opened and the bloody head of Tom Klasey appeared. He shouted, "They're gassing and clubbing us in here!" Without any hesitation, the Emergency Brigade sprang into action and shattered windows in the plant on Kearsley Street. When the police threatened to attack the pickets on the sidewalk, the Brigade threatened the police with their clubs. This is celebrated in the verse of Floyd Hoke Miller, "poet laureate" of Chevrolet Local No. 659 and a sitdowner in Plant 4:

> Did you hear the shrilling
> screams of angry women
> That dared the slugging blue
> coats with their lives
> And stormed the streets outside
> the factory gate
> Did you see them break the windows
> glass by glass
> And let escape the blinding,
> strangling force of gas
> In fighting female fury to
> succor endangered mates?[18]

When the action had concluded, Genora sent the Brigade back to the Pengelly Building, a few blocks away. She told her lieutenants to remain behind because the main strike action was at Plant 4 on Chevrolet Avenue. They immediately walked the half mile and arrived at the gate. One of the sitdowners instructed them not to let anyone past them: "We're having a hell of a time in here!"

Genora instructed one of the lieutenants to call headquarters for reinforcements. In what seemed a short time, the main corps of the Flint police came down the hill, to enter the plant. "Over our dead bodies," the women replied. The five brigade leaders clasped arms across the gate. "Well, we've got a job to do. Just stand aside," the police captain said. Genora said years later in interview:

> We were very determined. Well, naturally we couldn't hold out against them. They could have shoved us … or clubbed us … but at that point … the Brigade came marching down and they had the American flag flying at its head and they were singing "Solidarity" and those red berets bobbing like that and they reached the scene just in time. And so I said, "Set up the picket lines in front of the gate" … then the sound car rounded the corner and men started arriving … I climbed up in the sound car and started giving instructions.[19]

This episode was duly reported in the *New York Times* of February 1, yet in Kraus's *The Many and the Few* there is no account of the action that helped bring victory to the UAW.

As the siege of Plant 9 continued, Kermit Johnson and union supporters were locked in a struggle to oust the non-union forces and to barricade the huge doors of Plant 4. Turmoil reigned inside Plant 4. The strike leaders knew that success or failure hinged on this dramatic action. Writing long after the event, in the Chevrolet Local No. 659 union paper, Kermit Johnson attested to the drama of the action leading up to this moment. He described the degree of deception the union leaders practiced due to the fear that the union was infiltrated by company spies:

> I was remembering all these things and many others as I walked through the plant gate that afternoon, February 1, 1937. I was doing a lot of thinking. Everything that had happened in the past week was flashing through my mind over and over again. I thought about last night's final secret meeting held deep inside the South Fisher plant. What a farce that had been! I laughed to myself and felt like a conspirator when I recalled all the pretense we'd gone through to arrange a meeting for one despicable man, a stool pigeon. Thirty men had been secretly picked for that meeting by Bob Travis, Organizational Director, and his aide Roy Reuther, including Ed Cronk and myself from Chevrolet. The four of us, who alone knew the actual plans, put on a real show that night selling the right guy the wrong bill of goods. It seemed like a dirty trick to dupe so many good men, but to make the big fish swallow the bait, we had to have a lot of little fish nibbling. I was sure we

had convinced the stool pigeon that today at 3:30 p.m. the men in Plant 9 would stage a sit-down strike. I was sure because he asked so many pointed questions about strategy, and because others, taking a natural part in the discussion, helped to allay any suspicions he might have had.[20]

Kraus detours in his storytelling by leaving the reader with the impression that Kermit Johnson was irresponsible and perhaps even suffered from last-minute fear of his undertaking.[21] For whatever reasons, Kermit entered the plant on the second shift in time to shut the plant down. Kraus chooses to impugn Kermit by saying he overslept. But Walter Reuther had put the fate of the strike on Kermit's shoulders. It is far more likely that he didn't sleep much that night. Furthermore, he knew the action would start on the second shift: there was no reason to go to work for eight hours and then start the sitdown.

Sidney Fine's version is different again:

> Participants in the strike and those who have written about it have generally given either Bob Travis or Roy Reuther the principal credit for having devised the strategy that resulted in the UAW's seizure of Chevrolet No. 4. Travis himself has declared that Mortimer, Kraus, and he worked out the details of the maneuver, but he has said that his own thinking had been influenced by Kermit Johnson, who was to be designated the chairman of the strike committee in Chevrolet No. 4 and who had advised Travis that if the UAW planned to capture the plant it should try to create a diversion somewhere else. Travis insisted that Reuther took no part in the planning of the strategy, but he is certainly in error on that point.[22]

The notion that Travis, Mortimer, and Kraus—three outsiders with only a passing knowledge of Plant 4, or for that matter Roy Reuther—could have worked out the strategy stretches the imagination. In *Heroes of Unwritten Story*, Kraus admits to surprise at learning (from Fine's *Sitdown*) that Kermit Johnson is credited by Travis for the diversionary tactic. He chokes on the small piece of crow; nevertheless he insists that his slander of Kermit should be accepted as the correct version of this key event. According to Kraus, the strategy of capturing and barricading Plant 4 fell on the shoulders of three men: Johnson, Foster, and Kronk. Howard Foster was a tall six feet, well-built, carried himself well although a rather taciturn individual. Howard and his father worked in Plant 4 for several years. Although he was recognized as a member of the CP, he was so inoffensive that he never had any trouble, even at the height of the McCarthy period. Ed Kronk was built like a fire hydrant, his head topped with thinning sandy hair. He was a very gruff speaker but would make himself heard; with Howard you had to strain to hear him speak. In the seven years Foster was a member of Chevrolet Local No. 659, he spoke only rarely at union meetings; Kronk contributed even less. Kermit was the extrovert. He had a good baritone speaking voice. He was a bit taller than six feet and in his salad days rather slim but with a good frame. In a meeting Kermit sought center stage. He liked to join the crowd in the bar and tell stories which made him popular. He was a natural auto leader. Although he had faults, the public didn't see them.

Kermit Johnson had been nominated by Howard Foster for strike chairman. Foster, who had just been transferred, professed not to know anyone on the second shift, and would therefore be of little help in shutting down the plant. Ed Kronk was a typical example of a union Jimmy Higgins ready for any task. He worked in Plant 6 and therefore had minimal knowledge of Plant 4 personnel; he promised to bring along assistance. He duly arrived with twenty supporters.

What Kraus hides from us is the reputation that charismatic Kermit Johnson had attained with Chevrolet workers by his "rabble-rousing" at the mass meetings in the Pengelly Building. He was the ablest speaker among the GM workers, with no equal except Roy Reuther. Kermit could bring the crowd to its feet, one factor that explains his ability to lead in the shutdown of the plant.

Thus, according to Kraus, we are confronted with three leaders, two of whom lacked contacts of consequence. Kermit, for his part, had stature from the strike meetings but also from the years of building the meetings of the League for Industrial Democracy prior to the strike. These meetings attracted several hundred people, many of them Chevrolet workers. Most of the SP members were employed at Chevrolet, which also helped make it possible to implement the strike plan.

The fact remains that a small determined body of union men shut down a plant that employed four thousand workers. It was an extraordinary feat, and thus a turning point in the strike. Kraus sees fit in his book to impugn the reputation of the one man who made it possible. The unverifiable notion that Kermit may have overslept is totally immaterial in light of the successful action.

Each According to Their Ability

Another partisan of Kraus's history of the strike is Fraser M. Ottanelli. His book *The Communist Party of the United States* is a concoction of fact and fantasy and fails to breaks any new ground.

Communists were present at every stage and level of the confrontation: from its leadership down to the most menial tasks. Bob Travis was the chief UAW organizer in Flint; Henry Kraus was in charge of the union's paper as well as of publicity. Bud Simons, the head of the strike committee inside Fisher 1, was a Communist as were most of the committee members. Bob Travis played an essential role in devising the basically military strategy for the capture of the vital Chevrolet No. 4 engine plant in February. By enlarging the strike, this helped bring General Motors to its knees.

Outside the plant Communists also organized a network of support for the strikers. In Flint, Dorothy Kraus and Margaret Anderson formed a Women's Auxiliary of the UAW which organized a number of essential activities in support of the strike.[23]

Roger Keeran, in *The Communist Party and the Auto Workers Union*, supports the thesis of the key role of the party, not only in terms of its staff leadership, but also on the basis of its numerical strength in Flint. He cites Hy Fish, the Socialist Party organizer sent to Flint after the strike began, claiming the SP had only sixty-seven members in the entire state in auto, while the Communist Party had a thousand members in Flint alone. According to Genora, however, the SP had some forty members in Flint, while Detroit had three to four times as many.[24]

The CP in Flint was concentrated in the North End among those foreign-born. These northenders were members of the International Workers Order, an insurance organization and a fraternal society for the many ethnic groups. They often had difficulty with the language. They worked mainly in Buick, which played no role in the strike. Each one was a good Jimmy Higgins; they were foot soldiers. Native Flint auto workers tended to work in Chevrolet. This author knew each of the handful of CP members in Chevrolet. Like their political comrades in Buick, they were competent and respected, but average leaders. This in no way to denigrate their role in the union: each person contributed to the level of his or her ability.

The CP had no one to match Kermit Johnson in Chevrolet, and they had no one who could organize a thousand women, as Genora did, or who was able to play an independent union role. Those women who worked on kitchen duty made an enormous contribution, but it did not compare to the work of Genora and the Emergency Brigadiers.

In an article in the *Socialist Call*, Frank Trager claimed that "outside of Bob Travis all of the rank-and-file leaders are well-known Socialists."[24] Keeran thinks this is at variance with the reality. Here he follows CP leaders of the time, who thought it a boastful claim. Let history be the judge. Without Roy Reuther, Victor Reuther, Kermit and Genora

Johnson, this book would relate a different history of the 1937 GM strike. The Socialist Party leaders were more than a match for the Communist Party.

The CP asserts that the strike was under the aegis of Bob Travis. While it is true that he was the main public figure, his co-adjunct was Roy Reuther, a Brookwood Labor College graduate who had studied labor strategy at the school founded by A. J. Muste and other socialists. Roy enjoyed an independent standing in Flint and especially in Chevrolet because he had taught public education classes years before the strike.

Another criticism of CP-oriented writers is their failure to record the role of the Proletarian Party in Flint, with its large contingent in the Fisher Body 1 plant headed by Clayton Carpenter, Clarence Carpenter, Jay Greene, Monroe Blankenship, Bert Jones, Victor Van Etten, and many others, with long seniority standing in the plant. For example, the three leading Communists in Fisher would undoubtedly have had a more difficult time shutting down Fisher Body on December 30, 1936, without the support of this political group.

As important as the three CP leaders were in Fisher, in time the focus of union action shifted to the Chevrolet complex, which alone could bring the strike to a victorious conclusion. The facts are that the Socialists, Communists, Proletarian Party, and the Communist Party Opposition (Lovestoneites) functioned under the unwritten united front accord. This was one of the few occasions in recent labor history where the Communist Party joined in a genuine united front of the left. It took the strikes of 1934–1935 to teach the Communist Party that its program was failing. The Communist Party writers play down this period, but these events prepared and established the ground rules that led to the great victory of 1937.

Epilogue

The Auto Unions Today

The auto workers' unions' historic strikes of 1934, 1935, and 1936–1937 established industrial unionism as the fundamental form of organization. In the process, the unions integrated the concept of one union regardless of race, gender, or creed, on an equal basis; this solidarity led to a healthy relationship between the leaders and the members. Solidarity rested on the democratic participation of the entire membership. Respect of the picket line protected all workers while unions resorted to militant union action to overturn court injunctions and government intervention in support of the corporations. Leadership was earned; centralized leadership was frowned upon. The auto workers had suffered from centralization under William Green, William Collins, and Francis Dillon.

During the first ten years, 1935–1945, the union leaders failed to resolve tensions between the International Union leaders and the local unions. Members in the factories compelled the local union leaders to heed their complaints, while the International Union leaders, further removed from shop workers, heeded the complaints of the corporations. Pressure generated by the local unions offset that from management. Union members resorted to unauthorized strikes when the balance tilted against them.

Ongoing conflict gave dissident rank-and-file forces the opportunity to introduce issues that became the subject of great debates in the union at annual conventions. Some of these debates were reviewed in earlier chapters. However, not discussed were two particular issues that would affect the future arose at the October 1943 UAW Convention in Buffalo, New York. The first was the question of piecework, more euphemistically called incentive pay plan. The second, introduced by Walter Reuther, was the question of industry-wide bargaining.

In March 1943 the International Executive Board had adopted a motion reaffirming the auto unions' opposition to the introduction of piece-rate plans into plants that did not already have such programs. Piecework, considered another form of speed-up, was anathema in most locals. The union's position against incentive pay was formed in response to a national campaign by the Communist Party leader, Earl Browder. Browder appeared at a mass meeting in Detroit, and the CP took out full-page ads to support piece rates as a means of spurring production in war plants. George Addes and Richard Frankensteen spearheaded the campaign in the UAW. The issue was revived at the April executive board meeting of the UAW and tabled to be settled at the October convention.

During these same months the miners and John L. Lewis were locked in a titanic struggle with the coal operators and the government. Time after time the miners quit work. The government requested delays, and the union set new deadlines. Roosevelt issued an executive order removing draft deferments from the miners, and ordered the expropriation of union property and bank funds. Ignoring Roosevelt's draconian measures, the miners struck again. This went on for six months, ending with a complete victory for the 500,000-member miners' union. For the first time, wages of southern coal miners equaled those in the north.

The miners' militant actions inspired wildcat strikes in the auto plants, where supporters of Walter Reuther were unhappy with the no-strike pledge he and the other top officers had imposed on the union. Reuther participated in the debate over incentive pay plans. He tried to win back the militants he had lost with his support of the no-strike pledge:

> The decision you make here today will determine policy for the next twenty years....
>
> I say unless this union gets away from local wage negotiations and starts organizing and negotiating wages for the whole industry at one time to cover every worker at one time like they do in the coal fields....
>
> Our industry is suffering from a very chaotic wage situation. We have tremendous wage differentials going from ten to fifteen to thirty-five to forty cents an hour, differentials for workers doing the same job inside our union. What we decide here today, either we are going to go down the line on piecework and make that chaos and those differentials greater, or we are going to say it is about time we launch an industry-wide agreement and give workers the same pay for the same job no matter where he does that in the industry.[1]

Reuther went further in the hotly contested debate, to declare:

We have got to take labor out of competition. We have got to make them pay the same rate every place in this country where a fellow does the same job. That can only be done if we have an industry-wide wage agreement. Vote down piecework, vote down the minority report. Put this union on record and tell General Motors we are going to bury piecework once and for all and go out of here fighting for a master wage agreement covering all the shops based on equal pay and equal work for all jobs where ever that work is being done in our industry.[2]

The convention voted two to one against the piecework resolution. Reuther, of course, soon forgot about industry-wide bargaining when it was to his advantage to use one-at-a-time bargaining as a means of attaining presidency of the union.

While Reuther's attack on incentive pay contributed to the defeat of the Communist Party sponsorship of an issue already resolved in most auto plants, his remarks on industry-wide bargaining were met with silence. No one could raise any objections to the concept of equal pay for equal work so soon after the historic victory of the coal miners. Nevertheless the decline of the UAW in twenty-five years can be traced directly to Reuther's failure to fight for industry-wide bargaining.

When Reuther died on May 9, 1970, he left a union at peak strength, with 1.6 million members. Reuther's immediate successor, Leonard Woodcock, came from the same political school as Walter. Until the Second World War he had been in the Socialist Party. As late as the 1940 presidential campaign, he served on the SP national board. The International Board of the union continued to reflect the policies and views of the departed leader. After Woodcock came other board members who continued Reuther's policies. The union focused on the bread-and-butter issues that made auto workers among the highest paid industrial workers, whose fringe benefits included health insurance and a pension.

Despite its successes, the union nevertheless declined in numbers. At the time of writing it has approximately 750,000 members. The decline is partly accounted for by the secession of the Canadian Auto Workers with its 120,000 members. Furthermore, the membership total of the UAW disguises the true makeup of the union: auto workers are still a majority; nevertheless many members work in colleges, the health industry, and in retail business. The union has undergone a process of decreasing industrial proletarian composition.

Confronted by the decline in membership due to competition from foreign auto companies, automation, dispersal of the factories to low-wage areas, and a failure to organize, the union's leaders embarked on a new course. They turned away from their historic past; in fact they rejected it out of hand. With a myopic understanding of the new industrial reality, they launched programs to rescue the Big Three industrial giants by aping the Japanese auto companies' jointness programs, which have the same objectives as piecework without the monetary rewards. These Quality of Life programs—the name General Motors gave to the Japanese techniques—were designed to increase production. The auto corporations spent $900 million establishing their program, which established a new layer of workers in the plants who were the agents of the union leaders and the company. At union elections they campaigned for the union leaders representing the status quo. During the year they held meetings to explain the benefits of cooperation with management. In the huge GM complex, factories manufacturing the same product were put into competition, and the losing plant was shut down. The principle of union solidarity to protect all members was discarded by the union for short-term contractual advantage.

Piece-rate techniques to increase production were always considered anathema. Under piece-work programs the worker tallies his production at the end of the day. The company sets the minimum limit after a time study. If the worker produces a thousand pieces and he doesn't exceed the limit his pay remains the same but if at the end of the day he has exceeded the thousand by two hundred pieces his rate of pay goes up. The Quality of Life programs, however, worked on the principle that production could spiral upward without the monetary rewards associated with piece rates. Now consider a collective of workers numbering ten. Some of the representatives of the union under the jointness or supervision see that they can reduce by one the collective putting together front-end assemblies. The profits of the corporation have increased without any remuneration to the remaining nine, who have to work harder to make up for the redundant worker. As a result of the introduction of the jointness program, then, GM profits soared. The intensification of involved labor inevitably ended in the discharge of surplus workers.

These infamous programs, financed liberally by the corporations and signed up to by UAW leaders in the span of two decades, transformed the auto-labor landscape. The UAW union leaders accepted the despised two-tier wage system. Reuther's prediction of chaos if workers doing the same work received unequal pay came true. The union acquiesced to the sale of parts plants and the establishing of lower wage rates in the parts industry. Eventually the parts plants shifted to low-wage areas of the country. In 1996 the Bureau of Labor Statistics reported that 46 percent of workers in plants employing a thousand or more were represented by unions in the motor vehicles and equipment industry. However, it is impossible to provide accurate statistics as the majority of auto-parts plants employ fewer than a thousand staff and are not required to report. In 1974, before the advent of the Quality of Life programs, 76 per cent of the parts workers were organized. In 1994, according to a report drawn up at a UAW GM sub-council meeting in Chicago, the figure was 17 percent.

The adoption of the jointness program by the UAW leaders made them complicit in the destruction of the auto cities as production centers. Devastation of the inner cities of Flint, Detroit, Cleveland, and Toledo soon followed the closure of the factories. Particularly hard hit were the Blacks living close to the factories.

When the UAW instituted these programs, General Motors manufactured cars, radios, aircraft parts, trucks, military equipment, turbine engines for airplanes, refrigerators, space rockets, and many other products. General Motors had 112 factories in 67 U.S. cities. The corporation had 33 divisions, its own engineering school, research departments, a labor department, and all the trappings of a worldwide corporation. The annual GM report of 1996 asserts that GM cars and trucks are sold in 190 countries; the company assembles and manufactures parts in 50 countries; and the corporation aspires to lead the world in transportation products.

The labor observer's mind boggles at the audacity of union leaders attempting to solve the temporary problem of this industrial giant. The GM directors, for their part, never lost sight of their obligation to protect the class interest of the stockholders. The UAW leaders surrendered the principle of equal pay for the same work in the industry. They failed to protect the class interest of the auto workers in the way John L. Lewis had in the heroic fight against the coal operators during the war. The corporation gladly accepted the union's willing assistance, which was given even without a minimal quid pro quo. The fight for a thirty-hour week at forty hours' pay to reduce unemployment was abandoned. In a democratic union, leaders are deposed or they resign. The ruinous policies of the straitjacketed UAW brought no resignations, however.

General Motors continues on a relentless course that spells great trials ahead for the auto union. For a time, GM maintained a ratio of

80 percent U.S. production to 20 percent abroad. The ratio is now 50 percent at home to 50 percent abroad. The *Wall Street Journal*, April 4, 1997, reported a GM plan to build simultaneously four huge independent complexes in Brazil, Poland, Thailand, and China at a staggering cost of $2.2 billion. These plants will be supplied by local parts suppliers. The market in imported auto parts to the U.S. has grown to $250 million, and this is only the beginning. Engineers at the Delphi Automotive Systems Center in Mexico will serve markets in Mexico and anywhere in the world GM has installations—a significant cost-saving, if one compares the wages of an engineer in Mexico and in Detroit.[3]

The *Wall Street Journal* further reports that we may have seen the last of new plants constructed in North America—a great cause for alarm for Canadian and U.S. auto workers. General Motors executive Louis R. Hughes has announced the transformation of GM from transnational corporation to global entity, and he believes this has become the model for other global corporations. GM works with thirty thousand suppliers worldwide and dispenses $70 billion on this operation. Suppliers from the United States are diminishing as the cheaper suppliers come on line.[4]

The UAW's response has been to forge an alliance with the Steel Workers Union and the International Association of Machinists. A uniform contract date to enable unified strike action will take years to bring about. Restrictions imposed on labor by antiunion legislation going back more than five decades compel the unions to move at a tortoise pace, while the corporations, with great amounts of capital, institute new plants and policies at breakneck speed. The unions have spent tens of millions of dollars in their alliance with the Democratic Party. Yet the results of this alliance have only been more attacks on unions. Taft–Hartley, Landrum–Griffen, and NAFTA testify to the political disasters experienced by the unions.

In 1996 five international unions and other supporting union councils and locals met at a convention in Cleveland, Ohio, representing 1.5 million union workers, to form and launch a new party to represent labor and the country. The party program calls for the repeal of repressive labor legislation that has successfully impaired union organization in the United States. The intention of the Labor Party program is to aid all who work by hand and brain for wages. To date, the UAW, the Steel Workers Union, and the IAM have failed to endorse the new Labor Party. When the UAW reassesses its industrial policy, the union will also have to place on the agenda a failed political program.

Notes

Chapter 1

1. Harry Braverman, *Labor and Monopoly Capital: The Degradation of Work in the Twentieth Century* (New York: Monthly Review Press, 1974), 85.
2. Sidney Fine, *The Automobile Under the Blue Eagle* (Ann Arbor: University of Michigan Press, 1963), 28–29.
3. David Brody, *Dissent,* Summer 1997, 72.
4. Bert Cochran, *Labor and Communism: The Conflict that Shaped American Unions* (Princeton, N.J.: Princeton University Press, 1977), 66.
5. Fine, *The Automobile Under the Blue Eagle,* 233.
6. Philip A. Korth and Margaret R. Beegle, *I Remember Like Today: The Auto-Lite Strike of 1934* (East Lansing: Michigan State University Press, 1988), 8, 209.
7. Ibid.
8. Irving Bernstein, *A History of the American Worker 1933–1941: Turbulent Years* (Boston, Mass.: Houghton Mifflin, 1969), 220.
9. Oral history of James Roland, September 25, 1960, interviewed by Jack W. Skeels, under the auspices of the University of Michigan and Wayne State University Institute of Labor and Industrial Relations.
10. Art Preis, *New Militant,* series of three articles May 25–June 8, 1935 reviewing the 1934 and 1935 Toledo strikes; Fine, *The Automobile Under the Blue Eagle,* 275.
11. Edward Lamb, *No Lamb for Slaughter* (New York: Harcourt, Brace & World, 1963), 40. "When our entourage waded through the crowds of newspapermen, photographers, and others who had jam-packed the courtroom, we had to do a bit of nurse maiding for a very drunken Judge Stuart. It was really quite pathetic—the other judges had sidestepped the case and left Judge Stuart to face the defiant mob alone." During a visit to the ninety-year-old Ted Selander, he told me that the inspiration to fight the injunction came from Budenz, who had successfully fought them in two strikes: one in Kenosha, Wisconsin, and the other in Nazareth, Pennsylvania.
12. Korth and Beegle, *I Remember Like Today,* 12.
13. *New York Times,* May 24, 1934.
14. *The 1934 Electric Auto-Lite Strike,* produced by WBGU-TV (Bowling Green, Oh.: Bowling Green State University, 1995). The documentary shows

graphic film clips of the clashes between the strikers and the Guard. Emotion leaps out from one sequence, which shows strikers marching down the street toward the Guard, holding a strikebreaker naked to the world except for a necktie at his throat.

15. A. J. Muste, *The Nation*, June 1934, 640.
16. A. J. Muste, *New Republic*, June 6, 1934, 87.
17. Henry Kraus collection, Reel 5, Section 2, Reel 6 Section 6, in the Walter Reuther Library, Archives of Labor and Urban Affairs, Wayne State University.
18. Ibid.

Chapter 2

1. Art Preis, "Inside Story of the Toledo Strike," *New Militant*, June 1, 1935, 2.
2. A. J. Muste, *The Automobile Industry and Organized Labor* (Baltimore, Md.: The Christian Social Justice Fund, 1936), 40.
3. Art Preis, *New Militant*, May 11, 1935, 2.
4. Oral history of James Roland, September 25, 1960, interviewed by Jack W. Skeels, under the auspices of the University of Michigan and Wayne State University Institute of Labor and Industrial Relations.
5. Ibid.
6. Wetherald, vice president of Chevrolet, was married to Charles Raymond Albro's sister, and was thus an uncle by marriage to Genora Johnson Dollinger. During the 1937 sitdown strike, word was passed through the family offering Genora a good job if she gave up her union activity.
7. Henry Kraus collection, Walter Reuther Library, Archives of Labor and Urban Affairs, Wayne State University.
8. Henry Kraus, *Heroes of Unwritten Story: The UAW, 1934–39* (Urbana and Chicago: University of Illinois Press, 1993), 99:

   At the end of 1934 the American Workers Party, led by Muste, merged with the Communist League of America, followers of Leon Trotsky. Successful conduct of two of the three major strikes in 1934 largely effected the unification of the two parties. The new party became the Workers Party, under the leadership of James P. Cannon and A. J. Muste. Selander, Pollock and Preis were local supporters of this merged party.

9. Muste, *The Automobile Industry and Organized Labor*, 44.
10. *New York Times*, April 25, 1935.
11. Oral history of Joseph Ditzel, interviewed by Jack W. Skeels, under the auspices of the University of Michigan and Wayne State University Institute of Labor and Industrial Relations, 6.
12. Art Preis, *New Militant*, June 8, 1935.
13. "Chevrolet Strikers Stand Firm," handbill of the Workers Party, Henry Kraus collection, Walter Reuther Library, Archives of Labor and Urban Affairs, Wayne State University.
14. James O. Spearing, *New York Times*, May 3, 1935.
15. A. J. Muste, *The Nation*, May 29, 1935.
16. Louis Stark, *New York Times*, May 15, 1935.

Chapter 3

1. Flint sitdown strikers named the battle at Fisher Body 2 "the Battle of Bull's Run." The name was associated with Civil War history. Some labor historians changed the name many years later, thereby rewriting history. Chapters 12 and 14 below recount the events in this pivotal strike in greater detail.
2. Sidney Fine, *Sitdown: The General Motors Strike of 1936–1937* (Ann Arbor: University of Michigan Press, 1969), 280–82.
3. Ibid., 282.
4. *New York Times*, February 3–11, 1937.
5. *New York Times*, February 14, 1937.
6. Bert Cochran, *Labor and Communism: The Conflict that Shaped American Unions* (Princeton, N.J.: Princeton University Press, 1977), 130.
7. Henry Kraus, *Heroes of Unwritten Story: The UAW, 1934–39* (Urbana and Chicago: University of Illinois Press, 1993), ch. 15.

Chapter 4

1. There were two John Andersons in the UAW. Big John was the CP leader of Local No. 155. Little John Anderson, a Trotskyist, was from Fleetwood Local No. 174, which later became Fleetwood Local No. 15.
2. Oral history of Genora Johnson Dollinger, interviewed by Sherna Gluck, Feminist History Research Project of the Bentley Library, University of Michigan, and Wayne State University Institute of Labor and Industrial Relations, 1978.
3. Clayton W. Fountain, *Union Guy* (New York: Viking, 1949), 67.
4. Henry Kraus, *Heroes of Unwritten Story: The UAW, 1934–39* (Urbana and Chicago: University of Illinois, 1993), 357.
5. Ibid., 381. There was no mystery in leadership circles as to Lovestone's role supporting Homer Martin long before these disclosures. Nevertheless, the disclosures came as a shock to the membership.
6. Fountain, *Union Guy*, 84.
7. Ben Fischer, in *Socialist Call*, April 2, 1938.

Chapter 5

1. Ben Fischer, "Confidential Report of the Socialist Party (June 7, 1938) on the Inner Situation in the Auto Union," Henry Kraus papers, Box 6—film, Walter Reuther Library, Archives of Labor and Urban Affairs, Wayne State University.
2. Frank Marquardt, *An Auto Workers Journal* (University Park: Pennsylvania State University Press, 1975), 79.
3. Erwin Baur was a political associate of Cochran at Budd Wheel in Detroit. Oral communication with author, April–May 1996.
4. This reference is to Bert Cochran, *Founding of the Socialist Workers Party, Minutes and Resolutions 1938–39* (New York: Monad Press, 1982), 51.
5. Walter P. Reuther collection, Box 4 Folder 11, Walter Reuther Library, Archives of Labor and Urban Affairs, Wayne State University.

6. Henry Kraus, *Heroes of Unwritten Story: The UAW, 1934–39* (Urbana and Chicago: University of Illinois Press, 1993), 379.
7. Independent steel producers adamantly opposed to the CIO purchased machine guns, small arms, and tear gas to use against strikers. Peaceful pickets were assaulted in Cleveland, Massillon, and Youngstown; the most horrendous attack occurred at the infamous Memorial Day Massacre, where ten were killed and scores wounded.

   The CP's support for capitalist candidates like Governor Frank Murphy in Michigan and Roosevelt for president (even though the party had its own candidate, Earl Browder, on the 1936 ballot) reflected the party's emergence (by 1937) from its ultra-left Third Period, where the capitalist and even the left parties were anathema, into the People's Front era.
8. Oral history of Genora Johnson Dollinger, interviewed by Sherna Gluck, Feminist History Research Project of the Bentley Library, University of Michigan, and Wayne State University Institute of Labor and Industrial Relations, 1978.

Chapter 6

1. Sidney Fine, *Sitdown: The General Motors Strike of 1936–1937* (Ann Arbor: University of Michigan Press, 1969). General Motors was the largest single employer of the Pinkerton Detective Agency in the years immediately before the sit-down strike (38). Art Preis, *Labor's Giant Step* (New York: Pathfinder Press, 1964), 100. Ford employed eight thousand plant guard servicemen, many of whom were convicted felons (100).
2. By-laws of UAW Budd Wheel Local No. 306 Flying Squad, in existence 1937–1948. From the personal collection of Erwin Baur.
3. Bert Cochran, *Labor and Communism: The Conflict that Shaped American Unions* (Princeton, N.J.: Princeton University Press, 1977), 134.
4. Victor Reuther, *The Brothers Reuther and the Story of the UAW* (Boston, Mass.: Houghton Mifflin, 1976), 190.
5. Cochran *Labor and Communism*, 128.
6. Genora and Sol Dollinger collection, Walter Reuther Library, Archives of Labor and Urban Affairs, Wayne State University.
7. Oral history of Genora Johnson Dollinger, interviewed by Sherna Gluck, Feminist History Research Project of the Bentley Library, University of Michigan, and Wayne State University Institute of Labor and Industrial Relations, 1978.
8. John L. Lewis, address to the 1940 UAW Constitutional Convention, St. Louis, Missouri.
9. Preis, *Labor's Giant Step*: "An entry in Secretary of War Stimson's Diary dated November 25, 1941, reads: 'The question at the White House conference was how we should maneuver them (the Japanese) into the position of firing the first shot without allowing danger to ourselves'" (134).

Chapter 7

1. Woodward Avenue in Detroit divides the city north and south to the Detroit River. One block to the east was the beginning of the Black East

Side ghetto. Yet not a restaurant would serve a Black on Woodward Avenue. The SWP undertook a campaign to eradicate restaurant discrimination on Woodward Avenue. Led by Jessie and Ernest Dilliard, Genora (Johnson) Dollinger, Larry Dolinski, Eleanor Foster and many others, including the future mayor of Detroit, Coleman Young, the restaurants were opened to all, regardless of color. Also participating was the NAACP youth group.

2. August Meier and Elliot Rudnick, *Black Detroit and the Rise of the UAW* (New York: Oxford University Press, 1979), 58.
3. Ibid., 59.
4. William Allen, in *Daily Worker*, March 13 and 23, 1941.
5. Keith Sward, *The Legend of Henry Ford* (New York and Toronto: Rinehart, 1948), 401–02.
6. William Allen, in *Daily Worker*, April 2, 1941.
7. *New York Times*, April 3, 1941.
8. Meier and Rudnick, *Black Detroit and the Rise of the UAW*, 99.
9. *Daily Worker*, April 4, 1941.
10. Meier and Rudnick, *Black Detroit and the Rise of the UAW*, 89.
11. *New York Times*, April 4, 1941.
12. *New York Times*, April 7, 1941.
13. *New York Times*, April 12, 1941.
14. Allan Nevins and Frank Ernest Hill, *Ford Decline and Rebirth: 1933–1962* (New York: Charles Scribner's Sons, 1962), 164. Meier and Rudnick, *Black Detroit and the Rise of the UAW*, 106.
15. Nevins and Hill, *Ford Decline and Rebirth*, 166.

Chapter 8

1. Telephone interview with the author, September 6, 1995. James Kalemis was a contributor to the *Punch Press* in the 1937 sitdown strike. The publication was published by students from the University of Michigan.
2. The suggestion of a salary limit may have come from the union to make the other restrictions more palatable. Hours worked in excess of the eight-hour day/forty-hour week were paid at time and a half; overtime worked on Sundays and holidays was paid at double time and termed "premium pay."
3. Harry Dahlheimer, *A History of the Mechanics Educational Society of America in Detroit from its Inception in 1933 through 1937* (Detroit: Wayne State University Press, 1951), 40.
4. Third Special Session, International Board, UAW–CIO, Saturday, March 28, 1942, Cleveland, Ohio; George Addes File, Walter Reuther Library, Archives of Labor and Urban Affairs, Wayne State University.
5. Nelson Lichtenstein, *Labor's War at Home: The CIO in World War II* (Cambridge and New York: Cambridge University Press, 1982), 99.
6. "Estimates based on U.S. Bureau of Labor Statistics and Department of Commerce figures show that in 1940 the average money income per member of the working population was about $1,155, while the cost of the government's 'minimum health and decency' budget—a minimum—was $1,958 in the same year. Since then the cost of living has risen over

11 per cent and further increases are expected..." R. J. Thomas report to UAW Seventh Constitutional Convention, August 3–9, 1942, Chicago.

7. Ibid.

8. Ibid. During most conferences of the UAW, a transcript was made which provided a verbatim record of the delegates' speeches. That was not the case with the War Emergency Conference, however. Only a selective record was made. For example, tabulations were recorded of speakers for and against. A synopsis of delegates' remarks replaced the practice of recording entire speeches and contributions from the floor. Some speakers' names are misspelled. It was, in effect, a hoax from beginning to end— intended to provide a legal veneer to illegal actions.

9. "We know that during the last war we had a bumper crop of war million-aires. We are not willing to tighten our belts to create another bumper crop ... our slogan is everything to win the war, but not one damned cent for corporations' profits." Walter Reuther to the 1942 UAW Seventh Con-stitutional Convention, August 3–9, 1942, Chicago.

10. UAW Local No. 599, *Headlight*, April 22, 1942.

11. Ibid.

12. Proceedings of the Seventh UAW Convention, August 3–9, 1942, 86–91.

13. Interview with author, September 17, 1995.

14. Telephone conversation with Bill Mazey, June 18, 1996. Bill recalls that Frankensteen, Addes and two other officers spoke for the International. A motion was made to restrict their time to ten minutes. Bill Mazey was the only speaker in opposition. At the conclusion the vote was unanimous against giving up premium pay.

15. During the Stalin–Hitler pact the CP slogan was "The Yanks Are Not Coming." William H. Hill is referring to the CP change in line.

Chapter 9

1. Sidney Fine, *The Automobile Under the Blue Eagle* (Ann Arbor: University of Michigan Press, 1963), 153.

2. B. J. Widick, *Detroit: City of Race and Class Violence* (Chicago: Quadrangle Books, 1972), 72.

3. Oral history of Genora Johnson Dollinger, interviewed by Sherna Gluck, Feminist History Research Project of the Bentley Library, University of Michigan, and Wayne State University Institute of Labor and Industrial Relations, 1978.

4. Frank Marquardt, *An Auto Worker's Journal* (University Park: Pennsylvania State University Press, 1975), 106.

5. Nelson Lichtenstein, *Labor's War at Home: The CIO in World War II* (New York: Cambridge University Press, 1982), 130.

6. Ernest Mazey could never be employed in Briggs: his reputation as a militant leader of a city employees' union went before him, and in any case Briggs would not have hired another brother of Emil Mazey. Local No. 212 was an amalgamated local. A small unit of the local was the Huck Manufacturing Company. Ernest managed to get hired by this plant and thus became a member of the local.

7. Genora Dollinger, "I Warned Reuther," *American Socialist,* February 1954, 23.
8. Editorial, "Must We Have Government by Violence Instead of by Law?", *Detroit Free Press,* October 19, 1945.
9. "Thugs Beat CIO Woman," *Detroit Times,* October 16, 1945.

Chapter 10

1. Doctor Sweet had purchased a home in a predominately white neighborhood. He was not the first Black to break the covenants of a prejudiced white society, but unlike others, Dr. Sweet, his relatives, and friends armed to defend his property. In a clash organized by the powerful Detroit Ku Klux Klan, a white neighbor across from the Sweet home was killed in the resulting gunfire. Dr. Sweet, his wife, brother, and others— eleven in all—were charged with first-degree murder. Among the attorneys representing Dr. Sweet, relatives, and friends, arranged by the NAACP, were Clarence Darrow, Arthur Garfield Hayes, and Walter Nelson. The defendants were tried before an all-white jury and the case ended in a hung verdict. See B. J. Widick, *Detroit: City of Race and Class Violence* (Chicago: Quadrangle Books, 1972), 6.
2. Ibid., 121.
3. Victor Reuther, *The Brothers Reuther and the Story of the UAW* (Boston, Mass.: Houghton Mifflin, 1976), 298.
4. Jack Strohm, "Perrone and Renda Tied to Anti Unionism," *Detroit Free Press,* January 7, 1954, 7; see also Reuther, *The Brothers Reuther,* 276.
5. Reuther, *The Brothers Reuther,* 297.
6. Strohm, "Perrone and Renda Tied to Anti Unionism."
7. Reuther, *The Brothers Reuther,* 297.
8. Information uncovered by Ralph Winstead and given to Senior Inspector Slack of the Michigan State Police September 28, 1951. Victor Reuther collection, Box 8, Folder 26, Walter Reuther Library, Archives of Labor and Urban Affairs, Wayne State University. The names of those listed as present at the meeting came from Ford, Chrysler, Briggs, and Michigan Stove.
9. Strohm, "Perrone and Renda Tied to Anti Unionism."
10. Statement made by Ritchie to Gerald K. O'Brien, the Wayne County prosecuting attorney.
11. Foster Hailey, "Reuther Witness Flees to Canada—Now Denies the Named Assassin," *New York Times,* January 10, 1954, 1, 54.
12. Strohm, "Perrone and Renda Tied to Anti Unionism."

Chapter 11

1. Emmett Moore, *Militant,* January 20, 1948; "GM Victimizes Tucker Veteran Union Militant," *Militant,* February 2, 1948. In the Genora and Sol Dollinger collection, Walter Reuther Library, Archives of Labor and Urban Affairs, Wayne State University.
2. Art Preis, *Labor's Giant Step* (New York: Pathfinder Press, 1964), 314–15.
3. Ronald Edsworth, *Class Conflict and Cultural Consensus: The Making of a Mass*

Consumer Society in Flint, Michigan (New Brunswick, N.J.: Rutgers University Press, 1987), 206; Preis, *Labor's Giant Step*, 332–33.

4. Victor Reuther, *The Brothers Reuther and the Story of the UAW* (Boston, Mass.: Houghton Mifflin, 1976), 257.

5. Proceedings of the Eleventh Constitutional Convention of the UAW, November 9–14, 1947, Atlantic City, New Jersey.

6. Frank Marquardt, *An Auto Workers Journal* (University Park: Pennsylvania State University Press, 1975), 82.

7. *Militant*, February 1, 1947.

8. John Anderson, *Fifty Years of the UAW: From Sitdowns to Concessions* (Chicago: Bookmarks, 1985), 30; Martin Halpern, *UAW Politics and the Cold War* (Albany: State University of New York, 1988), 201.

9. David Brody, *Workers in Industrial America* (New York: Oxford University Press, 1980), 207.

10. Proceedings of the Eleventh Constitutional Convention of the UAW.

11. Ibid.

12. After the year-long Homer Martin fight most local union officers could distinguish between a CPer, a CPOer, a Socialist, and a Trotskyist.

13. Marquardt, *An Auto Workers Journal*, 112.

14. *Militant*, 1948.

15. In late 1937, when recession hit the auto industry, over 11,000 of the 40,000 GM workers were out of work in Flint. Genora and Kermit Johnson organized a WPA union of the men repairing streets, putting in sidewalks, and so on. One of the early participants was a young, articulate, ambitious and bright A.C. Sparkplug worker, Bob Carter. Going through hard times together cements a bond of friendship that is not easily broken; Bob and Genora remained friends even after he dropped out of the movement due to an injury suffered by his son. We moved to Detroit and Bob served in the Navy. After the war Bob held top positions in his local and became president of the CIO council. I often got Bob to introduce a resolution that was of political interest to the party. Bob was ahead of us and submitted eye-opening resolutions on behalf of the fifty thousand CIO members.

16. Edsforth, *Class Conflict and Cultural Consensus*, 208.

17. Ibid.

18. Reuther, *The Brothers Reuther*, 306.

Chapter 12

1. *Striking Flint: Genora (Johnson) Dollinger Remembers the 1936–37 General Motors Sit-down Strike*, told to Susan Rosenthal, with a Preface by Susan Rosenthal and an Introduction by Sol Dollinger (Chicago: L. J. Page, 1996).

2. The website http:/home.inreach.com/soldoll also contains three pieces on and by Genora.

3. On Genora's induction into the Hall of Fame of the Michigan Women's Historical Center in Lansing, October 1994.

Chapter 13

1. Letters in the Genora and Sol Dollinger collection, Walter Reuther Library, Archives of Labor and Urban Affairs, Wayne State University.

Chapter 14

1. William Serrin, *The Company and the Union* (New York: Alfred A. Knopf, 1973).
2. Henry Kraus, *The Many and the Few: A Chronicle of the Dynamic Auto Workers* (Los Angeles: Plantin Press, 1949); *Heroes of Unwritten Story: The UAW 1934–39*, Foreword by Nelson Lichtenstein, (Urbana: University of Illinois Press, 1989), xi.
3. John Steuben, *Strike Strategy* (New York: Gaer, 1950), chs. 12 and 13. The Mohawk Valley Formula to break strikes was developed during the Remington–Rand strike in the spring of 1936. It was endorsed and promoted by the National Manufacturers Association. Resolutions were mailed to its two million business and merchant list: (1) Union leaders to be labeled outside agitators. (2) The demands of the strikers to be discredited with mailings to the media. (3) Leaders of the community—civic, church, and merchant—to be organized into a citizens' committee. (4) The armed forces to be used in addition to police. (5) Back-to-work movements to be initiated.
4. Among the several thousand Flintites that responded to the alarming broadcasts of the Fisher Body 2 battle were Genora's father and mother. When the strikers threw the tear-gas canisters back at the police, the crowd had to rush into the restaurants on Chevrolet Avenue to escape from the gas.
5. Kraus, *The Many and the Few*, 138–39.
6. Roger Keeran, *The Communist Party and the Auto Workers Union* (New York: International Publishers, 1980), 173.
7. Ibid.
8. Victor Reuther, *The Brothers Reuther and the Story of the UAW* (Boston, Mass.: Houghton Mifflin, 1976), 157.
9. Sidney Fine, *Sitdown: The General Motors Strike of 1936–1937* (Ann Arbor: University of Michigan Press, 1969), 6.
10. Ibid.
11. Ibid.
12. Oral history of Genora Johnson Dollinger, interviewed by Sherna Gluck, Feminist History Research Project of the Bentley Library, University of Michigan, and Wayne State University Institute of Labor and Industrial Relations, 1978. The website http:/home.inreach.com/soldoll contains a transcript of Genora's 1987 speech at the fiftieth anniversary celebration of the Flint sitdown. She addresses Henry Kraus directly, taking issue with his account in *The Many and the Few*, in particular his sidelining of women's role in the success of the strike action.
13. Victor Reuther made this comment in his speech at the fiftieth anniversary of the sitdown strike in Flint on August 2, 1987.
14. Oral history of Genora Johnson Dollinger, interviewed by Sherna Gluck.
15. Fine, *Sitdown*, 248.
16. Genora's diary notes the arrival of Frank Trager in Flint in response to the letter sent to Norman Thomas. Diary in the Genora and Sol Dollinger collection, Walter Reuther Library, Archives of Labor and Urban Affairs, Wayne State University.

17. Kraus, *The Many and the Few*, 192.
18. Floyd Hoke Miller, in *Searchlight*, anniversary issue, February 11, 1959.
19. Oral history of Genora Johnson Dollinger, interviewed by Sherna Gluck.
20. Kermit Johnson, in *Searchlight*, anniversary issue, February 11, 1959.
21. Kraus, *The Many and the Few*, 192.
22. Fine, *Sitdown*, 267.
23. Fraser M. Ottanelli, *The Communist Party of the United States* (New Brunswick, N.J.: Rutgers University Press, 1991), 145.
24. For an inexplicable reason the Socialist Party leaders in Detroit insisted that party recruitment halt for the duration of the strike. The Communist Party operated under no such handicap.
25. Frank Trager, in *Socialist Call*, February 6, 1937.

Epilogue

1. Proceedings of the Eighth UAW Convention, March 1943, Buffalo, New York.
2. Ibid.
3. Rebecca Blumenstein, *Wall Street Journal*, April 4, 1997.
4. Ibid.

Bibliography

Books

Bernstein, Irving. *A History of the American Worker 1933–1941: Turbulent Years.* Boston, Mass.: Houghton Mifflin, 1969.

Bluestone, Barry, and Bluestone, Irving. *Negotiating the Future: A Labor Perspective on American Business.* New York: HarperCollins, 1992.

Budenz, Louis. *This Is My Story.* New York: McGraw Hill, 1947.

Cochran, Bert. *Labor and Communism: The Conflict that Shaped American Unions.* Princeton, N.J.: Princeton University Press, 1977.

Derber, Martin, and Edwin Young, eds. *Labor and the New Deal.* Madison: University of Wisconsin Press, 1957.

Dahlheimer, Harry. *A History of the Mechanics Educational Society of America in Detroit from its Inception in 1933 through 1937.* Detroit: Wayne State University Press, 1951.

Edsforth, Ronald, *Class Conflict and Cultural Consensus: The Making of a Mass Consumer Society in Flint, Michigan.* New Brunswick: Rutgers University Press, 1987.

El-Messidi, Kathy Groehn. *The Bargain: The Story Behind the 30-Year Honeymoon of GM and UAW.* New York: Nellen, 1980.

Fine, Sidney. *Sitdown: The General Motors Strike of 1936–37.* Ann Arbor: University of Michigan Press, 1969.

——. *The Automobile Under the Blue Eagle.* Ann Arbor: University of Michigan Press, 1958.

Fountain, Clayton. *Union Guy.* New York: Viking, 1949.

Glaberman, Martin. *Wartime Strikes.* Detroit: Bewick Editions, 1980.

Halpern, Martin. *UAW Politics and the Cold War.* Albany: State University of New York Press, 1988.

Howard, Tony, producer. *The 1934 Electric Auto-Lite Strike.* Video. Bowling Green, Oh.: WGBU-TV Bowling Green University, 1995.

Howe, Irving, and Widick, B.J. *The UAW and Walter Reuther.* New York: Da Capo Press, 1949.

Keeran, Roger. *The Communist Party and the Auto Workers Unions.* New York: International Publishers, 1980.

Korth, Phillip, and Beegle, Margaret, R. *I Remember Like Today: The Auto-Lite Strike of 1934.* East Lansing: Michigan State University Press, 1988.

Kraus, Henry. *The Many and the Few.* Los Angeles: Plaintin Press, 1947.

——. *Heroes of Unwritten Story: The UAW, 1934–39.* Urbana and Chicago:

University of Illinois Press, 1993.

Leuchtenburg, William E. *Franklin Roosevelt and the New Deal 1932–1940.* New York: Harper & Row, 1963.

Lichtenstein, Nelson. *Labor's War at Home.* New York: Cambridge University Press, 1982.

———. *The Most Dangerous Man in Detroit: Walter Reuther and the Fate of American Labor.* New York: HarperCollins, 1995.

Marquardt, Frank. *An Auto Workers Journal.* University Park and London: Penn State University Press, 1975.

Meier, August, and Rudwick, Elliot. *Black Detroit and the Rise of the UAW.* New York: Oxford University Press, 1979.

Moley, Raymond. *The First New Deal.* New York: Harcourt Brace & World, 1966.

Mortimer, Wyndham. *Organize: My Life as a Union Man.* Boston, Mass.: Beacon Press, 1971.

Mosher, Donald, ed. *The History of UAW Local 659: We Make Our Own History,* UAW Chevrolet Local 659.

Muste, A. J. *The Automobile Industry and Organized Labor.* Baltimore, Md.: Christian Social Justice Fund.

———. *The A.F.L. in 1931.* New York: Conference for Progressive Labor Action.

Nevins, Allan, and Hill, Frank Ernest. *Ford: Decline and Rebirth, 1933–1962.* New York: Charles Scribner's Sons, 1962.

Ottanelli, Fraser M. *The Communist Party of the United States.* New Brunswick, N.J.: Rutgers University Press, 1991.

Perkins, Frances. *The Roosevelt I Knew.* New York: Viking, 1940.

Preis, Art. *Labor's Giant Step.* New York: Pioneer Publishers, 1964.

Reuther, Victor, G. *The Brothers Reuther and the Story of the UAW.* Boston, Mass.: Houghton Mifflin, 1976.

Robinson, Jo Ann. *Abraham Went Out: A Biography of A. J. Muste.* Temple University Press, 1981.

Rosen, Elliot A. *Hoover, Roosevelt, and the Brains Trust: From Depression to New Deal.* New York: Columbia University Press, 1977.

Schlesinger, Arthur M., Jr. *The Coming of the New Deal.* Boston, Mass.: Houghton Mifflin, 1959.

Serrin, William. *The Company and the Union.* New York: Alfred A. Knopf, 1973.

Steuben, John. *Strike Strategy.* New York: Gear, 1980.

Sward, Keith. *The Legend of Henry Ford,* New York: Hadden Craftsmen, Rinehart, 1948.

U.S. Congress. Testimony of John L. Louis. 73rd Congr. 2nd sess., 1934.

White, Bob. *Hard Bargains: My Life on the Line.* Toronto: McClelland & Stewart, 1989.

Widick, B.J. *Labor Today.* Boston, Mass.: Houghton Mifflin, 1964.

———. *Detroit: City of Race and Class Violence.* Chicago: Quadrangle Books, 1972.

Periodicals

Business Week, July 21, 1934.

Commonweal, 20, no. 13 (July 1934).

Communist, 1934.

Daily Worker, March and April 1942.

Fortune, October 1934.
History of Region 2B (ed. Tom Whalen).
Labor Age, 1931, 1934, 1935.
Labor Action, March 1941, December 1941; 1946; 1947.
Militant, 1934, 1945, 1946, 1947.
Nation, June 6, 1934; May 29, 1935.
New Militant, 1935.
New Republic, June 6, 1934; July 25, 1934; October 1934.
New York Times, April 1934–June 1934; May 1935–June 1935.
Socialist Call, 1937, 1938, 1939.
Toledo Blade, May–June 1934.
Wall Street Journal, April 4, 1997.
Workers Age, 1937, 1938, 1939.

Archives

Walter Reuther Library, Archives of Labor and Urban Affairs, Wayne State
University. Repository of the oral histories of Joseph Ditzel, James Roland,
Genora Dollinger and many others.

Index

Abner, Willoughby 112
Addes, George 27
   and factional struggles in UAW 36,
     38, 48, 102
   and piece-work debate 190
   and Taft–Hartley bill 110
   and Toledo Chevrolet strike 20, 25
   and wartime labor agreement 71,
     73, 74, 77, 80–81
Albro, Jarvis 176
Allen, William 65, 67
American Federation of Labor (AFL)
   and Cleveland Fisher Body strike
     16–18
   and origins of UAW 3, 5–6, 27, 173
   Local No. 18384 3, 7, 8, 14, 15, 16,
     18, 19, 22–23, 25
   and Roosevelt 14
   and Taft–Hartley bill 111
   and Toledo Chevrolet strike 3, 18,
     20, 22–23, 24
   and unionization of Ford 66–67, 68
   and wartime labor agreement 77
American Socialist 159
American Workers Party 12, 13–14, 21,
   24
Anderson, Big John 36, 55
Anderson, Little John 38, 40, 47,
   109–10
   Fifty Years of the UAW 109
Automobile Workers Union 4–5
Auto Labor Board (ALB) 14, 17, 18–19
   20

Barringer, John 29
Battle of Bull's Run, Flint 28, 133–34,
   175–79

Baur, Erwin 46, 77
Bennett, Harry 63, 66, 67, 70, 84
Berry, Joe 116
Besson, Nellie 169
Bisaga, Cecile 91
Bishop, Melvin 87, 88, 98, 102, 108
Black workers 64–65, 67, 68, 142–43,
   169
   see also racism
Blankenship, Monroe 188
Bluestone, Irving 166
Bohlen, Ann 165
Boone, Bert 117
Briggs Manufacturing Company 4–5,
   82–104, 152–59
   anti-union violence at 83–84,
     87–104, 157–59
Brody, David 110
Brophy, John 180
Browder, Earl 190, 198 n7
Broun, Heywood 12
Brown, Donaldson 180
Budd Wheel Corporation 151–52
Budenz, Louis 10, 12, 13
Burling, Mr. 100
Butler, Marlon 118
Byrd, Richard 18

Cameron, James 165
Cannon, James P. 46, 196 n8
Capizzi, I. A. 69
Carpenter, Clarence 188
Carpenter, Clayton 50, 188
Carter, Bob 58, 116, 202 n15
Center, Melvin 35, 183
Central Labor Union (CLU) 6–7,
   11–13, 16

Chaplin, Charlie, *Modern Times* 125, 140, 182
Chapman, Donnel 114, 118
Chenot, Judge James E. 66
Chicago Tribune 170, 171
Churchill, Winston 111
Clampitt, Tom 106
Coalition of Labor Union Women 168
Cochran, Bert 32, 38, 39, 42, 45, 46, 47, 54, 56
Collins, William 17, 20, 189
Communist Party
  and capitalist candidates 38, 198 n7
  and Chrysler strike 34
  and factional struggles in UAW 44, 46, 51, 54–55
  and Flint sitdown strikes 126, 127, 174, 176–77, 180, 186–88
  and Lovestone 33
  and Ludlow amendment 42
  and piecework debate 190–91
  and W. Reuther 111, 117
  and Toledo Auto-Lite strike 13
  and Trade Union Unity League 4
  and wartime labor agreement 80
Communist Party Opposition 33, 188
Communist and Socialist leaders, rightwing attacks on 4, 22–23, 32, 34–35, 106, 108, 111, 117–18
  see also Taft–Hartley bill
Congress (formerly Committee) of Industrial Organizations (CIO) 27, 51, 145–46
  1938 Convention 55
Connolly, Bill 116
cost-of-living increases, debate on 114–19
Coughlin, Father Charles E. 5
Coyle, M. E. 19
craft vs. industrial unionism 5
Crellin, Jack 91, 116, 167
Crisis 64

Daily Worker 65, 117
Darrow, Clarence 201 n1
De Caux, Len 180
De Lamielleure, Albert 91, 98
'Death Watch' 59, 148–49
Debs, Eugene V. 7
DeLeon, Daniel 60
Detroit Free Press 90, 100, 104
Detroit News 167

Detroit Times 91, 116
Devitt, Joe 35
Dewey, James F. 70
Dilliard, Jessie and Ernest 198 n1
Dillon, Francis 20, 21, 22, 23, 24, 25, 27, 189
Ditzel, Joseph 20, 21, 22, 26
Dolinski, Larry 198–99 n1
Dollinger, Genora Johnson
  assault on 93–104, 157–58
  at Briggs 85–87, 88, 89–92
  and factional struggles in UAW 35, 36, 50, 55
  and Flint sitdown strikes 28, 37, 176, 177–79, 182, 183–4, 187–88
  interview with 123–60
  and making of documentaries 163–65, 168–72, 174–75
  and organizing of unemployed 43, 58, 59, 60
  and racism 198–99 n1
  and UAW celebrations 166–68
Dollinger, Sol 118, 151, 157
Domanski, Olga 168
Donoly, Frank 54
Dubinsky, David 33
Duncan, Sam 168
Dunne, Vincent R. 89, 102

Edsforth, Ronald 118, 119
Edwards, George 38, 110
El-Messidi, Kathy Groehn, *The Bargain* 118–19
Electric Auto-Lite Company 3, 6–15
Ellis, Don 168
Emshwiller, John R. 167
Equality of Sacrifice program 73–80

families, changes in working-class 144–45
Federico, Al 71
Feke, Frank 61
Fenster, Leo 112
Ferrazza, Jess 85, 86, 154
Field, Morris 46
Financial Times 165
Fine, Sidney 29, 180
  The Automobile Under the Blue Eagle 177
  Sitdown 174, 177–78, 185
Finnan, Larry 116
Fischer, Ben 38, 44, 45, 58

Fish, Fania 136
Fish, Hy 187
Flint, conditions in 123–24, 144
Flint Alliance 127–28, 138, 175, 181
Flint Auto Worker 107, 128
Flint Journal 128
Ford Facts 65, 66
Ford Motor Company 49–50, 63–70, 83
Foster, Eleanor 198–9 n1
Foster, Howard 185–86
Fountain, Clayton W. 37, 44
Frankensteen, Richard
    and electoral office 49, 90, 157
    and factional struggles in UAW 36,
        41, 43, 45, 48, 55, 63
    and Flint strikes 181
    and Ford organizing drive 68, 84
    and piecework debate 190
    and wartime labor agreement 71,
        73, 77
Fraser, Douglas 107, 172
Freedman, Louis 100, 101
Fry, John A. 98, 100, 102

Gadola, Judge Paul V. 28, 29
Gallery, Tom 88
Ganley, Nat 36, 55
Gebert, B. K. 55
Gelles, Catherine 169
General Motors
    anti-union activity of 83, 127–28,
        138
    and celebration of contract 166
    and globalization of production
        192–94
    negotiations with 40, 180–81
    recognition of UAW by 30–31, 142,
        181
    and wildcat strikes 40, 56
    working conditions at 124–26
    see also under strikes
Germer, Adolph 55, 180
Girdler, Tom 75
Gluck, Sherna 178
Goldfarb, Lyn 165
Goldman, Albert 42
Gosser, Richard 15
Gray, Lorraine 165, 166, 168–70
The Great Sitdown Strike (BBC) 163–65,
    174–75
Green, William 5–6, 14, 20, 22, 27, 67,
    68, 189

    and Taft–Hartley bill 111
Greene, Jay 188
Guardian 165

Hailey, Foster 103
Hall, Ed 36, 48
Hanford, Ben 174
Hapgood, Mary Donovan 136, 137
Harris, Bert 32, 35, 50
Hatcher, Lillian 169
Hayes, Arthur Garfield 10, 201 n1
Haywood, Allan 70
Headlight 71, 76
Henson, Francis 49
Hill, William H. 80, 81
Hillman, Sidney 49, 51
Holt, Edgar 146
Howe, Irving 107
Hughes, Art 54
Hughes, Louis R. 194

Independent Workers Association
    23–24
industry-wide bargaining 189–92
International Association of Machinists
    194
International Brotherhood of Electrical
    Workers 11–12
Industrial Workers of the World (IWW)
    4, 7, 126

Jacobs, Clarence 99, 103
Jenkins, Bill 54
Johnson, Al 65
Johnson, Genora *see* Dollinger, Genora
    Johnson
Johnson, Harrison 117
Johnson, Kermit
    and factional struggles in UAW 35,
        36, 55, 117
    and Flint sitdown strikes 37, 139–40,
        142, 176, 181–82, 184–86,
        187–88
    and organizing of unemployed 43,
        58
Johnstone, Art 110
Jones, Bert 188
Jones, Larry 117, 165
Joyce, Professor 107

Kalemis, James 71
Kantor, Robert 38, 68

Keeran, Roger, *The Communist Party and the Auto Workers Union* 176–77, 187
Kefauver Committee (U.S. Senate) 97, 99–104
Kelly, Nicholas 18
Kennedy, Thomas 61
Keracker, John 60
Klasey, Tom 35, 141, 183
Knudsen, William 17, 19, 36, 180
Kornbluh, Hy 107
Kraus, Henry 20, 33, 185
  Heroes of Unwritten Story 174, 178, 185
  The Many and the Few 174, 176, 178, 182, 184, 185–86
Krieger, Sheriff David 8–9, 10
Kronk, Ed 185–86
Krzycki, Leo 180

Labor Party (USA) 194
Labor's Non-Partisan Leagues 49
LaDuke, Ted 32, 35, 183
La Follette, Robert 83
Lamb, Edward 10, 12
Lasser, David 43
Lawrence, Bill 181
Lawrence, Roy 58
League for Industrial Democracy 126, 186
Lenin, V. I. 51
Leonard, Richard 43, 44, 45, 55, 77
Lett, Mark 167
Lewis, John L.
  and Chrysler strike (1937) 34
  and CIO 145
  and factional struggles in UAW 39, 40, 47, 48–49, 51
  and Flint sitdown strikes 29, 30, 31, 129, 180
  and Ford campaign 63
  and Labor Non-Partisan Leagues 49
  as leader of UMW 54, 57
  and Ludlow amendment 41
  and Taft–Hartley bill 111
  and wartime labor agreement 60, 61, 190, 193
Lichtenstein, Nelson 74, 87
Lindahl, James 80
Little, E. H. 75
Little, Jack 43–44
local unions, rights of 36, 38, 39, 51–52, 56–57, 107
Lovestone, Jay 32–35, 41–42, 48

Loyalty League 136–37
Ludlow amendment 41–42
Lynch, Mary 91
Lynd, Staughton 163

McCartney, Wilma 131
MacDonald, Gordon 88
McGill, John 43, 71–72, 76, 81, 108, 112, 113
'March of Labor' 16
Marquardt, Frank 46, 47, 86, 115
Marshall, Donald 68
Martel, Frank X. 68
Martin, Homer 27, 30
  and control over strikes 34–36, 39, 107
  and factional struggles in the UAW 31–52, 54, 56
  and negotiations with GM 40, 180, 181
  and unionization of Ford 66–67, 68
Mazey, Emil
  anti-Communism of 106
  and BBC documentary 164
  and Briggs beatings 94, 96–97, 100, 102, 103
  and factional struggles in UAW 36, 38, 47, 48, 51, 106
  and Genora Dollinger 85–86, 153–54
  and Ludlow amendment 42
  and organizing of Black and ethnic workers 64
  and rewriting of history 173
  and role of women 170–72
  and Taft–Hartley bill 113
  and unionization of Briggs 82
  and UAW celebrations 167
  and wartime labor agreement 78, 81
Mazey, Ernest 88, 89, 90, 94, 106
  and Taft–Hartley bill 109, 113
Mazey, William 78–80, 81
Mechanics Education Society of America (MESA) 73, 77
Michigan Stove Company 95, 97–98, 99, 100, 104
Miles, George 33
Militant 105, 116
Miller, Floyd Hoke 183
Miniger, Clem 6, 8–9, 12
Moore, Walter 35
Morosco, Gene 88

Morris, George Jr. 166
Morris, Ken 92, 95, 96–97, 106
Mortimer, Wyndham 27–28, 30, 176
    and factional struggles in UAW 36,
        39, 46, 48, 51
    and Ludlow amendment 41, 42
    role of, in Flint sitdown strikes 180,
        182, 185
Munger, William 33, 49
Murphy, Governor Frank 29, 30, 38,
    49, 134, 180, 198 n7
Murphy, Judge Gerald T. 94, 97
Murray, Pat 58, 59, 149
Murray, Philip 49, 51, 61, 69, 72, 79,
    112
Muste, A. J. 10, 12, 13, 14, 21, 24, 25,
    188

NAACP (National Association for the
    Advancement of Coloured People)
    64–65, 67, 146–47
National Labor Relations Board 66, 106
National Organization of Women 168
National Recovery Act 5
Nelson, Donald 73
Nelson, Walter 94
Neuenfelt, Judge Lila 66
New Militant 21
New Republic 12
New York Times 10, 25, 67, 103, 136,
    171, 184

Ogintz, Ellen 170
On Guard 86
Ottanelli, Fraser M., *The Communist Party
    of the United States* 186–87

Pagano, Joe 60
Palmer, Jack 114–17, 119
Parrish, Delia 168
Peet, Stephen 164–65
People's World 117
Perkins, Frances 12
Perrone, Gaspar 100
Perrone, Santo 95–104, 158
Perry, Tanner 65
piecework, opposition to 189–92
Pillsbury, Sara 168
Pitts, Ruth 135
Pollock, Sam 9, 10, 16
Porter, Russell 30
Pozzi, Jenni 163, 164

Preis, Art 18, 20, 21, 23
Pressman, Lee 30
Progressive caucus 36, 37–39, 44,
    45–47
Proletarian Party 4, 126, 188

Quality of Life programs 192–93

racism 64–65, 70, 142–43, 146–47
Ramsey, Thomas 8
Randolph, A. Philip 65
Raymond, Phil 4
Red-baiting *see* Communist and
    Socialist leaders, right-wing attacks
    on
Reisinger, Richard 73, 77
Renda, Carl 96, 97–98, 100–101, 104,
    158
Reuther, Roy
    and factional struggles in UAW
        33–38 *passim*, 43–44, 117
    and Flint sitdown strikes 127, 140,
        171, 177, 182, 185, 186, 187, 188
Reuther, Sophie 123
Reuther, Victor 36, 37, 38, 44, 55, 123
    The Brothers Reuther 103, 166
    and Flint sitdown strikes 134,
        175–76, 177, 178, 181, 187
    shooting of 97, 100, 158
    and Taft–Hartley bill 110
    and UAW in 1970s 166
Reuther, Walter 27, 49, 89
    and Briggs beatings 89, 94, 102, 103,
        159
    and control of UAW 51–52, 105,
        106–20, 160
    and factional struggles in UAW 31,
        36, 38, 40, 41, 44, 46, 48, 54, 55,
        56–57
    and Flint sitdown strikes 139, 140,
        181, 182, 185
    and industry-wide bargaining
        189–91, 192
    and rewriting of history 173
    shooting of 97, 100, 101–2, 158
    and unionization of Ford 63, 68,
        84–85
    and wartime labor agreement 71,
        73, 77, 81
Rigby, Charles 6–7, 10, 12, 13, 15
Ritchie, Joseph 103
Robinson, Dean 100, 102

Roland, James 9, 10, 18–19, 20, 21, 22, 24, 25, 26
Roosevelt, F. D. 12, 14, 29, 38, 198 n7
    and wartime labor agreement 57, 60–61, 72, 75, 77, 78, 81, 190
Rosenthal, Susan 123
Rothe, Nick 95–97
Roy, Bill 35, 182
Roy, Tekla 132

Saginaw, unionization of 136–37
Schwake, Fred 19, 22, 25
Selander, Ted 10, 12, 195 n11
Serrin, William, *The Company and the Union* 173
Shachtman, Max 107
Sheffield, Horace 65
Sides, Everett 117
Silver, Frank 88, 158
Silver, Paul 54
Simons, Bud 35
Smith, John Thomas 180
Smith, Matthew 73
Snowden, Roy 84–85, 87, 88, 95–96, 158
Socialist Appeal 41, 42
Socialist Call 58, 127, 187
Socialist Labor Party 126
Socialist Party
    and Briggs strike 4
    and factional struggles in UAW 38, 44, 45–46, 54, 106
    and Flint sitdown strikes 35, 126–27, 139–40, 182, 187–88
    and Ludlow amendement 42
    and Reuther 55
    and Toledo strike 8, 21
    and UAW leadership 168, 191
Socialist Workers Party 93, 106, 107, 108, 114, 116, 198–99 n1
speed-ups 4, 125
Stalin, Josef 33, 51
Stark, Louis 25
Steel Workers Organizing Committee 30
Steel Workers Union 194
Stevens, Fred 133
Stone, Eve 33, 49
strike(s)
    Briggs (Detroit, 1933) 4–5
    Chevrolet Transmission (Toledo, 1935) 16, 18–26

Chrysler (1937) 34
Cleveland Fisher Body (1934) 16–18
Flint sitdown, against GM (1937) 28–31, 126–46, 174–88
Ford River Rouge (Dearborn, 1940–41) 63–70
Toledo Auto-Lite (1934) 3, 6–15
wildcat 31, 39, 40, 56–57
strike bulletins 21–22, 23
Strike Truth 20, 22
Strohm, Jack 100
Stuart, Judge Roy R. 8, 9, 10
Sugar, Maurice 41–42
Sunday Mirror 165
Sweet, Dr. Ossian H. 94

Taft, Charles 12, 13
Taft–Hartley bill 105–6, 108–13
Tappes, Shelton 65, 107
Taylor, Bill 49
Taylor, Frederick Winslow 4
Taylor, William 67
Taylor, T. N. 22
Teamsters 68
Terkel, Studs 170
Thomas, Norman 41, 42, 139, 182
Thomas, R. J.
    and factional struggles in UAW 36, 43, 50, 51, 102, 108
    and Taft–Hartley bill 110, 113
    and unionization of Ford 63, 70
    as UAW president 52, 54, 89
    and wartime labor agreement 71, 73, 74–75, 76–77, 78, 81
Toledo Bee 12
Trade Union Unity League (TUUL) 4
Trager, Frank 139–40, 182, 187
Travis, Robert
    and factional struggles in UAW 33, 34–35, 36
    role of, in Flint sitdown strikes 27–28, 127, 171, 176, 177, 180, 181, 182–83, 185, 188
    and Toledo Chevrolet strike 19, 21, 26
Trotsky, Leon 33, 42, 107
Trotskyists 38, 42, 46–47, 109
Tucker, Ray 105–6
Tuttle, Judge Arthur J. 69

unemployed, organizing of 43, 57–60,
147–49
Unemployed League 8–10, 13, 16
United Automobile Workers
(UAW–CIO)
and Black community 64–65
decline in membership of 191
factional struggle in 31–40, 41–52
formation and growth of 27, 30–31
leadership and membership 109
1977 celebrations 166–68
Local No. 12 (Flint Unemployed) 15,
43, 147–49
Local No. 156 (Flint) 32, 33, 34, 37,
43–44, 137
Local No. 174 (Detroit) 56–57
Local No. 212 (Detroit) 82–104,
152–57, 164
Local No. 306 (Detroit) 54
Local No. 599 (Flint) 71, 72, 76
UAW Conventions
1935 (Detroit) 27, 173
1936 (South Bend) 27
1937 (Milwaukee) 38–39
1939 (Cleveland) 50–51
1940 (Cleveland) 60, 63
1942 (Chicago) 73, 76–80
1943 (Buffalo) 189–91
1946 (Atlantic City) 112
1947 (Atlantic City) 105, 110–13
United Automobile Worker 33, 49
United Mine Workers (UMW) 54, 57,
129
Unity caucus 36, 37–39, 43–50, 54–55

Van Etten, Victor 188
Van Wagoner, Governor 69, 70
Van Zandt, Roscoe 143, 169
Vega, Art 87, 158

Wage Earner 106
Walker, Coburn 116

Walker, Sybil 'Teeter' 135, 169
Wall Street Journal 167, 194
War Emergency Conference (1942) 73,
74–76
Watts, Janet 165
Weinstone, William 55
Wells, Walter 48
Wetherald, Charles 19
White, Walter 64, 65, 67
Widick, B. J. 83, 107–8
Widman, Michael 63, 64
Wilkins, Roy 64, 65
Wilson, C. E. 36
Wilson, Charles 75
Winstead, Ralph 97, 98–99, 102, 104,
159
With Babies and Banners 166, 168–72,
174–75
Wolcott, Sheriff Tom 28
Wolman, Leo 18
women
employment of, during war 151–52,
153, 156
role of, in Flint strike 130–38,
169–72
working conditions of 124
Women's Auxiliary of Flint 28, 130–32
Women's Emergency Brigade 134–38,
140–42, 165, 168–72, 183–84
Woodcock, Leonard 166, 168, 191
Workers Age 42
Workers' Alliance 43, 59
Workman, Claude 58
Works Project Administration (WPA)
57–60, 146–48
World War Two, labor agreements
during 57–58, 60–62, 71–81, 151
see also Ludlow amendment

Young, Coleman 198–99 n1

Zimmerman, Charles 33